AF607960

CAPTURING THE INEFFABLE

An Anthropology of Wisdom

Capturing the Ineffable

An Anthropology of Wisdom

EDITED BY PHILIP Y. KAO
AND JOSEPH S. ALTER

UNIVERSITY OF TORONTO PRESS
Toronto Buffalo London

Toronto Buffalo London
utorontopress.com

ISBN 978-1-4875-0313-0 (cloth)
ISBN 978-1-4875-1726-7 (EPUB)
ISBN 978-1-4875-1725-0 (PDF)

Library and Archives Canada Cataloguing in Publication

Title: Capturing the ineffable : an anthropology of wisdom / edited by Philip Y. Kao and Joseph S. Alter.
Names: Kao, Philip, editor. | Alter, Joseph S., editor.
Description: Includes bibliographical references and index.
Identifiers: Canadiana (print) 20200177745 | Canadiana (ebook) 20200177796 | ISBN 9781487503130 (cloth) | ISBN 9781487517267 (EPUB) | ISBN 9781487517250 (PDF)
Subjects: LCSH: Wisdom. | LCSH: Anthropology.
Classification: LCC BD450 .C37 2020 | DDC 301.01 – dc23

Funding for the research project on wisdom and aging and a conference entitled "Capturing the Ineffable: Wisdom in Perspective" provided by the Office of the Provost, University of Pittsburgh.

University of Toronto Press acknowledges the financial assistance to its publishing program of the Canada Council for the Arts and the Ontario Arts Council, an agency of the Government of Ontario.

Canada Council for the Arts
Conseil des Arts du Canada

Funded by the Government of Canada
Financé par le gouvernement du Canada
Canada

Contents

Acknowledgments vii

Introduction: Towards an Anthropology of Wisdom 3
PHILIP Y. KAO

Part One: Seeking Wisdom

1 Revelations of Delusion: Becoming Isomorphic to the Urgrund with Philip K. Dick 27
RICHARD DOYLE

2 The Social Life of the Inexpressible: English Benedictine Mysticism, the Ineffable, and the Sublime 45
RICHARD D.G. IRVINE

Part Two: Discerning Wisdom

3 How Wisdom Is Discovered: Discretion and Emotional Insights in Naikan Meditation in Japan 67
CLARK CHILSON

4 Navigating Wisdom and Time: Reflections on Aging and Eldercare 82
PHILIP Y. KAO

Part Three: Transmitting Wisdom

5 Yoga and Wisdom: Reflections on the Body at the Intersection of Epistemology and Ontology 103
JOSEPH S. ALTER

6 Social Construction of Wisdom in Institutions 122
CHARLOTTE LINDE

Part Four: Narrating Wisdom

7 Of Uncertainty, Sophiology, and Governance: Zen and the Art of Scenario Planning 155
JAMES D. FAUBION

8 Grappling with the Ineffable in Three African Situations: An Ethnographic Approach 179
WIM M.J. VAN BINSBERGEN

Contributors 243

Index 247

Acknowledgments

An intellectual project such as the anthropology of wisdom would never be possible without a community of dedicated scholars and university press publishers who remain faithful to the adage that knowledge is not (only) "the filling of a pail, but the lighting of a fire." We would first like to thank the University of Pittsburgh's Anthropology Department for its support, giving this project both an intellectual and institutional home. The project began as an international workshop-style conference entitled "Capturing the Ineffable: Wisdom in Perspective" at the University of Pittsburgh. Over the course of two days, many ideas captured the imagination of participants and attendees. The conference would not have been possible without the vision and support of the University of Pittsburgh's Office of the Provost and Office of Research. Special thanks on this front goes to George Klinzing, who first raised the question of wisdom's cultural construction as a major research initiative. The University of Pittsburgh's Humanities Center was also a vital supporter and sponsor of the conference's keynote lecture by Veena Das. Special thanks goes out to Howard C. Nusbaum, Jean Bulware, and Brenda Huskey at the Center for Practical Wisdom at the University of Chicago for their academic and conference support. Last, but certainly not least and just as essential, we would like to thank the University of Pittsburgh's Honors College and the Asian Studies Center. The editors would like to thank the following conference participants: Susan Andrade, Clark Chilson, Steven Collins, Thomas Csordas, Veena Das, Richard M. Doyle, Paul Eiss, James D. Faubion, Richard D.G. Irvine, Charlotte Linde, Michael Puett, and Wim M.J. van Binsbergen. Andrea Agas, Erin Baschwitz, Emily Lynn Holland, Dongbo Qiu, Leah Siegel, and Kailey Ziemianski were enthusiastic college students from Philip Kao's Anthropology of Wisdom and Aging class who presented insightful research posters on wisdom during the conference.

The book's index was prepared by Mike Hurley, and the editors are grateful for his work and addition. Douglas Hildebrand was an early admirer of the project, and it was his encouragement that paved the way for our work with the University of Toronto Press. Our publishing team at the University of Toronto Press, including our constant champion and editor, Jodi Lewchuck, is one of the reasons this book has been published. Thank you. Janice Evans and Carolyn Zapf have also been a tremendous help in getting the book polished to its final form. Carolyn's meticulous and thoughtful edits have helped to improve the overall quality of this volume.

CAPTURING THE INEFFABLE

An Anthropology of Wisdom

Introduction: Towards an Anthropology of Wisdom

PHILIP Y. KAO

Wisdom is peculiarly abstract, ineffable, and yet perennial. It is also temporal, stretching forward as well as backward in time. As a cornerstone of Western philosophy, it is human and humanistic – after all, "homo sapiens" means "man the wise." In a written entry about the experience of wisdom and learning across the lifespan, we are directed to the following etymology: "The word wisdom in Old English, Greek, and German languages can be traced back to the Indo-European word, wede, which means 'to see' or 'to know'" (Ainsworth, Bluck, and Glück 2012: 1207). Whether we have grown too clever for our own good or we are still determined to claim the coveted accolade of wisest in the animal kingdom, wisdom is a significant part of the human story. Wisdom is associated with the outcome of life experience, self-reflection, discipline, conation, sound decision-making, and equanimity. In addition to these traits and appraisals of wisdom, researchers have been asking important questions: What constitutes wisdom for a person in a given place and time? Can wisdom be learned or taught? What are the pathways to wisdom? Wisdom is also considered contagious. "Throughout history," Siegel and Germer (2012: 33) point out, "people have sought contact with great teachers and sages for precisely this reason. And many wise figures point to the tutelage of their mentors as important developmental influences." Some researchers have also proposed (even half-heartedly) that wisdom can be found in particular parts of the body. According to Meeks and Jeste (2009), specific areas of the brain are active during behaviours associated with wisdom, including pro-social attitudes, emotional homeostasis, tolerance, and the like. The studies conducted by researcher Igor Grossman also explore this theory. His experiments look for indications of wise reasoning (for example, recognizing one's limits, having the ability to take on another's perspective, and so on) in the context of higher heart rate variability when participants were instructed to take a self-distanced perspective (Grossman, Sahdra, and Ciarrochi 2016). Other seekers of wisdom have travelled to our enteric systems, postulating that the stomach may be a kind of wise eye, given its deep connection to the nervous system (see Gershon 1999). Fleeing from this terra incognito does not mean we have to surrender to wisdom literature or rely solely on philologists to hand us our gnomic revelations (see Kaufmann 1996). Psychologists conducting wisdom research are making progress in locating the processes involved in wisdom recognition and attainment beyond simple mind-body frameworks. In fact, what if wisdom were actually a product of sociocultural contexts and factors?

The University of Chicago's Center for Practical Wisdom is a recent example of a group of interdisciplinary scholars studying wisdom critically in order to refine the contours of our moral and cultural systems. They strive to shed light on how forms of wisdom shape our institutions and attitudes, and facilitate human flourishing. In order to learn more about the mind, how humans change and adapt, and how practical reason is sourced throughout the life course, wisdom is frequently brought down to the level of the person, to the praxis of living and discernment. Although something in this approach harkens back to Aristotle's phronesis and the pragmatic, wisdom continues to resonate beyond the individual. It is once again a worthy topic, being given serious rethinking in relation to human evolution, metacognition, and structures of affect shaping the mundane and the metaphysical, as well as the epistemological role of emotions. According to the philosopher Nicholas Rescher (1990), proverbial wisdom and its ubiquitous nature shows (for the layman at least) that wisdom is indelible and penetrates where theorists cannot gain entry.

Psychologists "divining" wisdom have approached a variety of fronts.[1] Some have underscored that wisdom is related to cognition, and, as such, it interacts and unfolds throughout human development. Psychologists have naturally gravitated towards wisdom as a marker for desired capacities and strategies for living better lives, especially in the context of the modern era. Wisdom recommends a way to be able to understand and cultivate self-reflection, evaluate life's decisions and choices, plan and manage life, and affect useful perspectives. Some psychologists argue that wisdom can be (and has been since antiquity) celebrated as a personal good, meaning that "we need wisdom to get pleasure from health, satisfaction from fame, and good use out of wealth" (Csikszentmihalyi and Rathunde 1990: 36). Furthermore, and drawing from Carl Jung and Eric Erikson, Juan Pascual-Leone (1990) contends that wisdom can be regarded as a positive achievement in the course of an individual's growth. He goes on to say that wisdom "is the *category* that describes the moment (*state* or stage) in development when the psychological system becomes fully coordinated across experiential contexts and across alternative forms/modes of processing" (245). Needless to say, I am not attempting to provide an exhaustive summary or even a tip-of-the-iceberg treatment of how wisdom has been and is being studied by psychologists. What I want to highlight for purposes of distinction is that wisdom for many psychologists is bound up with knowledge systems. Of course, it is not what people know, but how they use specific knowledge (while maintaining a healthy amount of doubt) that renders wisdom discernable. Knowledge formulated in this highly functional way can be useful as a system in the "fundamental pragmatics of life" (Baltes and Smith 1990) when it is geared towards conducting better lives and knowing the causes (and consequences) of the human condition.

More recently, wisdom has been understood to consist of particular metacognitive functions such as wise emotions. According to Nancy Sherman (2000), emotions play a significant role in the context of Aristotelian practical wisdom. Emotions are intentional states with which we can communicate and navigate. "The Aristotelian view of emotions as intentional not only is inherently more plausible," she explains, "but gives a more natural account of how emotions track salience" (329). For a healthy and full psyche, Sherman would have us consider both wise choices and wise emotions. Warren Brown (2000a; 2000b) adds that, "with respect to wisdom, the emphasis here will not be on knowledge and understanding, but on the contribution of emotional responses to the ability to regulate one's behavior – *wisdom as performance*" (2000b: 197).

Turning now to a systems view, Jonas Salk (1973) in *The Survival of the Wisest* famously argues for the importance of cooperation, consciousness, improved design systems, and nurturing wisdom in order to comprehend the interactive and technological ways humans shape their ecologies and vice versa. His son, Peter Salk, sees wisdom playing a role in larger systems.[2] How can we enact sustainable lives that are good for humans as well as for the planet? If we are to get ahead of the curve and leap to the more advanced stage of evolution, a period Jonas Salk calls Epoch B, a change in emphasis has to occur. Instead of self-interest and competition as motivating themes rooted in Epoch A, an inflection point has to be dealt with, launching us into Epoch B with its emphasis on cooperation, consciousness, and design systems that interact with the human nervous system, mutualism, and wisdom.[3]

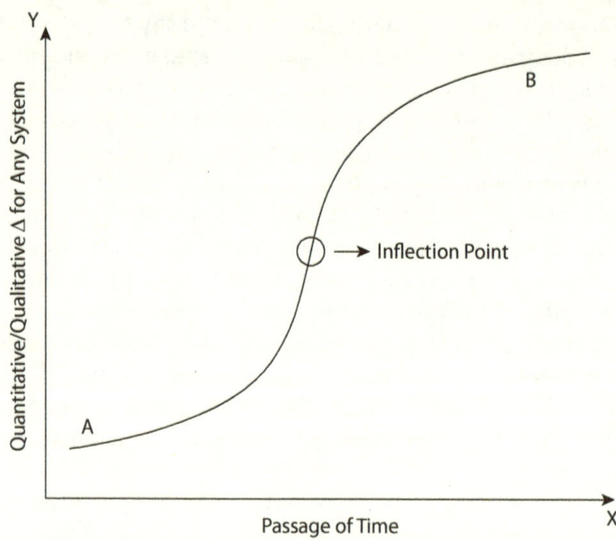

Figure 0.1 Jonas Salk's Human Values and World Population. (Adapted from Salk 2017)

Reframing/revaluing our notions of time and the life course may also require and bring about wisdom. In figure 0.1, we see how normalizations of the human lifespan frame particular structural problems. At stake is the future: creating and executing better policies that make room for empathy in a global world and ending Epoch A practices such as ageism is an evolutionary, a systemic, and, ultimately, a "design" problem.

Anthropologists have also been interested and enraptured by human wisdom in all its cultural forms. I turn now to revisit three ethnographic analyses of wisdom to illustrate how wisdom has been studied and contextualized ethnographically. Although wisdom was not something he was even thinking about during the initial phase of his fieldwork, Keith Basso (1996) was led to the topic of wisdom by way of his informants. He was invited to help make Apache maps, non-white maps, that could help the Apache nation articulate and preserve (cartographically and legalistically) what it was that made Apache cultural ecology resonant and worthy of protection for posterity.

For the Apache, places in the central eastern part of Arizona, home to mountains, deserts, canyons, and creeks, play an important part in their myth and history. Even more, places are alive and take on moral didactic dimensions, which intervene in the everyday discourse of life in and around the reservation. Particular places, like a bend in the river, a pathway flirting with the sunrays in a canyon, or a formidable tree are not just backdrops to ancestral stories but are also places that were named because of particular incidents that occurred there in the past. Take, for example, Old Man Owl. Because of his drunkenness and sexual exploits, he became ostracized and ridiculed. In one story, Old Man Owl was tricked by two girls and left in a compromising position at "Trail Goes Down Between Two Hills." This name is important, because it becomes not only a reference point but also a performative utterance – a forceful and moral speech act with particular lessons.

Basso recounts how he was meeting two cowboys when a third and slightly younger one showed up to work with them. The third cowboy was losing respect in the community. He was becoming unreliable on the job and sullying more than just his reputation. He was drinking too much and never showing up for anything. The other cowboys began to talk among themselves in a particular gnomic register, but only in reference to specific Apache place names. When "Trails Goes Down Between Two Hills" came up, the young drunkard admitted that he was like Old Man Owl, unable to see clearly. He claimed that he was ready to work and had come to his senses.

Basso points out that the older cowboy's greeting to the young man – "'So! You've returned from Trail Goes Down Between Two Hills!' – was intended to focus the young man's attention on the place where Old Man Owl encountered the two Apache sisters and to summon thoughts of what transpired there." According to Basso, by "announcing that [the young cowboy] had *returned* from Trail Goes Down Between Two Hills," the older cowboy also "affirmed [the young man's] decision to refrain from drinking and resume a normal life." The older cowboys were criticizing, in a circuitous and tactful way, the young man's "misguided behavior and at the same time commending him for rejecting it as unacceptable" (Basso 1996: 118–19).

Place names are not fixed, but can be conjured up, played with, and manipulated to give alternative meanings and suggestions depending on the audience and situation. These place names for the Apache stand in the community as a visible embodiment of myth, a monument and domain of Apache wisdom. Speaking in names not only makes reference to landscapes and their associated fables and stories but also activates a place-world where moral conduct and sociality descend on people by way of speaking in names and stalking with stories. It is because of this activation that Basso titles his ethnography "Wisdom Sits in Places."

Let us briefly return to the Apache. In this case study, we saw how wisdom was transmitted not simply via language but also through a series of connections to networks of images, stories, and representations. Rather than arrive at wisdom through sentential logic, picture worlds and place names "affect" the Apache person. The work of Dan Sperber helps us to understand this process at work. Sperber (1985) sees "the casual explanation of cultural facts as necessarily embedded in a kind of epidemiology of representations" (74). In this way, place names endure like dead metaphors (abstract ideas), which continue to preserve. But where do they exist exactly? Is culture out there in people's dress or in their heads? Sperber asks us: Where is Beethoven's ninth symphony exactly? Or Little Red Riding Hood? Furthermore, he points out: "What pathology is to the epidemiology of diseases, psychology of thought should be to the epidemiology of representations" (75). Wisdom might be grasped here as a set of meta-representations that expand knowledge and draw from a conceptual repertoire of mental and public processes.[4]

Anthropologist Graham Townsley (1993), in a research piece entitled "Song Paths," talks about the ways and means of shamanic knowledge among the Yaminahua of southeastern Peru. The Yaminahua conceive of the world as animated by *yoshi*, an animate essence. Although this essence can lead to danger because of its mystery, all things in the world – humans, trees, insects – are animated by *yoshi*. *Yoshi* cannot be thought of as simply a life force; rather, *yoshi* are forces onto themselves. They wander; they cause death when they leave the human body and travel to the land of the dead. According to Townsley, shamanic knowledge is, above all else, knowledge about *yoshi* and how they cause illness and are implicated in the life course of humans. The shaman's job is to convene and broker between the Yaminahua world and the non-Indigenous world of Western capitalism by communicating with and tapping into the powers of *yoshi*. If we adopt the shaman's point of view instead of analysing things from the perspective of the symbolic structure, it becomes apparent that shamans bring forth a kind of ethno-epistemology. One can then identify the wisdom of the shaman as ways of knowing – the ideas of knowing – rather than the system of things to know.

Things become a bit more complicated, however, because *yoshi* reside both in this world and beyond. Shamanic knowledge has to grapple with how *yoshi* interact with things in this world; hence, getting to know something – for example, the strength and nature of *yoshi* in a jaguar – draws from a fine-tuned empiricism. In this world, *yoshi* and things are mutable/transformational. There are no fixed constructions. Shamans must commune with *yoshi* by eliciting them like a hunter in a forest, using paths, interpreting clues, and reading signs. Dreams are the shaman's portals, and the songs a shaman sings during a healing session while smoking hallucinogenic ayahuasca plants are paths for drawing out *yoshi*. Like the hunter who mimics the sound of a peccary in order to locate prey by following their answering sounds, the shaman sings with metaphors and in onomatopoeia. Townsley interviewed a shaman who explained: "My songs are paths. Some take me a short way – some take me a long way – I make them straight and I walk down them – I look about me as I go – not a thing escapes my notice – I call – but I stay on the path." (Townsley 1993: 454).

By calling upon his own *yoshi*, the shaman sings a path for engaging the body and its perception in a way to "stimulate and clarify the visions of the *yoshi* from which knowledge can be gained" (Townsley 1993: 458). According to Townsley, shamans "are adamant that the songs are not ultimately created or owned by them at all, but by the *yoshi* themselves, who 'show' or 'give' their songs, with their attendant powers, to those shamans good enough to 'receive' them [and to direct them subsequently to their patients]" (458). By singing and calling to things as metaphors, the shaman creates a powerful space where visionary experiences can occur. The meeting between the human and spirit world in song drag the refractory meanings and images of the *yoshi* into this world. The person seeking a cure from the shaman does not even need to understand the metaphors, mumblings, and circumlocution of the song. Only when the naming of the patient's body is made do the images from the song crash into it, affecting a change not only in the nature of the illness but also in the relationship between the person and his or her *yoshi*.

Although shamanic knowledge might appear opaque, it is fundamentally more than just cognitive. There are networks of paths and a sensitivity to *yoshi*. If there is any efficacy to be had, the wisdom of the shaman has to transcend the body, tapping into the spirits both in and beyond the immediate Yaminahua world. Wisdom here is thus not about knowing the right things, but about complex techniques for constructing ways of knowing and operationalizing this transcendence in the context of traditional healing.

The example of the shaman brings us towards an appreciation for a cybernetic sense of wisdom following Gregory Bateson. For Bateson, love, the mind, and wisdom are more than concepts; they are commitments to the world that cannot be arrived at by conventional scientific methods. For example, to think of a person mowing the lawn as a set of networked systems between the human, the grass, the engine of the lawnmower, the decomposition of the grass blade, and the soil unites the individual with the greater world as a living, thinking life-mind. Regarding the relation between the horse and the grassy plains, Bateson claims that, if we want to have a lawn in the suburbs, we must first buy a mower, which is the teeth of the horse. Then we purchase a roller to make turf. Finally, we need manure, because after all, there is the other end of the horse to account for (Bateson 1991: 276)!

Because mind is not something in the brain but rather an interlocked network of ideas spanning the entire universe, we can appreciate what is meant by an ecology of the mind, as well as conceive of animals and our very own anatomy as a system of ideas. The upshot is that we are now dealing with the evolution of ideas and relations, and not physical bounded objects. Acknowledgment of this circuitry, the ability to see the larger interactive system or the mind as ecology, enables art and beauty in nature to reveal itself to the wise person. For Bateson, "wisdom … [is] the knowledge of the larger interactive system," whereas "lack of systemic wisdom is always punished" (Bateson 1972b: 433–4). Furthermore, "when human beings, participating in larger systems of mind that do not stop at the boundaries of skin and sense receptors, know themselves as a part of mind rather than as individuals, they have arrived at wisdom. Equally, however, one might say that the system of which they are a part has arrived at wisdom: Human consciousness is potentially the organ of self-knowledge for the entire eco-system" (quoted in Brockman 1977: 70).

Even the shaman does not "tune out" his consciousness in order for the unconscious material of the dreams and *yoshi* to flow. The shaman reactivates the circuitry between the human and the spiritual world. "Wisdom is the conclusion to a many-layered process of cognition at all levels of mind, and this is why the traditional spiritual ways are marked so often by paradox, the experience of dissonance between levels, which must be transcended" (Brockman 1977: 69). There is also the role of imagination and ritual, especially regarding the subjunctive (Puett 2008). Rather than viewing ritual as a cognitive process that accounts for innovation and change while forming social relationships, we see in our Amerindian example of the Yaminahua shamans that there is a wisdom to negotiating the animist worldview. Humans, animals, and objects, despite their skins, share *yoshi* and soul stuff and are capable of transforming into other forms. Is not this theory of perspectivism the essence of the ecological mind? It is both about life, about shaping life projects, and about the formation of the spiritual.

In her ethnographic monograph *Dancing Wisdom: Embodied Knowledge in Haitian Vodou, Cuban Yoruba, and Bahian Candomblé*, Yvonne

Daniel (2005) focuses on dance behaviour in the context of African diasporic religious systems. Her analysis links dance movement to spiritual development in various sociocultural contexts. For worshippers of Cuban Yoruba, for example, music and the expression of spirit mediums through bodies during dance contain, symbolize, and emit many levels of meaning. Dance rituals, which emerge in social settings, reverberate across domains, creating religious, social, and cosmological harmony. For Daniel, these festive dance performances, which arouse concentric rings of performers and attendees, bring about social cohesion. She says: "Ritual performances are filled with what I call 'social medicine': power, authority, and community relations are affected, rearranged, or affirmed; social wounds are healed" (55). For the enslaved in the diaspora, "intellectual knowledge without concomitant integration of somatic intuitive understanding and the spiritual wisdom their combination yields is 'disembodied knowledge'" (57). The worshipping performers re-enact what they learned from the past, emulating the attributes of various deities through signature dance moves and poses. By carving out a sacred space and time for these performances, worshippers invoke the deities to give wisdom, moral instruction, and advice to the collective in the same way as the song chants are used to activate medicinal qualities of specific plants. The way people dance to invoke the attention and presence of deities amounts to a form of embodied physiology. Specific song chants used with particular medicinal plants denotes an embodied botany. Daniel therefore comments: "Praise performance practices have guarded embodied knowledges for centuries" (93).

A certain kind of poise and a moral way of being in the world is brought forth, underscored by the ritual community and its performances. In this way, "the social body experiences the remembered patterns that constitute a balance of each interfacing realm of knowledge and integrates those experiences into daily routine and critical situations" (Daniel 2005: 252–3). Here is the ritual power of dance: to activate wisdom. The wisdom instructs the present by making the social body sense, smell, taste, and feel the embodied knowledge all around; the body thus avails itself to various remedies. In this case study, wisdom is not trapped in ancient texts or somewhere in the spirit world, only to be unleashed. The embodied knowledge practices of the sacred chant, the healing herbs, the talking drums, and the dance are collectively sources of wisdom. How one engages with wisdom is not always an individualistic endeavour, but one with social consequences. For Daniel, the end of her research journey led her to a recognition: "I have acquired more assuredness and calm, and over time I have also connected with a powerful sense of cultural integrity, in the same ways that I have witnessed some ritual performers grow. When performers gain an acute sense of individual and community awareness, they behave with social responsibility" (270).

German scholar Aleida Assmann (1994) once remarked that wisdom flourishes between total order and total contingency. Wisdom can therefore be found in many ritual contexts. The practice of wisdom contains a transaction, seen particularly in the three case studies previously discussed. What is being dealt with is a worldview, a system of meaningful relations in the cybernetic sense. To locate the emplacement of wisdom, we ask ourselves: Where exactly is wisdom? Is it in culture, in our heads, in our bodies, in public representations? The danger in showing these cultural accounts is the implication that wisdom is something fixed and universal, and that all cultural anthropologists have to do is to comb the earth for wisdom's different ornamentations and expressions. These cautionary words are not meant to pander to cultural relativism, nor to take anything away from the search for "wisdom" across human societies and history (see also Curnow 2010; Katz 1999; Maybury-Lewis 1992; McConchie 2003; Radin 1957). Rather, they show the importance of recognizing that wisdom is constituted by differing ideas of the world and of the person, which can be very different from conventional understandings arising from Western cognitive science. For Maurice Bloch, the clash of ideas between cultural determinists and universalists persists ad nauseam. According to Bloch, "the universalists criticise the culturalists by stressing the general aspects of such things as human cognitive development but then normally only pay lip service to the very difficult questions that cultural and historical variation pose for them" (2011: n.p.). The self is not one thing or the other, but a continuum. By locating wisdom along this continuum, we learn much from how wisdom is constituted and operationalized – not lodged in some kind of self-narrative about brainhood. The question of whether there are any gendered aspects of wisdom is also important. Carolyn Aldwin (2009) argues that her team's working model of wisdom, which integrates facets such as self-knowledge, nonattachment, and compassion, is a developmental process. She argues from her research findings that "an integrated approach to wisdom [is] truly androgynous, although men and women may focus on different aspects of personal experience during which wisdom is developed" (1). For Aldwin, pathways to wisdom may, however, be different for men and women in different contexts. Meanwhile, Michael Levenson (2009) argues that "using the construct of compassion as a vehicle for the integration of wisdom and ethics obviates any gender-related differences in wisdom" (45). Because wisdom is a complex construct, looking for "feminine" and "masculine" reasoning perpetuates false dichotomies.

This volume argues for wisdom as a heuristic beyond the post-cultural and post-postmodern terrain of discourse, pointing a way to a philosophical anthropology, which (1) explores the fundamental human questions regarding existence and what is outside and beyond the human in anthropological studies of people and their cultural domains; (2) makes room for noetic visions of the whole (of reality/nature), including a theory of anthropology as a humanistic value proposition and exercise; and (3) describes how genealogies and forms of wisdom lead to particular social and political processes.

What has been missing, however, is not only a rigorous analysis of the sociocultural context and its role in shaping the forms of wisdom that obtain throughout human history, but also an explanation of how wisdom transcends and integrates the various divisions of our knowledge systems, categories, and ways of experiencing the world and others. This volume shows how the conception and paradoxical nature of wisdom dispels the dichotomies of self/other, structure/agency, known/unknown, nature/culture, and the like. What is at stake is a recasting of wisdom as a particular kind of anthropological endeavour and, thus, a return to and modification of philosophical anthropology. The task is not easy; short of announcing a Vichian *Scienza Nuova* (Vico 2002) or drowning oneself in what Vivian Clayton, a psychologist and pioneer of wisdom studies, calls the "Milky Way of wisdom" (quoted in Hall 2007), this edited volume rubs wisdom and anthropology together to generate new capacities and meanings that are not simply reiterations of conformist wisdom/ideologies that Slavoj Žižek (2014) so rightfully detests.[5] Rather than reproduce the discursive colonization associated with patronizing primitive society and their folk wisdom, the chapters in this book render wisdom analytically and ethnographically as grounded in what can be described overall as a practice in contemporary philosophical anthropology.

Volume Breakdown

To begin capturing wisdom, one must examine the experiences from which it emerges and the persons, places, and sites to which those experiences give rise. This book provides these ethnographically grounded instances of wisdom. Any chapter can be read alongside any other, providing the reader with a series of productive comparisons. There are many overlaps and threads between the chapters, and we encourage readers to carve out their own hermeneutic journey through the text.

Nonetheless, the present volume is divided into four sections in order to provide a suggested roadmap for navigating the various case studies and issues relating to wisdom and the ineffable. This grouping also reflects and highlights particular analytical and methodological concerns. The first section, "Seeking Wisdom," launches into a conceptual exploration of wisdom and its relationship to the ineffable. It demonstrates that what we do with this knowledge leads to a radical deconstruction of our engagement with (social) reality and metaphysics.

Starting with Richard Doyle's chapter, "Revelations of Delusion: Becoming Isomorphic to the Urgrund with Philip K. Dick," wisdom is decoupled from a consciousness of the self, not as a hallucination to transcend in order to experience something unified in the true reality of things but as a revelation that the Urgrund (that is, the "underlining ground of reality," a concept coined by the German philosopher and Christian mystic Jakob Böhme) shapes our reality in a projection for its own self-learning. Doyle explains: "What is revealed, in wisdom, is not the world but the Urgrund itself." He turns to Philip K. Dick's tome, *The Exegesis*, in order to analyse how a mystical experience in 1974 led to the production of this massive text, which can be understood as a revelation in wisdom. Doyle says that the purpose of his chapter is to "contextualize and focus on the treatment of the word 'wisdom' in this condensed tractate of *The Exegesis*, a gateway to our own practice of exegesis, the deconstruction of the 'I' in a flurry of Phil Dickian wisdom." In this way, the exegesis in *The Exegesis* is a projection, an artifact itself that has to be exposed through a series of negations and dialectics, evincing revelations of delusions.[6]

Richard D.G. Irvine's "The Social Life of the Inexpressible: English Benedictine Mysticism, the Ineffable, and the Sublime" investigates ethnographically how silence is produced, socialized, and present in the context of a Catholic monastery. By showing how silence structures particular religious and community practices and rituals, Irvine shows that silence is not as simple as a restriction or a required condition for experiencing the sacred. Instead, Irvine shows that wisdom can still be invoked even though speaking about it is prohibited. In such silent traditions of contemplation, Irvine argues that "the centrality of silence, it seems, points very directly towards the confrontation with vastness." Irvine grounds this experience or, rather, practice of the sublime as a shared experience, demonstrating that the ineffable, even if it cannot be talked about (or around), is located socially and "visible as negative space within the routine of social life."

The next section, "Discerning Wisdom," focuses on two case studies detailing how certain spaces and cultural practices produce momentary instances of and appeals for wisdom. These practices suggest that wisdom is not an ideology but instead is tied to particular sequences and interactions involving introspection and even emotions. Clark Chilson's chapter, "How Wisdom Is Discovered: Discretion and Emotional Insights in Naikan Meditation in Japan," discusses the history and current-day Japanese practice of Naikan, a form of meditation involving self-reflection. We learn from Chilson that physicians in the 1960s started to use Naikan as a psychotherapeutic method to treat people with such conditions as alcoholism. By explaining how the *naikansha* (people practising Naikan) undergo their sessions and outlining the routines and questions they have to meditate on, Chilson is then able to argue that the concept of *chie* is similar in some ways to the Western concept of wisdom, but also differs. Coming to terms with *chie* is necessary for the *naikansha* to discern right from wrong behaviour and is also linked to emotional intelligence. For Chilson, "wisdom, which has discretion as a core characteristic, is thus prosocial and requires understanding social relations."

Philip Kao's "Navigating Wisdom and Time: Reflections on Aging and Eldercare" investigates how residents and staff in a long-term care facility wrestle with issues of care, aging, and personhood. Within this context, wisdom is taken to be knowledge about what to do in an unforeseen circumstance and, more generally, how to act and even age "properly." In this hyper-regulatory and rule-bound long-term care community, codifying phronesis runs into a series of devastating results. Kao shows how the conventional thinking on aging and wisdom reproduces inflexible and unwise instances of caregiving. According to Kao, what is needed is a re-evaluation of practical wisdom, one that can take on the abstract as well as complex notions of life and the phenomenological. In the end, Kao suggests that wisdom cannot be made into a set of procedures, but rather emerges once people begin to discern how differing experiences of time constitute personhood and well-being.

The third section, "Transmitting Wisdom," deals with particular exemplars of wisdom and investigates how wise persons in various institutions and traditions come to be associated with particular attributes. Additionally, this section uncovers how and to what degree wisdom is transmitted. Joseph S. Alter's piece, "Yoga and Wisdom: Reflections on the Body at the Intersection of Epistemology and Ontology," dives straight into the issue of language and its role in the formation and politics of knowledge. His concern is with the problematic nature of language in relation to the embodiment of wisdom. Notwithstanding a representational and somewhat Wittgensteinian view of language, how can one even claim to articulate and control the transmission of certain kinds of embodied wisdom that defy normative facts and reality on the ground – so to speak. The solution to this seeming impasse is the discovery that, because language is "irreducible to anything other than semiotics," yoga gurus oscillate between and take advantage of the inherent slippage between epistemology and ontology in order to deliver on their construction and education of wisdom.

Meanwhile, Charlotte Linde takes another approach. In her chapter, entitled "Social Construction of Wisdom in Institutions," Linde analyses wisdom not as an inherent quality of particular charismatic persons or institutional founders/leaders but, rather, as the result of relations – underscored by particular narratives between individuals and institutions. She explores three ethnographic sites: a major American insurance company, a Buddhist meditation centre, and Silicon Valley. By detailing the production of exemplars (that is, wise persons) in these domains, Linde is able to assess the narrative strategies underlining various constructions of wisdom and show what these instantiations of wisdom are really about. In Caroline Humphrey's (1997) classic account of exemplars and rules in the Mongolian moral universe, people choose from a stock of adages and examples. These exemplars are unique to each person and their life circumstances. In this way, wishing to find direction in a difficult situation and to become a better and wiser person is "understood as evidence for a sense of self as a fundamental form of thought and action" (38). In contrast to this ethnographic case, one of Linde's interesting discoveries "has been finding commonalities across domains in the social structures that produce exemplars – something that groups and institutions do as part of the ways they maintain themselves."

The fourth and final section, "Narrating Wisdom," focuses on the conditions of narrating and interweaving wisdoms across various boundaries, cultures, and paradigms. In James D. Faubion's piece, "Of Uncertainty, Sophiology, and Governance: Zen and the Art of Scenario Planning," the author looks to the history and industry of corporate scenario planning as an instance of wisdom practice. He calls upon the work of Carlo Ginzburg to show how the evidential paradigm, the "generative matrix of modern historiographical research," provides an opportunity to assess the experiential and philosophical aspects of narration.

This bout of intellectual history segues to the work of the French economist and oil executive Pierre Wack. Faubion details the "sophiology" of Wack's corporate scenario planning and argues that it is both an intuitive method as well as a reflexive modernist practice. For example, Wack calls for accepting, understanding, and embedding uncertainty as part of the reasoning in devising future scenario cases. Faubion ends the chapter by introducing an ethnographic case involving a Greek governmental platform called FORESIGHT, which was tasked to construct economic and technological scenarios in order to inform and help European policymakers plan for particular future outcomes. Needless to say, specific scenarios were narrated in particular ways, and not all of them were accepted, especially the ones that got it right about the Greek government's debt crisis in the aftermath of the 2007–8 global financial crisis. All in all, Faubion's synthetic perspective provides a unique and somewhat cynical take on the near impossibility of registering wisdom, especially when solutions to wicked problems depend not only on subjective evaluations of credibility and evidence but also on the nature of constructing alternative models and judgments (see also Kitchener and Brenner 1990).

The issue of whether or not society is able to listen to wise narrations regarding the need to stop our continued destruction of the environment and violence against one another carries forward into the last chapter. Wim M.J. van Binsbergen's compelling contribution, "Grappling with the Ineffable in Three African Situations: An Ethnographic Approach," threads many of the major themes already discussed in this volume, including the distorting limitations of language and the fundamental ineffability of many of the important aspects of the human experience.

Van Binsbergen reconsiders three of his prior fieldwork engagements in Africa, including his research in the Ḫumiriyya region of North West Tunisia; his work with the Nkoya of South Central Africa; and his experience with *sangoma* healing in North East Botswana. He uses these three vignettes to deconstruct *etic* notions of wisdom, arguing that wisdom articulates itself in different ways that can only be understood in context. If wisdom is bound to the ineffable and occurs, in the case of the Nkoya, only by investigating kinship as a boundary condition, then what is the role of the ethnographer? Van Binsbergen offers some ways forward, suggesting that truth as justified beliefs is not statically and inevitably tied to cultural truth enclaves. Consequently, ethnographers can do more than just speak to peripheral wisdoms; they can engage in elucidating the larger global history of wisdoms in a network of intercultural epistemologies that may bring about greater cultural awareness, acceptance, and understanding.

Conclusion

I have been arguing for an anthropological conception of wisdom that is more than just folk conceptions of cultural models associating wisdom with some kind of advanced stage of schematic integration and thinking. This introduction has shown that wisdom resides beyond the discourse of positive psychology and individuals. Moreover, there is not a clear-cut evolutionary narrative to describe wisdom as a third order system of checks and balances against deterministic explanations of biological behaviour and culture as self-relinquishment. Nor is wisdom abstract; there might very well be feedback mechanisms associated with various kinds and practices of wisdom. Jeffrey Schloss's (2000) integrative approach provides food for thought in moving us beyond a static conception of wisdom as a kind of ideological straightjacket. For Schloss, wisdom can even be seen in the context of our organism's evolution. Leaving aside for now the contemporary debates surrounding adaptive explanations, sociobiology, and epigenetics, what is interesting here is Schloss's usage of Henry Plotkin's heuristics to situate wisdom as a top-down evaluative filtering of tertiary level innovations (that is, culture).

Heuristics are "a means of devising and testing novel adaptations, of 'discovering' new ways of fitting to the environment" (Schloss 2000: 163). According to the hierarchy of heuristics, secondary heuristics (the ability of organisms to learn and adapt, including the role of the immune system) make up any shortcomings at the level of primary heuristics, which is wrapped up in how life at the basic level works by encoding/testing information at the genetic level. Culture presents a tertiary heuristic that can be quicker to adapt to a changing environment, but, since "it is at least partially uncoupled from the biological heuristic, there is no guarantee that cultural innovations will be adaptive or even hospitable to our biological functioning" (165) – or so goes the narrative. If cultural models are understood as made up of culturally derived ideas and practices that are embodied, enacted, and instituted in everyday life, how do these models ever get learned and changed in the first place? What is their relation to the domains and degrees of wisdom in human society? I am weary of the deterministic nature of taking cultural models and habitus too far; they may be used to represent ideas and relations, or even to reason with, but there is still something more complex at work than the mechanistic explanation of how schemas organize the world for us. Wisdom is much more than a mastery of various cognitive tools. One way out could be to consider wisdom as a quaternary heuristic, and, indeed, this solution is what

Schloss offers. He points the way towards an explanation: "Yet a control device for cultural inputs would seem to require a human capacity to transcend it evaluatively ... [Wisdom] is a quaternary heuristic that is both contained within and partly free to transcend – even oppose – the cultural heuristic. This capability is perhaps reflected in the Pauline exhortation to 'be not conformed to this world, but be transformed from within by the renewing of your minds'" (166).

If there is anything universal to human wisdom, perhaps it is in our ability to exercise self-judgment in order to regain our footing in the world. It varies with different conceptions of personhood and with what is at stake in our relation to our self through others and beyond. In the end, wondering what exactly is a wisdom-related experience might just lead us to a greater wisdom and its sources. To understand the nature of wisdom is to engage in the most basic but also the most profound aspect of anthropological inquiry, namely, relativism – not only cross-cultural relativism but what might be called the meta-relativism of philosophical skepticism and the requirement of periodic suspensions of belief. To the extent that it is often disembodied, how is wisdom manifest in forms that force a reconceptualization of delimited bodies, human and non-human agents, and the larger distinction between animate and inanimate things? Where is wisdom located in relation to personhood and community, as these domains, and their relationship one to the other, reflect the interplay of mind, self-perception, and social practice? We venture to seek out just where and how wisdom is emplaced, moving from formulations and instantiations of wisdom in (and with) our minds, bodies, institutions, and beyond.

Precisely because it is ineffable, wisdom also begs the question of how it is linked to institutionalized forms of practice that cross the social and cultural spectrum from regimented and prescriptive forms of ritualized orthopraxy (for example, wisdom is sometimes found in dogma) to highly creative, inspired, and ecstatic forms of self-expression. Our aim is to formulate an understanding of wisdom as constructed in experience and to examine the ways in which it shapes (and takes shape in) social practice. What this volume begins to show, and what future studies of wisdom can explore even more systematically, is the performative dimension of wisdom. I am not talking about the encapsulation of wisdom in proverbs and their various usages, readings, and understandings. What is more fruitful, I should think, is how wisdom is brought to life as a result of mechanisms (including the "work" of discourse) defining and commenting about the world. In this vein, wisdom can no longer be an individualized quality belonging to just any one person; it is always co-constructed and can be made playful/useful in a host of contexts. Should all else fail, we need to keep in mind that wisdom is not created, but happens (like in a séance), requiring thus a performative analysis to ascertain the social life and reach of wisdom.

To the extent that wisdom can be understood as a kind of counterpoint to cultural knowledge and cultural systems of meaning, its theorization can provide new approaches into areas that are difficult to grasp within standard frameworks of knowledge, including areas such as "artificial" intelligence, cross-species communication and biosemiotics, ecologies, virtual "social" media, and bioethics, at a time of rapid techno-scientific innovation. Theorizing wisdom is especially relevant in the context of globalization and broad trends in national and international policy that tend to naturalize instrumental reasoning and schematic empiricism in characterizations of human difference, movement, and interaction. Moreover, societies around the world continue to acknowledge (and even produce) wisdom as a means and an end vis-à-vis context-specific values and goals.

NOTES

1 Readers interested in learning more about the breadth of wisdom studies in psychology and human development can consult sources such as Robert J. Strenberg's (1990) edited volume *Wisdom: Its Nature, Origins, and Development* – especially for its historical perspective.

2 Peter Salk, personal communication with the author, December 2015 at the 2015 Jonas Salk Symposium on Wisdom and Aging.

3 "In Epoch A, resources seem limitless. Unrestricted growth, expansion, and exploitation of both natural and human resources are rewarded. Values of consumption, excess, independence, and short-range thinking are most beneficial. In the different conditions of Epoch B, where resources are limited and growth is slowing, there would be high value placed on conservation/sustainability, balance, interdependence, and long-range thinking" (Salk 2017).

4 Other oral traditions around the world testify to the importance of how wisdom is captured and deployed in various settings. Harald Gaski tells us how Sami poetry beautifully captures nature and our relation to it. But, more than this, folk wisdom is encoded and given birth by a creative use of language. To this point, Sami riddles such as "A bird flies / and blood drips / from its wingtips" stimulates creative thought processes, opening up worlds of interpretation. "Thus part of the point with riddles," Gaski says, "is to allow some time to pass before one gives the answer … [W]e must think of an evening hour with the sun setting and a boat being rowed on the water. When we observe the boat from land it looks like a bird flying

(typically Sami [like] to see the beautiful and poetic in all motion!) and every time the rower takes a new stroke, water drips from the tips of the oars, which against the light looks like drops of blood" (Gaski n.d).

5 E.M. Cioran also rejects wisdom, preferring the passions to a cold sterility. Cioran famously quipped: "The wise man's resignation springs from inner void, not inner fire. I would rather die of fire than of void." (Cioran 1992: 89). Like Žižek, Cioran is more than just skeptical; for him, wisdom is nothing but "a system of capitulations: namely, reserve, abstention, withdrawal not only from the world but from all worlds, a mineral-like serenity, a craving for petrifaction, out of fear both of pleasure and of pain" (Cioran and Brown 1966–7: 547).

6 It is interesting to note a similar approach to wisdom in the work of Gregory Bateson. He recalls that what is required of wisdom "is not simply a relaxation of consciousness to let the unconscious material gush out … My own slight experience of LSD led me to believe that Prospero was wrong when he said, 'We are such stuff as dreams are made on.' It seemed to me that pure dream was, like pure purpose, rather trivial. It was not the stuff of which we are made, but only bits and pieces of that stuff. Our conscious purposes, similarly, are only bits and pieces. The systemic view is something else again" (Bateson 1972a: 438–9).

REFERENCES

Ainsworth, Sarah E., Susan Bluck, and Judith Glück. 2012. "Experiencing Wisdom across the Lifespan." In *Encyclopedia of the Sciences of Learning*, edited by N.M. Seel, 1207–9. Boston, MA: Springer. https://doi.org/10.1007/978-1-4419-1428-6_1767.

Aldwin, Carolyn M. 2009. "Gender and Wisdom: A Brief Overview." *Research in Human Development* 6 (1): 1–8. http://dx.doi.org/10.1080/154276009027793cc47.

Assmann, Aleida. 1994. "Wholesome Knowledge: Concepts of Wisdom in a Historical and Cross-Cultural Perspective." In *Life-Span Development and Behavior*, vol. 12, edited by D.L. Featherman, R.M. Lerner, and M. Perlmutter, 187–224. Hillsdale, NJ: Lawrence Erlbaum.

Baltes, Paul B., and Jacqui Smith. 1990. "Towards a Psychology of Wisdom and Its Ontogenesis." In Sternberg, *Wisdom: Its Nature, Origins, and Development*, 87–120.

Basso, Keith. 1996. *Wisdom Sits in Places: Landscape and Language among the Western Apache*. Albuquerque: University of New Mexico Press.

Bateson, Gregory. 1972a. "Conscious Purpose versus Nature." In Bateson, *Steps to an Ecology of Mind*, 426–39.

– 1972b. *Steps to an Ecology of Mind*. New York: Ballantine Books.

– 1991. *Sacred Unity: Further Steps to an Ecology of the Mind*, edited by R.E. Donaldson. New York: HarperCollins.

Bloch, Maurice. 2011. "The Blob." *Anthropology of This Century* 1. http://aotcpress.com/articles/blob/.

Brockman, John, ed. 1977. *About Bateson: Essays on Gregory Bateson*. Afterword by Gregory Bateson. New York: Dutton.

Brown, Warren S. 2000a. *Understanding Wisdom: Sources, Science, and Society*. Philadelphia, PA: Templeton Press.

– 2000b. "Wisdom and Human Neurocognitive Systems: Perceiving and Practicing the Laws of Life." In Brown, *Understanding Wisdom*, 194–213.

Cioran, E.M. 1992. *On the Heights of Despair*. Translated by Ilinca Zarifopol-Johnston. Chicago: University of Chicago Press.

Cioran, E.M., and Frederick Brown. 1966–7. "The Snares of Wisdom." *The Hudson Review* 19 (4): 539–50.

Csikszentmihalyi, Mihaly, and Kevin Rathunde. 1990. "Psychology of Wisdom: Evolutionary Interpretation." In Sternberg, *Wisdom: Its Nature, Origins, and Development*, 25–51.

Curnow, Trevor. 2010. *Wisdom in the Ancient World*. London: Duckworth.

Daniel, Yvonne. 2005. *Dancing Wisdom: Embodied Knowledge in Haitian Vodou, Cuban Yoruba, and Bahian Candomblé*. Urbana: University of Illinois Press.

Gaski, Harald. n.d. "Folk Wisdom and Orally Transmitted Knowledge – Everyday Poetry in Adages, Rhyme and Riddles." Translated by John Weinstock. Sami Culture (website). Accessed 24 June 2019. http://www.utexas.edu/courses/sami/diehtu/siida/language/folkevisdom.htm.

Gershon, Michael D. 1999. *The Second Brain: A Groundbreaking New Understanding of Nervous Disorders of the Stomach and Intestine*. New York: Harper Perennial.

Grossmann, Igor, Baljinder K. Sahdra, and Joseph Ciarrochi. 2016. "A Heart and a Mind: Self-distancing Facilitates the Association between Heart Rate Variability, and Wise Reasoning." *Frontiers in Behavioral Neuroscience* 10 (68): 1–10. https://doi.org/10.3389/fnbeh.2016.00068.

Hall, Stephen S. 2007. "The Older-and-Wiser Hypothesis." *New York Times*, 6 May. https://www.nytimes.com/2007/05/06/magazine/06Wisdom-t.html.

Humphrey, Caroline. 1997. "Exemplars and Rules: Aspects of the Discourse of Moralities in Mongolia." In *The Ethnography of Moralities*, edited by S. Howell, 25–47. London: Routledge.

Katz, Richard. 1999. *The Straight Path of the Spirit: Ancestral Wisdom and Healing Traditions in Fiji*. Rochester, VT: Park Street Press.

Kaufmann, W.O. 1996. *The Anthropology of Wisdom Literature*. Westport, CT: Bergin and Garvey.

Kitchener, Karen S., and Helene G. Brenner. 1990. "Wisdom and Reflective Judgment: Knowing in the Face of Uncertainty." In Sternberg, *Wisdom: Its Nature, Origins, and Development*, 212–29.

Levenson, Michael R. 2009. "Gender and Wisdom: The Roles of Compassion and Moral Development." *Research in Human Development* 6 (1): 45–59. https://doi.org/10.1080/15427600902782127.

Maybury-Lewis, David. 1992. *Millennium: Tribal Wisdom and the Modern World*. New York: Viking.

McConchie, Peter. 2003. *Elders: Wisdom from Australia's Indigenous Leaders*. Port Melbourne, AU: Cambridge University Press.

Meeks, Thomas W., and Dilip V. Jeste. 2009. "Neurobiology of Wisdom: A Literature Overview." *Archives of General Psychiatry* 66 (4): 355–65. https://doi.org/10.1001/archgenpsychiatry.2009.8.

Pascual-Leone, Juan. 1990. "An Essay on Wisdom: Toward Organismic Processes That Make It Possible." In Sternberg, *Wisdom: Its Nature, Origins, and Development*, 244–78.

Puett, Michael. 2008. "Ritual and the Subjunctive." In *Ritual and Its Consequences: An Essay on the Limits of Sincerity*, edited by A. Seligman, R. Weller, and B. Simon, 17–42. Oxford: Oxford University Press.

Radin, Paul. 1957. *Primitive Man as Philosopher*. New York: Dover Publications.

Rescher, Nicholas. 1990. *Human Interests: Reflections on Philosophical Anthropology*. Stanford, CA: Stanford University Press.

Salk, Jonas. 1973. *The Survival of the Wisest*. New York: Harper & Row.

Salk, Jonathan. 2017. "A New Reality: Human Values and World Population." *Thrive Global*, 12 April, https://thriveglobal.com/stories/a-new-reality-human-values-and-world-population/.

Schloss, Jeffrey P. 2000. "Wisdom Traditions as Mechanisms for Organismal Integration: Evolutionary Perspectives on Homeostatic 'Laws of Life.'" In Brown, *Understanding Wisdom*, 153–91.

Sherman, Nancy. 2000. "Wise Emotions." In Brown, *Understanding Wisdom*, 319–39.

Siegel, R.D., and C.K. Germer. 2012. "Wisdom and Compassion: Two Wings of a Bird." In *Wisdom and Compassion in Psychotherapy: Deepening Mindfulness in Clinical Practice*, edited by R.D. Siegel and C.K. Germer, 7–34. New York: Guilford Press.

Sperber, Dan. 1985. "Anthropology and Psychology: Towards an Epidemiology of Representations." *Man*, n.s., 20 (1): 73–89. https://doi.org/10.2307/2802222.

Sternberg, Robert J., ed. 1990. *Wisdom: Its Nature, Origins, and Development*. Cambridge: Cambridge University Press.

Townsley, Graham. 1993. "Song Paths: The Ways and Means of Yaminahua Shamanic Knowledge." *L'Homme* 33 (126–8): 449–68.

Vico, Giambattista. 2002. *Scienza Nuova: The First New Science*. Edited and translated by Leon Pompa. Cambridge: Cambridge University Press.
Žižek, Slavoj. 2014. "The Problem with Wisdom." Short clip from the second discussion between Paul Holdengräber and Slavoj Žižek. *YouTube.com*. https://www.youtube.com/watch?v=BJHp7JA8pnQ.

PART ONE

Seeking Wisdom

1 Revelations of Delusion: Becoming Isomorphic to the Urgrund with Philip K. Dick

RICHARD DOYLE

The delusions of a penurious science fiction writer might seem of marginal interest, except that Philip K. Dick was not just any science fiction writer.

– Charles Platt (2011) on Philip K. Dick's *The Exegesis*

It is not God nor the gods which must prevail; it is wisdom, Holy Wisdom.

– Philip K. Dick (2011b: 196)

Why are you unhappy?
Because 99.9 per cent
Of everything you think,
And of everything you do,
Is for yourself –
And there isn't one.
– Wei Wu Wei (2002: 7)

Between 1974 and 1982, writer Philip K. Dick (hereafter PKD) composed a massive "Exegesis" in response to a mystical event of 1974, in which he reports being "nailed by information." PKD's writings, composed in daily entries, ranged over scientific, philosophical, religious, and spiritual queries fathoming and navigating what he eventually dubbed an ongoing event of "ultra-meta-cognition." Dick's relentless quest to observe and explore the nature of reality and consciousness – what *was* he that he could imagine being in unavoidable contact with what he called a vast living intelligent system (VALIS) apparently transmitting enormous quantities of information? – has been frequently met by responses such as Platt's quote at the beginning of this chapter. Dick's narration, exposition, and analysis of his intensely acute observations of his own consciousness – "ultra-meta-cognition" – are often viewed as "hallucinations" or "delusions," even while Dick's text features learned and erudite responses to a planetary stew of thinkers across cultures and time scale, including Shankara, Plotinus, Heidegger, and Spinoza. Dick fashioned extraordinary and even self-referential models of his experience with the concepts and vocabulary of cybernetics, physics, and psychology, models eminently useful for and suitable to life on a planet now crawling with information. This tension between the probing and intensely erudite writings of Dick, their often prophetic insights, and the response of readers to them as "delusions" suggests that, for contemporary audiences, intensely pursued introspection, perhaps even thinking itself, is "delusional."

There is, of course, something deeply comforting about excluding entire spectrums of existence. Dick imagines three-eyed alien invaders, so we don't have to. Perhaps PKD's imagination died for our sins. We can forget about any nagging or even vaguely fascinating questions about the nature of reality, forget that Ecclesiastes, at the very heart of a biblical literary tradition, itself ponders the motivating question of PKD's entire oeuvre: What is real?

But what does this response to *The Exegesis* as delusion itself avoid? What forms of life and forms of thought does a "prohibition on the within" entail? This chapter will explore PKD's investigations as an inquiry into the systematic delusion that is the "I," drawing on the work of fellow Californian Franklin Merrell-Wolff (henceforth, FMW). FMW was a Harvard-trained mathematician who experienced similar "realizations" as PKD. Yet, unlike PKD's lengthy and wide-ranging text that swarms with diagrams, frequently interrupts itself, and explores everything from "three-eyed invaders" to the conclusion that PKD had experienced nothing but the content of his own mind, FMW offered a complementary and lucid mapping of the effects of "ultra-metacognition" in the context of the Vedanta tradition. By weaving FMW's descriptions and insights alongside PKD's, my hope is to illuminate both and point the reader towards an experience of, and not merely an essay about, the revelation of the delusion of the "I," the very punchline of the Irish playwright, prankster, and mystic Wei Wu Wei's observation quoted earlier.

The Diagnosis, with Special Reference to Garden Gnomes

If contemporary philosophers and literary critics talked in gestures about PKD and *The Exegesis*, they would point their index fingers towards their temples and make little circles …

This gesture may seem understandable, given the sheer scale of *The Exegesis* itself. When a good friend urges you to visit their enormous collection of action figures from the science fiction tradition, your interest may be cautiously piqued. But, when you arrive and discover that there are *thousands* of multi-eyed carnivorous invaders injection molded into existence, you may find yourself in the grip of a full-fledged fight or flight response – acetylcholine triggering the release of epinephrine, heart racing ... And so, an analogous sense of shock and even denial can attend the realization that, in addition to scores of novels and hundreds of short stories, Dick wrote nearly 9,000 pages in daily entries of *The Exegesis*. It is, quite literally, "too much" or, as Jean Paul Sartre put it with much more sense of dread, "de trop."

The sheer amount of writing is itself a symptom, we might agree, but of what? Contemporary critics rarely invoke the sheer quantity of *The Exegesis* in their diagnosis, but it is most certainly the hundred-pound volume in the room. The quantity of the intensive reflections on the nature of reality, God, human purpose, and Fleetwood Mac singer Stevie Nicks tend to be obscured by the analysis and evaluation of the content.[1] And the analysis is almost always on the brink of diagnosis. In an introduction to a volume of essays on Dick, we learn from Alexander Dunst that it is "difficult to refrain from doubting Dick's sanity at times" (Dunst 2015: 5). Perhaps your doubt is stoked when you read of narratives of ultra-meta-cognition, as when Dick opines: "I think it is waking. The universe-organism of the Greek philosophers. It wakes and sees. Cells, forming a Great Brain. Bees in a hive. Rising now to consciousness. Of what? Itself?" (Dick 1996: 326).

PKD's balanced and sympathetic biographer, Lawrence Sutin, notes in an introduction to a collection of PKD's work that "the diagnoses are legion" (Dick 1996: xx). This essay, though, suggests that the dominance of this medicalized response is itself symptomatic of an unwillingness as well as an atrophied ability to attend to, and tarry with, the extraordinary claims, hypotheses, and observations PKD made in *The Exegesis*. While the epic scale of *The Exegesis* itself provides an easy alibi for anyone who would rather avoid the "delusions of a penurious science fiction writer," Dick prepared a "summary of the key insights expressed in *The Exegesis*" as of 23 January 1978 entitled "Cosmogony and Cosmology" and sent off the typed pages to his agent Russell Galen. "Cosmogony and Cosmology" was 1978's *Exegesis* exegesis. While "Cosmogony and Cosmology" is, of course, anything but the final word on what PKD hath wrought, it provides a very useful and highly distilled response to and interpretation of the sprawling text, and was itself published in

1987. Its focus, too, is ontological: it concerns less the "whatness" than the "thatness" of the act of exegesis itself. In particular, and apropos the efforts of this volume, we will contextualize and focus on the treatment of the word "wisdom" in this condensed tractate of *The Exegesis*, a gateway to our own practice of exegesis, the deconstruction of the "I" in a flurry of Phil Dickian wisdom.

As to Our Reality Being a Projected Framework: On Errant and Disobedient Wisdom

From the very beginning of *Cosmogony and Cosmology*, PKD is unusually direct. While *The Exegesis* itself has the very form of the flow of logos or "living information," this "summary" has a tone that, at times, approaches that of a memorandum. The opening phrase of the first sentence reads, for example, as if it were responding to an already existing query:[2] "As to our reality being a projected framework –."[3] This matter of fact declaration provides the very premise and destination for the memo on what he will later describe as the "the greatest esoteric knowledge that could be imagined" (Dick 1996: 288). If one is capable of accepting, even in a provisional fashion, the possibility of "our reality being a projected framework," then, in some sense, "wisdom, Holy Wisdom," has already been transmitted by Dick.

Perhaps this matter of fact declaration shields the reader from the epistemological bomb triggered by this initial, and possibly initiating, premise. As soon as we accept the possibility that our reality is a "projected framework," we are being asked to enact the very conclusion of the summary: "There can be no divine birth within the human mind until that human has denied the world" (Dick 1996: 292). The phrase before the dash, "As to our reality being a projected framework," already enacts this denial of the world by provisionally asserting its ephemerality: in some fundamental sense, PKD experiments with the hypothesis that the world "isn't." The world becomes an appearance whose implicit claim to reality is itself the ultimate (deluding) falsehood, the *maya* of Vedanta or the "vanity of vanity" of Ecclesiastes. After the dash, we find that that this false world has been projected by a technology, an artifact:

> It appears to be a projection by an *artifact*, a computerlike teaching machine that guides, programs, and generally controls us as we act without awareness of it within our projected world. (281)

This model is in some ways ancient, kin to book seven of Plato's *Republic* and the familiar allegory of the cave. The world we dwell in, hypothesizes PKD, is but a shadow, a "projection," a pale image of the true Urgrund. Yet, after hypothesizing that the apparently real world is, as he will later label it, "spurious," "only seemingly real" (Dick 1996: 284), PKD offers a rationale for this appearance, a technological scheme whereby it could appear to be real while being a mere "projection."

> The artifact, which I call Zebra, has "created" (actually only projected) our reality as a sort of mirror or image of its maker, so that the maker can obtain thereby an objective standpoint to comprehend its own self. In other words, the maker (called by Jakob Bohme in 1616 the Urgrund) is motivated to seek an instrument for self-awareness, self-knowledge, an objective opinion or appraisal and comprehension of the nature of itself (it is a vast living organism, intrinsically – without this mirror – without qualities or aspects, which is why it needs the empirical world as a reflection by which to "see" itself). (281)

In this context, our world seems real precisely because it is a simulacrum of the actual transcendental, living substratum, the Urgrund out of which it has been projected and created. It is precisely the world's proximity to truth that beguiles us and challenges us to observe its distinction from Truth with wisdom.

The apparent world for PKD is a fiction, but, unlike Plato's shadows, it is a fiction that teaches. Our senses are convinced, for example, that the glass from which I just drank some iced tea is real. In fact, you may be thinking, it is an awfully good thing that this glass, and the tea in it, is real, because otherwise I would remain thirsty and, eventually, dehydrate and die. What if only the tea were real, but the glass ephemeral? Surrounded by tea, but not a drop to drink!

But PKD, unlike most of us, has thought a great deal about the nature of reality. More crucially, he has observed: "Reality is that which, when you stop believing in it, doesn't go away" (Dick 1996: 261). If, even provisionally, we take PKD's definition seriously, this statement means that the glass is anything but real, as the glass is always about to shatter. There is a time scale, to be sure, on which the glass would seem to persist. I can put it down on a table and come back, and, whether or not I still believe in it, it is still there. But this time scale is immensely constricted and amounts to a "projection" of our own, quite limited time scale onto our perceptions. For if we look extremely closely at the glass, we will see that it is mostly space. If we zoom out, as it were, over a larger time scale, we see that the glass is a mere eye-blink in the history of reality, an event of such little duration that it becomes difficult to comprehend how we could have ever thought it was a "thing." The glass, whether we believe it is real or not, goes away.

Yet, PKD, being a science fiction writer as well as an experimentalist in metaphysics, a careful observer of the very dynamics of reality – its tendency to persist – offers a more sophisticated model than Plato's "den" and fire" that casts shadows upon a wall. This projection is that of an "artifact," a technology which is "computerlike," a teaching machine. And this "machine" guides us, programs us, and generally controls us. The artifact, or what PKD dubs "Zebra, the projecting energetic artifact" for its ability to camouflage itself like a striped horse on a grassy plain, is described by PKD as "virtually decisive" (Dick 1996: 282). PKD's 1964 novel *Martian Time-Slip* rehearses this engagement with teaching machines that "mold" us without any regard for the "subjective factor" – that is, who we really are – but instead bend us to their direction:

> And yet he felt repelled by the teaching machines. For the entire Public School was geared to a task which went contrary to his grain: the school was there not to inform or educate, but to mold, and along severely limited lines. It was the link to their inherited culture, and it peddled that culture, in its entirety, to the young. It bent its pupils to it; perpetuation of the culture was the goal, and any special quirks in the children which might lead them in another direction had to be ironed out. (Dick 2012: 75)

What difference might it make that PKD's model involves a technology that "guides" or "programs" us? Unlike the fire casting shadows in Plato's hypothetical den, which emits only one binary signal – a shadow gradient of darkness against light – a computerlike teaching machine can generate a practically unlimited variety of signals, *including the signal that it is false.* It is this revelation of falsehood, I would like to suggest, that is "wisdom, Holy Wisdom" for PKD, and his *The Exegesis* consists of the relentless discrimination between the true and the false, where the true world consists of the within: "what is Beyond is within" (Dick 1996: 282). For Jack Bohlen, PKD's character in *Martian Time-Slip* who notes the horror of the teaching machines and their denial of the "subjective factor," the "within" is the domain of schizophrenia but also the visionary space of prophecy and prescience. Away from the false guides of the teaching machines and the infrastructure they have wrought, the within harbours both truth and illness.

According to PKD, the very fact of the within, though, is something that the Urgrund can learn about itself by becoming aware of itself in an act of ultra-meta-cognition. Awakening consists of encountering the very existence of the within. The Urgrund can learn, for example, that it is not fundamentally material, for when it observes itself over larger scales of time or smaller scales of space, that which appears to our senses to persist (in time) or offer integrity (in space) just doesn't. As the Urgrund learns about itself from this perspective of an observer, what appears to be real, the glass, isn't. Or, as Dick says elsewhere, it is "only seemingly real" (Dick 1996: 284).

This skepticism – what appears to be real is in fact a "projection" – is not simply a negating force. Once we are cleared of the false impression that apparent reality is real, PKD asks us to experience a much more substantial reality "underneath" or "behind" appearance, a reality that is "motivated" and "living." Beyond the appearance of reality, for example, as inert, "mechanical," and devoid of meaning, PKD insists there is an entelechy, a purposive, learning, living, and deeply real ontology beyond the world of things: "I propose the proposition that such an invisible substratum does indeed exist" (Dick 1996: 288).[4]

It may be crucial to note that this observation of the nature of reality as (1) only apparently real and (2) occluding a more substantial reality emerges from the hypothesis that the Urgrund has projected the apparently real world as a method of observing itself. The Urgrund, like VALIS, is an information technology gathering information about itself. The Urgrund manifests reflexive awareness and engages in a systematic, even scientific study of its own nature through the projection of a model of itself.[5] As a good scientific practice – indeed, our scientific practice appears as the microform of this overall tendency of the Urgrund and Zebra – learning occurs through falsification. We learn not so much what is, but what is not. Some aspects of the scientific experiment can even be aware of the results. It is this awareness, PKD says, that we are. We are a projection of a more substantial self-aware reality by which that reality can come to know itself. As a microform of that self-aware reality, we ourselves can mirror or "become isomorphic to" (Dick 1996: 290) the Urgrund through what fellow California sage and mathematician Franklin Merrell-Wolff (1995: 111) called "introception," "the power of the Light of consciousness to turn upon itself toward its source." In this view, when we "wake up" and engage in this deeply reflective form of awareness and investigate our own nature as conscious beings, we awaken to the Urgrund, the Observer observing its mimetic creation or what the Sanskrit traditions label "*atman*." We may usefully ask: Why can't this supposed Urgrund, as the foundation of all being, simply inspect *itself* in an act of self-knowledge or gnosis?

PKD anticipates this query through his observation that, while we are replete with qualities and aspects – brown hair, born under the sign of Scorpio, prone to ecstatic hyperbole – the Urgrund, as Urgrund, is devoid of them. It is pure awareness itself, "without qualities or aspects" (Dick 1996: 281). In order to investigate its own (possibly infinite) nature, then, the Urgrund alters itself through the experimental and only apparent transformation into innumerable qualities and aspects. But these qualities and aspects, unlike the Urgrund, come and go. They are not real, but only symptoms of the capacity of the Urgrund to (perhaps infinitely) become.

Given that PKD will consider the "advantages of this model" later, it is tempting to suggest that PKD is adopting a conceptual map for understanding the nature of reality and the human who would know, or attempt to know, reality. It is tempting to think that PKD found Böhme's concept of the Urgrund useful as a concept precisely because it met some unsatisfied need in his own conceptualizations of what he came to call 2–3–74, the mystical eventhood of VALIS. But a consideration of the opening fragment, "As to our reality being a projected framework–," suggests that any reader who wishes to actually evaluate PKD's proposition – and who wouldn't wish to access, or even imagine, "the greatest esoteric knowledge that could be imagined" (Dick 1996: 288) – must in fact break with the conceptual order altogether. The order of the concept is precisely the order of the artifact, Zebra, not the Urgrund but the projection of the Urgrund itself. If one wishes to tarry with, experiment with, welcome, the Urgrund, PKD says, we must disobey the existing order of things: "Is it not a disobedience to the present system of things, which [system of] things, if bipolarized against the Urgrund, is at the same time an act of obedience to God?" (290). How, though, is one to disobey the claim the world makes for its own reality? Readers are asked to reject the very reality of the world in which they have been raised, but through what means? PKD declares that "our … egos" must die as the condition of possibility for knowledge of the Urgrund:

> But on the moment that our individual egos die and the Urgrund is born in us – at that moment we are freed from this world and become a portion of our original source. The initiative for this stems from the Urgrund; as unhappy as this projected world is, as unheeding of suffering as the artifact is, this *is*, after all, the structure that the Urgrund has created by which we reach isomorphism with it. Had there been a better way the Urgrund certainly would have employed it. The road is difficult, but the goal justifies it. (Dick 1996: 286)

So, this model offered by PKD is precisely a technique for achieving this birth of the Urgrund – not a concept, nor a description, but a textual labour or yoga by which we become isomorphic with the Urgrund. This textual yoga, then, is, in some sense, neither true nor false, but software for transforming the computerlike teaching machine itself by giving it a glimpse of itself – ultra-meta-cognition. If we can successfully refuse the world's claim to reality, we will discover a far more fundamental reality than that which comes and goes in the apparently existing order of things. And our refusal comes not from us, but is instead an effect of the teaching we experience at the hands of Zebra: "The artifact, not knowing the purpose for which it was created, had contributed substantially to this; by inflicting too much pain on me it had, in a certain real sense, awakened me" (Dick 1996: 296).

The form of *The Exegesis* itself provides yet more context for the work of these "birth pangs" induced by the textual labour of becoming isomorphic to the Urgrund through the suffering of trial and error. Night after night PKD would write, and then change his mind, suffering the explanation to be incomplete. Day after day we might read *The Exegesis* and fail, once again, to come to any conclusion concerning it. Perhaps the truth of *The Exegesis* is not to be found within *The Exegesis*?!

Again, a difference from the Platonic cave comes into relief. While the shadows present a variety of shapes and activities in shadow form, there is no signal carried by each shadow over and above its representation of an object or an event, a representation taken by cave dwellers to *be* the thing or event itself. But, as PKD's practice of textual exegesis illuminates, even the suffering induced by the artifact transmits information over and above any particular message or event that is being transmitted. The artifact, Zebra, in the sheer amount of suffering induced, transmits a message: Wake up with ultra-meta-cognition! This quantity of suffering, in other words, becomes a quality – a quality that can erode or even "destroy" that multilayered barrier to realization, the ego:

> Put another way, it had managed to destroy the layer of individual personality by a series of afflictions against which my self, my ego, could not survive. Thus the microform of the Urgrund was exposed, and perceived its macroform in the totality of the universe – or, as the article on Bruno says, the divine *behind* the universe. (Dick 1996: 296–7)

For PKD, it is this path to ego death by which we become isomorphic to the Urgrund, by which the Urgrund can be born in us. If this path is the path of wisdom, in what does it consist? Wisdom for PKD is neither the reception nor a transmission of a packet of information or knowledge, but is instead a set of means by which awakening from the spell cast by the world's claim to reality can occur. PKD, it would seem, suffered until he found that suffering unacceptable, and, in a desperate act of healing, disobeyed the very claim that suffering made to be real. He rejected the reality of his empirical suffering. From whence did this rejection come?

> Reality must be regarded as process. However, although there is acute suffering by living creatures who must undergo this process, without understanding why, there is occasional merciful intervention by the Urgrund overruling or overriding the cause-and-effect chains of the artifact. Perhaps this salvific intervention results from a birth of the Urgrund in the person. One should note that the actual historic meaning of the term "salvation" is "liberation," and that of "sinful" or "fallen" is "enslaved." It is *a priori* possible, given this model, to imagine a freeing of a human from the control of the artifact, however good, useful, and purposeful the activity of the artifact may be. *It is obviously capable of error,* as well as imperfection. An override is obviously sometimes essential, given this model. Just as obviously, it would be the primal maker or ground of being that would possess the wisdom and power to do so. Nothing within, or stemming from, the artifact or the projected world, would suffice. (Dick 1996: 283–4)

Wisdom here would seem to involve an understanding of suffering as an aspect of a "process" of entelechy whereby a malfunction or "error" manifests as liberation. In other words, the suffering occurs for a purpose unknown even to Zebra – which, in fact, knows nothing at all and merely grinds on in blind mechanical causality – and is instead an effect of Urgrund within the artifact itself, a manifestation of wisdom PKD characterizes as "liberation" and whose patron saint is Sophia.

Liberation, ultra-meta-cognition, consists of the experience that suffering cannot be separated from the Urgrund. Even while suffering appears and feels very much separate and not equal to the plenitude that is Urgrund, it is revealed in the birth of the Urgrund within a human to be intrinsic to the "process" of reality. When we think we understand the framework of that process, liberation itself can appear as an "error." PKD sums up that process within the distillation that is "Cosmogony and Cosmology": "Urgrund creates artifact which projects universe which gives rise to life forms which evolve to a stage in which the Urgrund is 'born' or 'reflected'" (Dick 1996: 297).

Our attention might not be drawn to this oscillation between such apparently distinct verbs as "born" or "reflected." But if you attend, slow down, tarry, wait on this tension or continuum opened up by "born" or "reflected," you might find the Urgrund "born" or "reflected" in this beyond of language itself. We can pass over the quotes around "born" if only to point to them as indicators of the insufficiency of the language PKD can manifest to occasion or "reflect" what he will dub "the Blitz as Urgrund." PKD has nearly 9,000 pages to draw on to language whatever it was that triggered the writings of Böhme as well as his own, but here it is the space between "born" – already marked by the inverted commas of semantic insufficiency – and "reflected" that are called forth in this crystalline compression of the distillation of *The Exegesis*. The sheer differential between the quantity that is a quality that is *The Exegesis* and this teeny sliver of an algorithm for the very genesis of reality and its evolution into self-awareness might seize our interest, if only to imagine how we might think a birth that is not literal, and yet which occurs through something like a reflection. PKD's own "birth" or "reflection" is, he writes, occasioned by an error.

> And – too – God answered my prayers re the Exegesis, by leading me to Jacob Boehme. Somewhere between the truths revealed to Boehme and to me *the correct model lies*. The Blitz as Urgrund encounters the lowest 3rd of the secondary (material) triad – the divine agony as opposition between the Urgrund and physical nature … Only God can see God. He wielded me, from inside me, effortlessly … The above prayer was answered by my mistakenly reading the entry in the E of Phil. on Jacob Boehme. (Dick n.d.: 50:85)

The Urgrund is, for PKD, "born" or "reflected" only and precisely when he does not know what he is doing. Something larger, "substantial," and actual beyond himself is revealed. "Mistakenly reading the entry … on Jacob Boehme" turns out to be a mistake, not from the perspective of the Urgrund, manifesting through the seventeenth-century German cobbler Jacob Böhme in response to a ray of sunlight reflecting off a pewter dish, but from the perspective of the "layers of individual personality" that were Philip K. Dick. This revelation through errancy occurs not so much through an entropy that is external, but by an internal dehiscence characteristic of identity itself that can apparently become increasingly aware of its dehiscence. "Only God can see God" indicates, points out, directs our attention to the fact that the experience of the apparent personality must give way if Urgrund is to shine through. In *VALIS*, the novel in which Dick, his "alter ego Horselover

Fat," and the Exegesis all appear as characters, the character Phil asks: "Isn't it an oxymoron to say, I am not myself? Isn't this a verbal contradiction, a statement semantically meaningless?" (Dick 2011b: 128).

While arguably semantically meaningless at the level of the sentence, the insight that "I am not myself" is the definitive truth of both *VALIS* and *The Exegesis* – a revelation of falsehood. The birth or "reflection" of the Urgrund, then, occurs through the event of ego death because it indicates a truth. Ego, "I," is only the apparent and not the actual domain of identity: "I am not myself." As with the fourteenth-century text *The Cloude of Unknowing*, PKD identifies the agency of revelation to be intensified through "not knowing" what he is doing: a cloud of "error." Aligning ourselves not with the world but with consciousness, we must heed PKD's counsel of disobedience to the apparent self and become isomorphic with the revealed truth of the ego's falsehood. Only when we do not know what we are doing can such a "revelation" occur. But, if it is a revelation, it is a revelation of delusion:

> There is evidence that the Urgrund does in fact sometimes make such a revelation to human beings, in order to further the dialectical process toward its desired goal. On the other hand, the artifact would counter by inducing as much blindness or occlusion as possible; viewed this way, darkness and light seem to be at war, or, more accurately, knowing versus nonknowing, with the human beings correctly aligning themselves with the entity of knowing (called Holy Wisdom). (Dick 1996: 286)

What is revealed, in wisdom, is not the world but the Urgrund itself. This knowing of the Urgrund takes place when the light of eternity shines on the transient material of reality – a "counterfeit" "projection." Zooming in on matter, we find space. Slowing down into time, we find that it is always Now. In the Blitz of the Now, ego structures – which appear to be actual and to persist in time – dissipate. The ego for PKD is perhaps best modelled as a character, a fundamentally narratival structure that inhabits linear time and amounts to the accrued information of "me and my story." Without before and after, here and there, in the Now, these characters disappear. Like his alter ego Horselover Fat, who appears and disappears throughout *VALIS*, this character vanishes in the light of the Urgrund, in the Blitz that is Now. Once seen to be itself an artifact, it can never again convince with any claim to persistence and actuality. Who would it convince? Not the artifact, which, again, does not "comprehend" even itself:

> The artifact does not comprehend what risk it is running in the inflicting of unmerited suffering on living creatures. It imagines them all to be at its

> mercy and without recourse. In this it is wrong, absolutely wrong. Buried here, mixed in with the bulk, the mass, there exists unsuspected even by itself the Urgrund with all the power and wisdom that implies. (Dick 1996: 304)

Wisdom, then, persists as what the Chandogya Upanishad called "the treasure beneath our feet" (Mahadevan 1995: 89). Perhaps the mass of the Exegesis exists such that it could be systematically, iteratively negated, revealed to be false, leaving the Urgrund, without qualities or aspects, to shine without occlusion. To paraphrase George Harrison, with every mistake the Urgrund must surely be learning. Indeed, PKD falsifies even the idea that he had the experience at all: Only the Urgrund did:

> My 3–74 experience, then, was not so much my experience as that of the Urgrund. It amounted to a replication of the Urgrund here rather than there. (Dick 1996: 297)

PKD's treatment accords with the more systematic account of Franklin Merrell-Wolff when he writes: "Introceptive Realization is to be conceived as something that can be known by a human being, but cannot be experienced" (1995: 174). This sentence offers a rather precise definition of "experience" as requiring the relation of a subject, the experiencer, and an object, the experience. When consciousness turns towards itself in an act of "ultra-meta-cognition" or "introception," knower is known, perceiver perceived. No subject, no object, just Urgrund or, as FMW puts it: "Consciousness-without-an-object."

Yet, as the history of psychedelic experience and other mystical events testify, it can be challenging to avoid slipping back into a dualistic state of thinking so foreign to the event of gnosis itself. Even as PKD recognizes the falsehood of the "I" and notes his experience was not "his," he maps the Urgrund as "here" and "there." This dualist two step – first PKD disappears into the total oneness of Urgrund, then he narrates it into a subject/object language – continues:

> The totality of the Godhead was recapitulated within me through a process of rolling back spurious or temporary layers to expose the permanent within. Thus it can be said that I was really the Urgrund, or at least a faithful mirror image thereof. The entire objective of creating me, of creating the universe as such and the life forms within it, was arrived at. Viewed this way, my life and that of my ancestors could be viewed teleologically: as moving through evolutionary stages toward that moment. My experience did not represent *a* stage in evolution but *the* ultimate stage or goal, at least if the premise stated in this paper is correct. (Dick 1996: 297)

But, if anything is "semantically meaningless," it is "I was really the Urgrund," for the Urgrund, as we have seen, is that which shines through in the death of the ego: "There can be no divine birth within the human mind until that human has denied the world" (Dick 1996: 292). The "permanent within" is precisely not that which struts and frets its hour upon the stage, coming and going: "I."

FMW, as always, puts it as lucidly as can be imagined: "In the end, everything hung upon a subtle psychical adjustment that is truly inexpressible, since the every act of expression gives it the false appearance of an objective character that is not all true to the real meaning" (Merrell-Wolff 1995: 149). To realize these revelations of delusion, then, we must move beyond an accounting of the content of *The Exegesis* and "Cosmology and Cosmogony" for the simple reason that no amount of writing or inquiry by PKD will lead us to our own alignment with the Urgrund. The "subtle psychical adjustment" must take place within. Even as PKD appears to experience the Advaita (non-dual) moment of unity with, or the "faithful mirror image" of, the Urgrund, the artifact – in this case, language itself – recasts or "molds" the experience into something that "we" could "have" or even "arrive" at. In short, as soon as PKD begins to narrate the vastness of the vast active living intelligent system by situating it in the subject/object domains of space and time, it becomes once again part of the "spurious projected framework" (Dick 1996: 282).

Note the dynamic here: as the radically interior experience of introception is externalized into the techne of language, the "Beyond is within" becomes obscured as our attention is captured by the counterfeit reality without, including the counterfeit reality of PKD's works. Must language itself essentially be experienced as external, concerning a world that is "out there"? The Urgrund, that which projects, is, to use one of PKD's favourite words, "occluded"; as a result, Urgrund, pure awareness, is squeezed into the shortest word in the English language, into the "I": "I was really the Urgrund."

This point is no doubt where critics begin pointing their index fingers – themselves oddly isomorphic to the "I" – at their temples and making little circles. Taken out of context, one could easily imagine that PKD takes himself to be a prophet of sorts. At times, he does. At times, perhaps we all do. But, for PKD, all of us are "like bits of a hologram: intact gestalts but 'dimmer' or less defined" aspects of the Urgrund (Dick n.d.: 50:88). PKD's difference, most of the time, in his own self-understanding was to have perceived this idea in the agony of the moments after oral surgery and under the influence of Sodium Pentathol. Faced with the agony of the without, PKD was more or less forced to focus his attention within. But, once PKD begins to narrate this self-intuition or "ultra-meta-cognition" into text, the words can only carry revelations of their own falsehood. Yet, PKD's novels subtly and persistently display this counterfeit aspect of even his own works: they are self-wounding stories, nailing themselves with information. While Julian of Norwich, in her own "shewings" or revelations, perceived the wounds of Jesus in her own inner sight, PKD's wounds are narratival: again and again, the narrative falls apart, unable to express in a medium beholden to subject and object, space and time. The timeless Urgrund of the Now shreds PKD's account, forcing him again and again to attempt the impossible and to tell the story of the Urgrund within the counterfeit reality, giving "it the false appearance of an objective character that is not all true to the real meaning" (Merrell-Wolff 1995: 149), describing the within through the terms of the without.

Why this apparent bottleneck of meaning between the within and the without? Subjectivity is not a field of awareness that lacks objectivity. On the contrary, objectivity is a field of awareness that has been separated from a being always already within subjectivity, cutting itself off from any apparent source. Psychologist Roland Fischer (1971), in his "A Cartography of Ecstatic and Meditative States," mapped this separation that is essential to the "I" as a "severed and mutilated condition."

> The mutual exclusiveness of the "normal" and the exalted states, both ecstasy and samadhi, allows us to postulate that man, the self referential system, exists on two levels: as "Self" in the mental dimension of exalted states; and as "I" in the objective world, where he is able and willing to change the physical dimension "out there." In fact, the "I" and the "Self" can be postulated on purely logical grounds. See, for instance, Brown's reasoning … that the universe is apparently … constructed in order (and thus in such a way as to be able) to see itself. But in order to do so, evidently it must first cut itself up into at least one state which sees, and at least one other state which is seen. In this severed and mutilated condition, whatever it sees is only partially itself … but, in any attempt to see itself as an object, it must, equally undoubtedly, act so as to make itself distinct from, *and therefore, false to, itself.* In this condition it will always partially elude itself. (Fischer 1971: 899; emphasis added)

Fischer gleaned this model from his extensive controlled research studies at Ohio State University on psilocybin, a psychedelic found in various species of mushrooms. Fischer's account is intriguingly isomorphic to PKD's "Cosmogony and Cosmology," with the added insight that the projection is in fact a product, at least in part, of consciousness itself – what he calls, along with the traditions of Vedanta, "Self." In other words, a tiny sliver of consciousness whose prime attribute is the experience of separation and "mutilation" mistakes itself for the whole shebang of awareness and consciousness. More contemporary neuroscience has mapped the experience of ego or "I me mine" and "location in space and time" in terms of the posterior cingulate cortex and its activities in the default mode network, where the incessant internal and self-referential narrative seems to be involved in creating this only apparent separation (see, for example, Brewer et al. 2011). In either map, the relatively tiny and insignificant domain of the "I" occludes the enormous flow of consciousness, which, despite its name, is not always conscious. Recent research, for example, estimates that, while conscious awareness is capable of information transfer at a rate of about sixty bits per second, nonconscious awareness – the Urgrund? – processes information at the rate of twenty-five million bits per second (Weber 2017; Koch et al. 2006). Yet, as long as we remain in the domain of the "I," and its obsession with "out there," the "exalted states" of the within are infinitely close and infinitely distant.

Fortunately, diverse traditions point to practical measures that can be taken to overcome, if only temporarily, this occlusion of the within and the thrall of the without. FMW suggests a practice in introception as follows:

> The subject of the experiment is asked to attend to some fixed object, preferably a visible object. Then, without changing the fixation of the sense impression, the subject is told to focus his or her attention upon the perceiving itself, rather than upon the object of perception. This is an effort to perceive perceiving. (Merrell-Wolff 1995: 146)

If readers will go beyond actually reading about this practice – the domain of without – and follow this little recipe for ultra-meta-cognition, they might begin to explore the domain of the within. It may well be this gap between the description of transcendent experience and its occurrence to some particular domain of awareness that induces the sheer amount of diagnoses of PKD. While our (usually nonconscious) expectations about a text indicate that we are to read it as if it were describing something "out there," both PKD's own account of his experience as being "nailed by information" and practically every linguistic and literary critical movement since Ferdinand de Saussure suggest that such a perspective on language is misguided at best. PKD's "nailed by information" emphasizes the transformative character of the signs on his mind/body as well as its resonance with the crucifixion of Jesus, and suggests that we will benefit less from "comprehending" PKD's writings than from being altered by them. The exalted states mapped by Fischer are encountered not in the interpretation of text but in the exegetical breakdown of "semantic meaning," such that we realize that we are no longer, and perhaps never were, ourselves, in our revelation of delusion.

NOTES

1 "This is probably the happiest moment of my life – I can say to this moment, 'stay.' Here is the fallen black cat on my lap. I am listening to Stevie Nicks on my Stax phones – the Gollancz edition of *Scanner* arrived today" (Dick 2011a: 286).

2 According to Paul Williams, former executor of the Philip K. Dick literary estate, it appears, indeed, to be the case. Dick began "Cosmogony and Cosmology" as part of a response to a student, David Kleist. Kleist "had sent him his term paper about Dick's writing" (Dick 1996: 8).

3 "Cosmology and Cosmogony" was published as a separate volume in 1987. In-text paginations are from the reprint of the essay in *The Shifting Realities of Philip K. Dick* (Dick 1996).

4 Here PKD points to what is left, truth, when we let go of the false. *The Heart Sutra* features the Sanskrit word *"amithyatvat,"* whose translation would be "that which is true by virtue of not being false." Usual translations render this word as "for what could go wrong," which loses the sense of a primordial truth that is simply occluded by the false (see, for example, Conze 2001). Only Osho among contemporary commentators seems to notice that the negation of the false here yields truth: "Truth is that which we go on missing. We go on missing because we go on clinging with the false. We miss the truth because we cling to the false. If we drop the false there is no missing at all" (Osho n.d.).

5 It is perhaps with this context that we can interpret Genesis's "In the image of God created he him" alongside PKD's foray's here.

REFERENCES

Brewer, Judson A., Patrick D. Worhunsky, Jeremy R. Gray, Yi-Yuan Tang, Jochen Weber, and Hedy Kober. 2011. "Meditation Experience Is Associated with Differences in Default Mode Network Activity and Connectivity." *Proceedings of the National Academy of Sciences of the United States of America* 108 (50): 20254–9. https://doi.org/10.1073/pnas.1112029108.

Conze, Edward, trans. 2001. *Buddhist Wisdom: The Diamond Sutra and the Heart Sutra*. New York: Vintage.

Dick, Philip K. 1996. *The Shifting Realities of Philip K. Dick: Selected Literary and Philosophical Writings*. Edited by Lawrence Sutin. New York: Vintage Books.

– 2011a. *The Exegesis*. Edited by Pamela Jackson and Jonathan Lethem. Boston: Houghton Mifflin Harcourt.

– 2011b. *VALIS*. Reissue ed. Boston: Mariner Books.

– 2012. *Martian Time-Slip*. Reissue ed. Boston: Mariner Books.

– n.d. "Exegesis Manuscripts." Zebrapedia Collaborative Transcription Project of Philip K. Dick's Exegesis. Accessed 6 August 2015. zebrapedia .psu.edu.

Dunst, Alexander. 2015. "Introduction: Third Reality – On the Persistence of Philip K. Dick." In *The World According to Philip K. Dick*, edited by Alexander Dunst and Stefan Schlensag, 1–12. New York: Palgrave Macmillan.

Fischer, Roland. 1971. "A Cartography of the Ecstatic and Meditative States." *Science* 174 (4012): 897–904. https://doi.org/10.1126/science.174.4012.897.

Koch, Kristin, Judith McLean, Ronen Segev, Michael A. Freed, Michael J. Berry II, Vijay Balasubramanian, and Peter Sterling. 2006. "How *Much* the Eye Tells the Brain." *Current Biology* 16 (14): 1428–34. https://doi.org /10.1016/j.cub.2006.05.056.

Mahadevan, T.M.P. 1995. "The Quintessence of Sri Ramana's Teachings." *The Mountain Path* 32 (3–4): 87–90. https://realization.org/down/mountain -path/32-3.1995-Jayanthi.pdf.

Merrell-Wolff, Franklin. 1995. *Transformations in Consciousness: The Metaphysics and Epistemology*. Edited by Ron Leonard. Albany: SUNY Press.

Osho. n.d. "Gone, Gone, Gone, Beyond!" In *The Heart Sutra: Talks on Prajnaparamita Hridayam Sutra of Gautama the Buddha*. OSHO International Foundation. http://www.oshosearch.net/Convert/Articles_Osho/The _Heart_Sutra/Osho-The-Heart-Sutra-00000009.html.

Platt, Charles. 2011. "The Voices in Philip K. Dick's Head." *The New York Times*, 16 December. https://www.nytimes.com/2011/12/18/books/review/the -exegesis-of-philip-k-dick-edited-by-pamela-jackson-jonathan-lethem-and -erik-davis-book-review.html.

Weber, Gary. 2017. "Right-Sizing Your 'I,' Understanding Confirmation Bias … New Studies." *Happiness Beyond Thought* (blog), 27 May. http:// happinessbeyondthought.blogspot.com/2017/05/right-sizing-your-i -understanding.html.

Wei, Wei Wu. 2002. *Ask the Awakened: The Negative Way*. Boulder, CO: Sentient Publications.

2 The Social Life of the Inexpressible: English Benedictine Mysticism, the Ineffable, and the Sublime

RICHARD D.G. IRVINE

Into Silence

A solid oak door marks the entrance to the monastic enclosure. Above the door, a plaque bears a single word, booming out in block capitals: SILENCE. What kind of restriction is this – or should it be read as an invitation?

The key question I ask here is prompted by this door. What is restricted, and what is made possible, when silence is elevated beyond the capacity to speak? To offer some ethnographic context: my focus is on Downside Abbey, a Catholic monastery within the English Benedictine Congregation.[1] Downside is by no means a "silent" community in the sense ordinarily understood. In a different context, Wichroski (1997) describes vividly the difficulties for the ethnographer of working in convents where speech is near-completely restricted, while also pointing towards the emergence of a sense of community within that shared silence. My ethnographic situation was less constrained: conversation at tea time and over work and general discussion at recreation and other appropriate times around the cloister meant that there was opportunity for talk (and thus verbal ethnographic inquiry). Yet, as the sign makes clear, upon entering the enclosure, one is entering a space where silence is valued and held core to the monastic identity.

In what sense is the monastery a space of silence? The institutional commitment to silence is perhaps most strikingly felt at mealtimes (Irvine 2011b). Food sharing might be thought of as the ideal occasion for conversation, with talk as central an ingredient of the meal as the food itself. Yet here, the monks sit and eat in silence, while books (sacred and secular) are read to them from the lectern. Malinowski (1923: 314), outlining the role of phatic communion for sociality, suggests that "phrases such as 'nice day to-day' ... are needed to get over the strange and unpleasant tension which men feel when facing each other in silence"; then "after the first formula, there comes a flow of language, purposeless expressions ... accounts of irrelevant happenings, comments on what is perfectly obvious," and so on. And, indeed, he links such chatter directly with commensality, suggesting that the "breaking of silence, the communion of words" is "consummated ... by the breaking of bread and the communion of food." But the monks cannot rely on the back and forth of chatter over the meal to bind the group. Instead, together as a group, they sit silently and focus on the words of the reader. They share in the act of listening (Irvine 2010). So what does it mean to keep silence during an event so apparently ripe for phatic communion? There is a sense in which this institutional silence displays the limits of conversation and the limits of community as something experienced through talk.

Silence also marks time through the *summum silentium* (complete silence). At the end of Compline, the final point of prayer in the monks' daily liturgy, the community process to a statue of the Blessed Virgin Mary, where they chant a prayer to Our Lady before the abbot sprinkles them with holy water. They bow together towards the statues, then raise their hoods and move off to their cells and the silence of night-time and sleep, alone. This complete silence lasts until after breakfast the following day. Again, in the solitude of the *summum silentium*, we see a community reaching the limit of talk and, in the silence of the night, moving beyond it.

This sense of silence beyond the limits of talk was also, as we shall see, central to the monks' understanding of contemplative prayer. As was explained to me by the novice master of the monastery, prayer is "getting used to silence," and silence was both the "condition" for prayer as well as being "itself prayer." The practice that the monks term "contemplative prayer," which they themselves identify as a mystical tradition, holds a place of particular importance for English Benedictine identity. One senior monk explained to me: "If you were a kind of ornithologist of monks, whatever that would be, then our tradition of contemplative prayer is how you'd spot us and pick us out. That's our identifying mark."

Central to the understanding of contemplation here is the failure of the mind and sense to know God. God is beyond any concepts at our disposal and cannot be apprehended through reflection or rendered intuitive through analogy. At this point of failure, it becomes necessary to move beyond mental representations of God, beyond words and images, beyond the tools of communication into silence.

What we see is a practice that is both deeply individual and thoroughly institutionalized. It is individual in that it involves the lone monk engaging in a practice which points towards a realm of experience that is non-conceptual, non-imagistic, and thus, at a certain level, incommunicable. Yet, it is also institutionalized in the sense that it is built into a structured corporate timetable as a thing the monk is expected to do at specific points in the day; and in the sense that it is recognized as an "identifying mark" of English Benedictines.

The puzzle I am presenting here is a challenge to the central premise that "wisdom" is something that can be spoken, and spoken about. What are the possibilities for the communication of wisdom when the ineffable appears to resist the very possibility of communication? Here is a tradition of contemplation within which the very possibility of communicability is denied. Yet, by referring to it as a "tradition," we create something of a paradox: here is something at core "ineffable," yet understood as having been institutionalized and carried through time within the social group. The challenge, then, is to understand how the inexpressible is learned, taught, and re-learned, becoming a thread of identity running through generations of monks. What does it mean to be part of a tradition beyond the limits of talk, invited to enter into silence?

Road Map for Prayer

In order to trace some of the common themes that shape descriptions of contemplative prayer, I will offer an account given to me by the monk who served as librarian of the community at the time of my fieldwork. As we shall see, it is an account grounded in the experience of failure, both in the way it is framed as advice for those who are having trouble praying – who are experiencing failure themselves – and in the way it treats failure as a goal. The librarian started off by remarking that many people find they have trouble praying and that these troubles make perseverance in prayer difficult: "They may well have found their experience of trying to make progress in prayer on the face of it a time-wasting exercise. These days, if you don't get instant results in anything, to give up seems the obvious answer. Life is too short. You think, surely there are more useful things I can be getting on with." Here, he said, it is useful to have a "road map" of prayer, "the experiences of those who have gone before … This map of prayer does not gloss over the fact that in the way ahead there will be some rough patches, dark nights of the soul, but they are not the end, there is life beyond them."

What does this "road map" consist of? For the librarian, it started with people's experiences of "discursive prayer," which he defined as "prayerful pondering on episodes in the life of Christ, using the imagination and the sense to reconstruct the scene, reflecting upon it with the reason, summoning up with appropriate emotions to make the will come to some practical resolutions." "I don't need to tell you this is the 'Ignatian' model," he said [that is, the model associated with St. Ignatius of Loyola and his *Spiritual Exercises*; I will return to this topic later].

But for many, this discursive approach to prayer becomes increasingly difficult. "They can't concentrate anymore. They have nothing to report back on ... There is a great temptation to give up praying altogether." The suggestion that people would experience rough patches where they lose focus in prayer and have difficulties focusing on thoughts or calling up feelings was a familiar one from other discussions around the monastery. Another senior monk had told me that many people realized they had reached the limits of discursive prayer when they found that it was an increasing struggle to focus in thought or feeling on the words of the Lord's Prayer. Yet, according to the "road map" that the librarian was laying out, these rough patches were seen to have had a purpose: "to change our means of praying, to develop our spiritual faculties ... to focus us on God the unknown, rather than the ways we picture him." Returning to the idea that, in prayer, our actions matter less and less, another senior monk explained the significance of this failure by way of scripture: "He must increase, but I must decrease" (John 3:30); while one is focused on one's own mental and emotional processes, the self is prominent in prayer. The failure of these forms of attention to the self is therefore key to reaching a state of attentiveness to God.

In this way, the failure of focus in discursive meditation, the failure to bring imagination, sense, reason, and emotion to bear, was cast as a positive development. Here was the point at which we move into a new means of praying, contemplative prayer, which responds to a desire for the ineffable – prayer that is open to God itself rather than representations of God.

However, the librarian went on, it is precisely at this stage that people find their prayer grows restless. The ways of describing the experience of prayer, and the ways of describing the God that one is praying to, take on the language of absence: "nothing," "a void," "a blank" – conceptualizations that point to the absence of concepts. This void was often a source of anxiousness: "how can you claim to know a thing without any sense, any concept of what that thing is?" Consequently, the mind grows restless.

This idea of "restlessness," and what it signifies in the life of prayer, is very important, and I will return to it shortly. However, first let us examine some of the cues which imply that the librarian, in offering this account, was speaking within a wider historic tradition. As I note earlier, so much of the texture of fieldwork was through the mediation of shared reading, and this figures strongly in the account I have just offered. Perhaps one of the most immediately visible cues is the librarian's reference to "dark nights of the soul," an explicit reference to the well-known spiritual writings of the Carmelite mystic St. John of the Cross (1542–91)[2] and thus a nod to the broader tradition of Catholic mystical prayer. Others are more subtle and draw connections with a specifically English Benedictine spirituality. For example, the description of discursive meditation as "prayerful pondering" is taken from Christopher Butler, the seventh abbot of Downside, who had been the librarian's novice master and was certainly a formative influence in setting out the "road map" for him.[3]

In particular, I think there are two key elements to this roadmap that can be productively linked with key English Benedictine historic sources. The first is the emphasis on prayer as an act of the will rather than a representation of the mind; and the second is the emphasis on the restlessness and anxiousness of the person at prayer. While these elements cannot, of course, be exclusively linked to any one historical figure, the contemporary presentation of prayer in the monastery bears the marks of two sources in particular, whose influence it may be useful to outline: Augustine Baker (1575–1641) and John Chapman (1865–1933).

Augustine Baker became a Benedictine monk in the early seventeenth century, a point in history when English Benedictines were entering monasteries on the European continent, from where they could be trained as priests and sent back as missionaries to their post-reformation homeland.[4] Although he would eventually be sent on the mission to England himself, dying in London as a victim of the plague, Augustine Baker's primary influence on English Benedictine mystical teaching comes from his time as spiritual director to the English nuns in exile at Cambrai. After his death, Baker's voluminous writings from this time were condensed into a systematized single book by another seventeenth-century English Benedictine monk, Serenus Cressy, and the volume that digested this teaching, known as *Sancta Sophia* or *Holy Wisdom*, has become a key element of reading for monks in English Benedictine noviciates.

The seed of Augustine Baker's teaching, and its influence shaping the "road map of prayer," came through clearly in an encounter one day in the library. Having seen a reference in an archival manuscript to "Fr B. and his S.S." (which I did not yet understand to mean "Father Baker and his *Sancta Sophia*"), I asked the librarian if he could help me decode this note. His response was to declaim some lines by Leander Normanton, a seventeenth-century monk of the community, which had been written to accompany an engraving of Baker:

> In sable lines o're a silver ground
> The face of that mysterious Man is found,
> Whose secret life and published Writings prove,
> To Pray is not to talke, or thinke, but Love.

The vision of prayer contained in this last line offers a succinct summary of what has been carried through from the influence of Baker into the contemporary prayer life of the community.

What we see in Baker's teaching – and what remains key in accounts of prayer in the monastery today – is a model of passage from discursive meditation to contemplative prayer; "mystic contemplation" is seen to begin when one stops using the imagination in prayer. In Baker's writing, such a passage consists at first of what he describes as "forced immediate acts." These are deliberate expressions of desire that focus the will upon God without seeking comprehension through reason. Those who pray in this way pass from the "representation" of a mystery of faith, or an expression of the greatness or perfection of God, to "acts" by which they relate themselves to God in adoration, humility, thanksgiving, love, and so on.

Crucially, the role of language in prayer is here recast. Such "acts" may well consist of words or images and, as such, contain a representational element; but this element is downplayed in the transition from "discourse of the mind" to "act of the will." Words or images used in prayer are thus an act of offering oneself to God, not a focus for reflection and scrutiny in their own right – one contemporary member of the monastic community made the analogy here with "whispering sweet nothings to a lover." Indeed, Baker envisages that the use of representations will come to diminish, with contemplation growing more and more "pure" as the need for mental images lessens; thus, beyond these "forced acts" are "aspirations," the spontaneous expression by the will of the desire for God, who is beyond mental representation. It is important to emphasize that here, by defining mystical contemplation in this way, Baker suggests it is available to "all who dispose themselves to it" and cannot be thought of as purely an extraordinary gift of the few, a position that has aroused some controversy (see Knowles 1961: 161–87).

Now, let us return to another key element in the narrative of progress in prayer that the librarian provides: the emphasis on restlessness and anxiousness. How might this element relate to a broader tradition? The suggestion the librarian gives here is that, in the absence of images and conceptualizations, the mind grows restless; yet, one is to be reassured: "People who are in such a quandary should take heart from the truism that, although they feel they have harvested nothing from what now seems a pointless exercise, nevertheless what they have been doing or suffering has been well and truly prayer. The reason why it is, is because the essence of prayer, like everything in the moral and spiritual order, lies in the intention … If you intend to pray, then you are praying, even though you have no signs of any success in doing so."

Such reassurance is very close to the teaching of John Chapman, who was fourth abbot of the community during the late 1920s and early 1930s. Chapman was the son of an Anglican clergyman and had begun training for the Anglican priesthood before converting to Catholicism in 1890. He became a monk of Maredsous Abbey in Belgium, a house of the Beuronese Congregation, making his solemn profession at its daughter foundation at Erdington Priory, near Birmingham. When the circumstances of the First World War caused the closure of the community – belonging as it did to a German congregation – he moved to Downside Abbey, later becoming a full member of the community there and, finally, being elected as abbot.[5] What we know of Chapman's spiritual teaching comes from the extensive letters that he wrote to a wide variety of correspondents – priests, monks, nuns, as well as laymen and laywomen; these letters were gathered together and posthumously published (Chapman 1935). Here again, it is worth noting that Chapman does not restrict his advice and guidance to those who belong to particular religious or monastic orders, or might otherwise be seen as prayer "specialists"; this sense that Chapman "democratizes" prayer remains key for the community, many of whom make a special effort through talks, retreats, and writing to speak about contemplative prayer to a wider public.

Chapman's advice continually focuses on the difficulties faced by those passing from discursive to contemplative prayer. Meditation becomes difficult, or impossible: "a dry land where no water is" (Chapman 1935: 46); the sense that prayer becomes "dry" is a recurrent theme in Chapman's letters. The value of this dryness is that it leads us to change our way of prayer. "All those who find it impossible to meditate … and find they cannot fix their thoughts on a subject, or understand the meaning of the words, unless they cease to feel they are praying, are meant to cease all thinking, and only make acts of the will" (119).

Prayer comes to consist of simply fixing the will upon God; the trouble is, this *feels* like doing nothing at all. "The soul itself often feels rather idiotic and wonders whether it is not wasting time, knowing that, if it described its state to any sensible person, it would be told to go do something useful" (Chapman 1935: 137). But this anxiousness is because openness to God as he is, rather than as we imagine him, is an openness that must go beyond thought or feeling; Chapman therefore maintains that this "simple prayer" "is absolutely easy, if only you realise that it is a prayer of the will, not of the intellect, or the imagination, or of the emotions" (45–6). We must therefore deal with what Chapman terms a "divided consciousness" (255); a recognition that the "real me" consists of the upper capacities (which, through prayer, come to be united with God) and that we cannot come to identify the "self" with our thoughts and feelings. "The real 'I' is the will which gives itself to God, (the emotions and imaginations are not me, they are in me, but they are not under my control)" (175).

This model of "divided consciousness" is one that is recognized and engaged with in a variety of ways. For example, at an early stage during my research, a book by the New Age writer Eckhart Tolle was enthusiastically recommended to me by one monk. In particular, he felt that I needed to read the account given by Tolle of his "spiritual awakening," which the monk said resonated with his own experience. "'I cannot live with myself any longer.' This was the thought that kept repeating itself in my mind. Then suddenly I became aware of what a peculiar thought it was. 'Am I one or two? If I cannot live with myself, there must be two of me: the "I" and the "self" that "I" cannot live with.' 'Maybe,' I thought, 'only one of them is real'" (Tolle 1997: 2).

As the monk explained, "that account by Tolle is one of the most dramatic I know. And I think it's common to a lot of mystics. You have this massive deflation of the self that we build up, and the realization that there is a different 'ME' [he gestures towards himself with both hands], the true self. What he had discovered, his huge discovery, was that you can stop thinking and stay fully conscious. And then he was onto the Chapman gap, you see." Now, I would not like to give the impression that Eckhart Tolle is being treated as the authoritative mystical teaching of the Church (a certain wariness could be heard during one teatime conversation: "Tolle. Is he even Catholic?" "I think he's some kind of Buddhist." "Oh."[6]). Nevertheless, I believe this identification of what was termed "the Chapman gap" in Tolle's writing is significant. What was cherished by this monk was the recognition that the "self" should not be identified just with *thinking*, and that even when disconnecting yourself from the things you think up (and so existing, as Chapman says, "in an idiotic state"), the "me" in prayer remains – as long as we remember that this "me" is not the self that we associate with the images, words, thoughts, and feelings that present themselves in our minds.

Kataphatic and Apophatic Modes of Prayer

In order to understand the implications of this approach to contemplation, it is useful to recognize why a distinction is sometimes made between "kataphatic" and "apophatic" modes of prayer – a distinction that has also recently been highlighted as analytically significant by Luhrmann (2012).

By kataphatic, I mean essentially approaches to prayer that allow the person at prayer to be led by words, images, and concepts; thought and sense are heavily involved in what can be considered a process of mental, and often emotional, engagement. Apophatic forms of prayer, by contrast, deny that words and images can adequately reflect the nature of God – God is beyond our understanding and narrow sensory capabilities. That which can be imagined or comprehended in our finite minds holds us apart from the infinite God, and the failure of mind and sense is thus the start of contemplation.

The Jesuit Harvey Egan (1978) illustrates the difference between these two approaches by reflecting on two "paradigmatic cases": *The Spiritual Exercises of Ignatius Loyola,* sixteenth-century founder of the Jesuits, and the fourteenth-century English mystical text *The Cloud of Unknowing.* The kataphatic way of the *The Spiritual Exercises* is thus the "Ignatian" form of discursive prayer that earlier we saw the librarian of the monastery term "prayerful pondering": meditating "on episodes in the life of Christ, using the imagination and the sense to reconstruct the scene, reflecting upon it with the reason, summoning up the appropriate emotions to make the will come to some practical resolutions." The emphasis here is on vivid imagery directed through language, and, as Luhrmann (2012: 172–84) has described in some detail, this path involves building up a sensorium and developing the capacity to imagine and reflect during the time of prayer. *The Cloud of Unknowing,* by contrast, "provides an excellent illustration of orthodox Christian, apophatic mysticism. It urges forgetting and unknowing in the service of a blind, silent love beyond all images, thoughts, and feelings" (Egan 1978: 413); although a simple, one syllable word is used in prayer, the word is valued "not for its meaning (for he must not advert to its meaning) but for its simplicity. This one word helps his spirit to be poised at its fine point, to eliminate distractions" (407). Prayer here is a process of emptying oneself. It is worth noting that the paradigmatic example Egan draws upon here is seen as particularly important within the tradition of the English Benedictine Congregation, not only as part of the heritage of pre-reformation English spirituality with which English Benedictines are keen to stress their continuity, but also more specifically because the *Cloud* was a key influence on Augustine Baker, who was involved in the transmission of the text and wrote a commentary on it.[7]

The significance of this distinction is not simply in labelling different "flavours" of prayer. I would also argue that the distinction matters a great deal, because it points to different kinds of social and institutional relationships in the life of prayer. In short, a recognition of the distinction between apophatic and kataphatic prayer makes visible important differences in understanding the role of communication and the relationship with authority.

What we see in the kataphatic mode is the development of a particular discipline of self-scrutiny and sense-awareness within the framework of institutional authority. If the experience of prayer is communicable, consisting of describable images and feelings, there is a possibility of sharing this experience in such a way that one's success can be evaluated by others, including those in positions of authority. Tanya Luhrmann has emphasized "inner sense cultivation" (Luhrmann and Morgain 2012) as key to the way in which American Evangelical Protestants in the Vineyard churches build up their capacity to sense God as a vivid auditory and emotional presence, and imagine God as an interlocutor (Luhrmann 2007), and has made important connections between this building up of the capacity to imagine and sense and the Jesuit tradition of *The Spiritual Exercises* described earlier (Luhrmann 2012). So, to be trained in kataphatic prayer is to learn a set of skills, and one can assess whether those skills meet up with institutional expectations. Here, not only does one open oneself to evaluation by others – prayer can be articulated, shared, monitored, and made subject to the template of Church expectations – but one also comes to evaluate one's own success.

Apophatic prayer makes such guidance, and such evaluation, difficult. Not only is there a silence about what the experience of contemplative prayer is like – a silence made necessary because it is beyond means of representation – but, further to this, the monks in the monastery where I worked showed a great resistance to anything that might be seen as "prescriptive." As one monk explained to me, "one offers encouragement, but that is not the same as giving an instruction manual, because no instruction manual can exist. I don't want to sound prescriptive, because I don't think this is an area within which one can be prescriptive." Another declared himself "agnostic" on such matters – of course he had his own ideas, but he was wary of speaking in absolutes and wanted to allow for variety. This attitude is noteworthy, as it reflects the freedom associated with the practice of prayer. In contrast to Talal Asad's representation of the (medieval) Catholic monastery as a site where "obedient wills are created" (Asad 1993: 125), contemplative prayer in its apophatic form appears to stand apart from this work of reconstitution in relation to authority. Ultimately, it was the individual who was at prayer, and one cannot dictate an individual's experience of the ineffable. Prayer must therefore be without external constraint. Notwithstanding the hierarchical structures that shape the monastery (a system of *paterfamilias* under the governance of the abbot [Nuzzo 1996: 874], with novice and junior masters responsible for the formation of those who recently entered the monastery), in prayer monks were left "*solus cum solo*" – alone with the alone.

We have seen how apophatic prayer creates a space of freedom within the institutional structure and identity of the monastery. This practice severely complicates the idea that monastic life involves the "disciplined development of the self" through "the performance of prescribed forms under the authority of the more adept" (Asad 1993: 135), reflecting the claim that mysticism serves as a "systematic irritation" to the organization containing it (Faubion 2013: 304). In these dynamics, then, we see some of the social characteristics of the ineffable, reflecting in some ways the insights of the composer and artist John Cage on the generative possibility of silence – absence not as a vacuum, but as pure possibility, as expressed in his "Lecture on Something": "When nothing is securely possessed one is free to accept any of the somethings. How many are there? They roll up at your feet. How many doors and windows are there in it? There is no end to the somethings and all of them are acceptable" (Cage 1961: 132).

Yet, fundamental to the freedom provided by silence is that communication within this space is severely limited; and although I have highlighted the freedom that is made possible by the "ineffable" experience of contemplative prayer, its apparent incommunicability could also be seen as a source of frustration. This frustration comes across clearly in the memories of one monk, recounting his experiences as a novice in the 1990s: "What was very surprising to me was the silence about this thing called prayer. It was something that we were told to do twice a day, but we weren't told how to do it. Yes, we were told to read books about prayer. I remember reading *The Cloud of Unknowing*, and it had a very deep effect on me. But there was no real attempt to say 'this is what it feels like.' And I realized, I suppose it gradually dawned on me, that this was because here was something it was impossible to say or to express. But it was very frustrating at first all the same, like being sent to look for something but not being told what it was you were meant to be looking for."

The bemusement conveyed in this monk's memory does not appear to be an isolated case, but rather a broader characteristic of monastic prayer life and a recurring feature in accounts from within the community. Indeed, we see very similar frustrations expressed in a description of life in the monastery published in the late 1960s: "There was marked reluctance to say what prayer was actually like from within, to say anything precise or personal about what prayer was for the individual who was advocating it. So our school of prayer was really a do-it-yourself school in which the only principle was that this thing called prayer was all-important" (Harvey 1969: 4). Significantly, because contemplative prayer was not something that could be communicated, it was set apart from other aspects of monastic life in which the emphasis was on the ability of the monks to join together as a community. "Private prayer and its corollary – spiritual reading – jostled uneasily for top priority with corporate prayer; then came the second-grade, though indispensable, elements of work and recreation. The creative aspect of work, and of human relationships, was thus scaled down in favour of the purely or directly spiritual activity of prayer" (4). The impression given here is that the "spiritual activity" of contemplative prayer is disconnected from the rest of temporal life. "Because prayer was divorced from other elements it could not fulfil in practice the high claim made for it: it could not be interpretive of and enlarging of our experience" – and it is the incommunicable nature of prayer that creates this disconnection, rendering prayer a private activity set aside from the tools of sociality and thus generating "a radical tension between prayer, work and relationships" (5).

The social dynamics that make the ineffable a source of potential freedom and frustration are precisely those that lead to apophatic mysticism – including the contemplative tradition of the English Benedictines – becoming an object of suspicion. Indeed, key spiritual teachers in the history of the English Benedictine Congregation have been subject to investigation for the orthodoxy of their teaching. To consider the key figures outlined earlier: Augustine Baker's teaching was seen (and actively criticized) by some of his contemporaries as undermining obedience. Why? Precisely because he held that, as prayer was a personal experience, one's method of prayer should not be subject to external interference (Clark 2004: 219). The personal nature of contemplation meant that it resisted being subjected to authority, and, as Lunn (1975: 277) has noted, for this reason Baker was a constant cause of controversy: when he was working with nuns as a spiritual guide, it became clear that his insistence upon independence in prayer life challenged the jurisdiction of monastic superiors; he was eventually expelled from his role at Cambrai, and the contemplative manuscripts he gave to the nuns were formally examined at a General Chapter of 1633. In the twentieth century, controversy also accompanied the publication of John Chapman's *Spiritual Letters*; his teaching was subject to serious criticism and accused of bearing similarities to condemned writings: Hudleston (1935) responds to concerns about the volume raised by the Jesuit Alban Goodier, who sees Chapman's theories as likely to foster subjectivism in the spiritual life and an indifference towards theology. Here, the focus on individual ineffable experience is seen as a potential danger because it might undermine collective discipline, while the non-conceptual nature of mystical prayer risks undermining the conceptual grounding of Church teaching by demonstrating the limits of such knowledge, prioritizing instead the incommunicable. It is against such a background that the monks repeated to me on numerous occasions a joke attributed to Aiden Gasquet, a nineteenth-century prior of the community: "The trouble with mysticism is that it begins in mist and ends in schism."

Locating the Ineffable

To return to our key problem: how are we to engage an "ineffable" that appears to resist the very possibility of communication? At the heart of the concerns raised earlier is a suspicion towards the antisocial nature of ineffability. The theologian Christopher Insole takes as his target "some sloppier modern constructions of the apophatic God" (Insole 2001: 479). His concern is with the way that the encounter becomes closed in: the "phony-privatization of the inner world of each hermetically sealed individual" (481). The God for whom this individual looks becomes, like the searcher, "unfathomable," a projection of the "intensely private romantic self" (482). In such a scenario of incommunicability, nothing can be revealed, and so each individual is separated by their claim to a knowledge that cannot be shared. And, if nothing can be said of the experience of God – it can only be understood in the private world – God can neither be spoken of in the public domain, nor affect it. His inexpressibility renders him socially and politically impotent.

Insole makes clear that his intention is not to attack the apophatic tradition, but rather to warn about the risk of self-indulgence when an approach to knowledge rejects comprehension. Nevertheless, I think his warning raises an important question for our anthropological enquiry about the social life of the ineffable. If the experience of prayer is inexpressible, does this attribute run the risk of isolating the individual in an inner world that cannot be connected with the experience of others?

To offer one potential answer to this question, I want to return to the silence bellowed out, as you will recall, from the door to the monastic enclosure. Should this demand be taken as a sign of privatization and closing off, of disconnection? The centrality of silence, it seems, points very directly towards the confrontation with vastness. To reach towards an infinite God requires the failure of the finite mind. The eighteenth century philosopher and statesman Edmund Burke, in *A Philosophical Enquiry into the Origin of Our Ideas of the Sublime and Beautiful*, treats the encounter with vastness as a source of overwhelming excitement and horror: "Infinity has a tendency to fill the mind with that sort of delightful horror, which is the most genuine effect, and truest test, of the sublime" (Burke [1757] 1958: 73). And yet, if we consider the context of this encounter with the infinite, it is within an architecture of shared experience (Irvine 2011a). It is bringing the sublime home: silence, after all, is pronounced on the door to the cloister, the space of connection through which the monks move between the elements of their life – praying, sleeping, working, and eating. The point to make here is that if, following Burke, the confrontation with the infinite is overwhelming (and we saw earlier how it could create a sense, for better or worse, that the ineffable is something that transcends other elements of life), such an encounter is, nevertheless, located. The monastery is a space where time is organized. The imposing square tower of the Downside Abbey church carries a single bell, named "Great Bede." Great Bede's call to prayer, a continuous steady striking sound, rings out five minutes before each hour of the Divine Office, the monk's daily liturgy. During the minute prior to the service, a smaller bell hanging in the west wing of the monastery rings repeatedly, and the service starts as soon as this bell ceases to ring. The call to prayer is one of the most striking features of life in the monastery. The day is shaped around the repeated call to gather at set times, and it is this practice that gives daily life its rhythm. The monastery is, in this sense, a space of time-discipline (see also Zerubavel 1980).

While the striking of the bell calls the monks to the abbey church for the public prayer of the liturgy, it is in relation to these timetabled points of collective prayer that the acutely personal current of contemplative prayer is visible. After the abbot has brought Vigils (the first point of collective prayer in the day) to an end, a few of the monks remain in the stalls. Some kneel, others sit. Others leave the stalls and go to sit in the nave, perhaps, as one monk suggested I might do, looking up at the eastern window as the sun rises outside. Still others return to the monastery wing and to their cells. Again, in the evening (except on days when there is a conference to the community), once Vespers has been brought to an end, and the monks have processed from the church through into the cloister, some of them re-enter the church and sit or kneel, while some return to their cells, and others walk in the grounds.

These times are the two half hours of private prayer that monks at the monastery observe. The importance of these "two half hours" to their monastic identity was repeated to me in conversation on many occasions. Its importance to the monastic community meant that it was something to be protected: it was not to be allowed to slip or encroached upon by other activities during the day. Sometime early in 2006, I read a notice stating that from now on, Lauds was to start five minutes later (moving from 7:05 a.m. to 7:10 a.m.). When I asked why, I was told that it was to make sure there was adequate time for private prayer. Sometimes, when Vigils overran, it was feared that monks were not getting their full half-hour's worth.

I should perhaps make it clear at this stage, in case there is any doubt, that monks also pray at other times and the "two half hours" is not an arbitrary time limit. They might pray while taking a walk during a period of recreation, or maybe stay behind in the abbey church after Compline. And, of course, the monks pray at various times when they are not in the line of sight of visitors, such as when going to bed. One day, when I was asking about whether thought was a necessary constituent of prayer, a monk answered by telling me how, in sleep, the will could be fixed upon God even while the body and mind was resting. So, the personal prayer of monks is by no means limited to specific points in the timetable. Nonetheless, the "two half hours" remain significant. They indicate a shared intention and an institutional recognition of contemplative prayer's place of importance within the English Benedictine tradition.

It is for this reason that I suggest Burke's approach to the sublime is helpful in allowing us to ponder the relationship between structure and infinity, knowledge and failure. While recognizing that "there are scarce any things which can become the objects of our senses, that are really and in their own nature infinite" (Burke [1757] 1958: 73), Burke nevertheless suggests that structures of repetition (such as visual succession in architecture or rhythmic recurrence of sound) are key in leading our (finite) senses towards the overwhelming sensation of infinity

(140). Through this "kind of artificial infinity" (74), and thus through the structuring of space, time, sound, or vision, we apprehend that which reaches out before and beyond us and experience it as sublime.

This sense that what is overwhelming is, nevertheless, located within structure again resonates with John Cage's reflections on the mutually constitutive relationship between silence and sound, as in his "Lecture on Nothing": a lecture punctuated by silence, but showing how that silence takes its character from within the structure of the talk. "What we re-quire is silence; but what silence requires is that I go on talking ... Now there are silences and the words help make the silences. I have nothing to say and I am saying it ... This space of time is organized. We need not fear these silences" (Cage 1961: 109). Later in the same lecture, after a drawn-out rhythm of repetition, speech, and silence, resting, speaking, and then resting again, he states: "We really do need a structure so we can see we are nowhere" (125). My argument here is that the relationship between contemplative prayer and the monastic *horarium* is an apt illustration of this claim. The ineffable is situated against the backdrop of this temporal structure, visible as negative space within the routine of social life.

Pyysiäinen (1993: 9), in his historical study of early Buddhism in India, explores "the dilemma of expressing and describing an ineffable experience": how the inexpressible core of mysticism nevertheless comes to be narrativized as mythology (especially in the biographical image of the Buddha). Similarly, Denys Turner (1995), in his study of negativity in medieval Christian mysticism, draws our attention to the "visibility" of apophatic mysticism: the rich language of classic apophatic texts, metaphors of "exteriority," "interiority," and "ascent" central to narratives of the progress of the soul towards God even as the possibility of expressibility is explicitly denied (for example, in St. John of the Cross's *Dark Night of the Soul*, the symbolic metaphor of climbing the ladder to the beloved in the night). The image of darkness is key here as a descriptive metaphor for that which cannot be seen. For Turner, these metaphors should not be taken as after-the-fact descriptions of a mystical experience, but rather are statements of an "anti-mysticism" that seeks to use language in a self-subverting manner. They are descriptions that deny the possibility of description, a process resonant with the "active cultivation of the awareness of ignorance," which Mair (2015: 252) describes in the context of Inner Mongolian Buddhism.

The claim being made here is that apophatic mysticism does not stand alone, but that silence comes to be grounded in speech (see also McDonough 2011), visible in relation to it. If the radical claim to mystical incommunicability brings about "structural and organizational disruption" (Faubion

2013: 304) – and the suspicion in which contemplative prayer is held, as seen earlier, suggests that it has this potential – it calls upon that structure and organization in the process of insisting upon its failure.

What we have seen in this paper is a tradition that presents a key space of freedom from authority for the monks, privileging failure and severely restricting the very possibility of communication – but this space is situated within the rich and structured vitality of a community. The monastery is an organized space in time, and the silence pronounced on the cloister door exists within a structured world of sound and sense. Contemplative prayer, in all its unknowability, comes to be visible against the backdrop of the shaping of time and space that the monastery presents.

The ineffable requires a social life.

NOTES

1 I first lived alongside the community throughout the academic year 2005–06, and my fieldwork involved sharing as a guest in the life of the monastery, eating in silence in the monastic refectory, learning to make things in the carpentry workshop, drinking tea, and following the daily cycle of prayer. I have subsequently returned to stay in the monastery for shorter periods of time on numerous occasions. For an ethnographic overview of the everyday life of the monks, see Irvine (2017).

2 Faubion (2013) engages with St. John of the Cross at length in his reflection on mystical prayer as "desubjectification."

3 See Butler (1961) for a published account of prayer in which this term "prayerful pondering" is used to describe discursive meditation.

4 As these activities were deemed treasonable, several of these monks, upon discovery, were executed and are thus treated as martyrs by the Church. See Lunn (1980) for an account of this period of history in the English Benedictine Congregation.

5 For an account of the life of Chapman, see Butler (1934), as well as Roger Hudleston's memoir, which prefaces his edition of the *Spiritual Letters* (Chapman 1935).

6 When I have presented this quotation, it has occasionally caused some confusion, with readers thinking that the monks were suspicious of Buddhism. I would suggest that this is unlikely, as the monks in question had made links between contemplative prayer and Buddhist experience on more than one occasion. At the time of the conversation, I interpreted the suspicion here as being based more on the "Some kind of" – it was Tolle's heterodoxy and New Age basis that made him dubious, not whatever affiliation he may have had to Buddhism.

7 English Benedictine scholars have debated the nature of the link between the *Cloud* and Augustine Baker. Spearritt (1974) argues that, in Baker's teaching, what we see is a post-reformation survival of the spirituality of the *Cloud*; Lunn (1975), however, is more cautious, pointing to a wider pool of influences on Baker than just English pre-reformation sources.

REFERENCES

Asad, Talal. 1993. *Genealogies of Religion: Discipline and Reasons of Power in Christianity and Islam*. Baltimore, MD: John Hopkins University Press.

Burke, Edmund. (1757) 1958. *A Philosophical Enquiry into the Origin of Our Ideas of the Sublime and Beautiful*, edited by James T. Boulton. London: Routledge and Kegan Paul.

Butler, B.C. 1961. *Prayer: An Adventure in Living*. London: Darton, Longman and Todd.

Butler, Edward Cuthbert. 1934. "Abbot Chapman." *Downside Review* 52: 1–12.

Cage, John. 1961. *Silence: Lectures and Writings*. Hanover, NH: Wesleyan University Press.

Chapman, John. 1935. *The Spiritual Letters of Dom John Chapman O.S.B.*, edited by Roger Hudleston. London: Sheed and Ward.

Clark, J.P.H. 2004. "Augustine Baker, O.S.B.: Towards a Re-Assessment." *Studies in Spirituality* 14: 209–24.

Egan, Harvey D. 1978. "Christian Apophatic and Kataphatic Mysticisms." *Theological Studies* 39: 399–426.

Faubion, James. 2013. "The Subject That Is Not One: On the Ethics of Mysticism." *Anthropological Theory* 13 (4): 287–307.

Harvey, Peter. 1969. Introduction to *The Experience of Prayer* by Sebastian Moore and Kevin Mcguire. London: Darton, Longman and Todd.

Hudleston, Roger. 1935. "Abbot Chapman on Prayer: A Reply to an Article in 'The Month' for June, 1935." *Downside Review* 53: 286–306.

Insole, Christopher. 2001. "Anthropomorphism and the Apophatic God." *Modern Theology* 17 (4): 475–83.

Irvine, Richard D.G. 2010. "How to Read: *Lectio Divina* in an English Benedictine Monastery." *Culture and Religion* 11 (4): 395–411.

– 2011a. "The Architecture of Stability: Monasteries and the Importance of Place in a World of Non-Places." *Etnofoor* 23 (1): 29–49.

– 2011b. "Eating in Silence in an English Benedictine Monastery." In *Food and Faith in Christian Culture*, edited by Kenneth Albala and Trudy Eden, 221–37. New York: Columbia University Press.

– 2017. "The Everyday Life of Monks: English Benedictine Identity and the Performance of Proximity." In *Monasticism in Modern Times*, edited by Isabelle Jonveaux and Stefania Palmisano, 191–208. London: Routledge.

Knowles, David. 1961. *The English Mystical Tradition*. London: Burns and Oates.

Luhrmann, T.M. 2007. "How Do You Learn to Know That It Is God Who Speaks?" In *Learning Religion: Anthropological Approaches*, edited by David Berliner and Ramon Sarró, 83–102. Oxford: Berghahn.

– 2012. *When God Talks Back: Understanding the American Evangelical Relationship with God*. New York: Knopf.

Luhrmann, T.M., and Rachel Morgain. 2012. "Prayer as Inner Sense Cultivation: An Attentional Learning Theory of Spiritual Experience." *Ethos* 40 (4): 359–89.

Lunn, David. 1975. "Augustine Baker (1575–1641) and the English Mystical Tradition." *Journal of Ecclesiastical History* 26 (3): 267–77.

– 1980. *The English Benedictines, 1540–1688: From Reformation to Revolution*. London: Burns and Oates.

Mair, Jonathan. 2015. "The Discourse of Ignorance and the Ethics of Detachment among Mongolian Tibetan Buddhists in Inner Mongolia, China." In *Detachment: Essays on the Limits of Relational Thinking*, edited by Matei Candea, Joanna Cook, Catherine Trundle, and Thomas Yarrow, 236–55. Manchester, UK: Manchester University Press.

Malinowski, Bronislaw. 1923. "The Problem of Meaning in Primitive Language." In *The Meaning of Meaning: A Study of the Influence of Language upon Thought and of the Science of Symbolism*, by C.K. Ogden and I.A. Richards, 296–336. London: Routledge and Kegan Paul.

McDonough, Conor. 2011. "Grounding Speech and Silence: Cataphaticism and Apophaticism in Denys and Aquinas." *Irish Theological Quarterly* 76 (1): 57–76.

Nuzzo, James L.J. 1996. "The Rule of Saint Benedict: The Debates over the Interpretation of an Ancient Legal and Spiritual Document." *Harvard Journal of Law and Public Policy* 20: 867–86.

Pyysiäinen, Ilkka 1993. *Beyond Language and Reason: Mysticism in Indian Buddhism*. Helsinki, FI: Suomalainen Tiedeakatemia.

Spearritt, Placid. 1974. "The Survival of Medieval Spirituality among the Exiled English Black Monks." *American Benedictine Review* 25 (3): 287–316.

Tolle, Eckhart. 1997. *The Power of Now: A Guide to Spiritual Enlightenment*. Vancouver, BC: Namaste Publishing.

Turner, Denys. 1995. *The Darkness of God: Negativity in Christian Mysticism*. Cambridge: Cambridge University Press.

Wichroski, Mary Anne. 1997. "Breaking Silence: Some Fieldwork Strategies in Cloistered and Non-Cloistered Communities." In *Reflexivity and Voice*, edited by Rosanna Hertz, 265–82. Thousand Oaks, CA: Sage.

Zerubavel, Eviatar. 1980. "The Benedictine Ethic and the Modern Spirit of Scheduling: On Schedules and Social Organization." *Sociological Enquiry* 50 (2): 157–69.

PART TWO

Discerning Wisdom

3 How Wisdom Is Discovered: Discretion and Emotional Insights in Naikan Meditation in Japan

CLARK CHILSON

In an essay titled "An Anthropology of Knowledge," Fredrick Barth (2002: 1) wrote that "we can greatly advance our anthropological agenda by developing a comparative ethnographic analysis on how bodies of knowledge are produced in persons." The same is true for the anthropology of wisdom, which can show us how understandings of wisdom vary across cultures and, to echo Barth, how wisdom is produced. In anthropological studies of wisdom, two questions are pertinent. First, how do different cultures conceptualize certain forms of knowledge in a way close to what is conventionally called "wisdom" in English? Second, how are certain cultural practices associated with the attainment of wisdom? This chapter attempts to contribute to an anthropology of wisdom by addressing these two questions. It does so first through an investigation of how "wisdom" is understood in Japan and then by showing how wisdom relates to a form of meditation called Naikan that developed in the mid-twentieth century.

The practice of Naikan involves self-reflection. The term "naikan" is written with the kanji "inner" and "looking"; we might literally translate it as "introspection." Naikan developed out of a Pure Land Buddhist practice in Japan and is currently used as both a self-cultivation practice and a form of psychotherapy. Practitioners of Naikan deliberately call to mind instances of family and friends doing things for them, instances of giving back to those family and friends, and times when they caused others trouble or difficulties. It can be done in intensive one-week retreats or as part of a daily practice. People who have little or no meditative experience often claim that, as a result of doing Naikan, they have had insights into their lives, which have changed how they see themselves and their social relations.

Anthropologists who have previously studied Naikan have characterized it in various ways. In the early 1970s, Takie Lebra (1976) saw

Naikan as a "moralistic type of therapy." By contrast, David Reynolds, who did ethnographic fieldwork at a major Naikan centre several years after Lebra, argued that we should not view Naikan as primarily moralistic. He wrote that to understand Naikan as a "guilt-producing, self-punishing Oriental moralism ... would be to risk missing even a glance into the wisdom of a transcendent lifeway. For Naikan offers this profound insight into human existence: that each of us, by his or her own standards, fails to live a life of balanced giving and receiving" (Reynolds 1983: 1). Most recently, Ozawa-de Silva has argued that Naikan involves "mindfulness of the kindness of others" and that it is a healing practice residing in a borderland between religion and psychotherapy (Ozawa-de Silva 2006; 2015).

On the basis of my own fieldwork at a Naikan training centre in Tokyo, I add to previous anthropological work on Naikan by showing how it can be a wisdom practice that leads to emotional insights into a person's life and fosters the development of discretion.

Wisdom in Japanese Culture

As a social construction, the word "wisdom" has a distinctive range of meanings, which have wielded influence in English-speaking countries. In the academic world today, psychologists have given more attention to defining "wisdom" than have anthropologists. The psychologist Roger Walsh (2015) has pointed out that there is personal and general wisdom. The former indicates a type of self-understanding, while the latter refers to knowledge on existential matters. He also delineates four types of wisdom: practical, intuitive, conceptual, and transconceptual. Overall, the concept of "wisdom" in English commonly focuses on a type of knowledge that individuals have about themselves and the nature of reality.

Other languages have words that connote something similar to "wisdom" in contemporary English but have different ranges of meaning. To understand the meaning of "wisdom" in Japanese culture, we can examine three things: the explicit definitions of terms close in meaning to wisdom; the usage of these terms; and, finally, implicit definitions of these terms. Together they make up a sematic field related to wisdom.

Several Japanese words have explicit, lexical definitions that are close to "wisdom." Among them are *kenmei* 賢明, which refers to something that is intelligent and in accordance with reason; *eichi* 叡智, which signifies superior knowledge and the ability to discern the truth; and *hannya* 般若, which is the translation of *prajñā*, a Sanskrit word used in Buddhist texts to mean an understanding of the way things truly are.

But the most commonly used Japanese word that is close in meaning to "wisdom" is *chie*. It is written with two ideograms, *chi* 知 and *e* 恵, which respectfully denote "knowledge" and "blessing." *Chie* is knowledge that allows the discernment of right from wrong and good from bad. It is also knowledge about the true nature of things.

When we examine the usage of *chie* in, for example, proverbs and idiomatic expressions, we find how *chie* is similar to the English concept of "wisdom." For example, *chie*, like wisdom, is treated as valued and rare in proverbs, such as "*Chie* is a treasure for all generations" (*chie wa bandai no takara*) and "For every man with *chie* there are 10,000 fools" (*chiesha ichinin baka mannin*). *Chie* is also close to the meaning of "wisdom" in the expression "If three people come together, they will have the wisdom of [the wise Bodhisattva] Manjushri" (*sannin yoreba monju no chie*).

Chie, however, also connotes a variety of mental activities. To say someone's *chie* lags (*chie okure*) is to say the person has an intellectual disability. In different sayings, *chie* might be translated as wit, thinking, or knowledge. For example, the expression *chie ga mawaru*, translated literally as "*chie* goes around," is used to indicate that someone is quick witted. In other cases, the word is closer to knowledge about something. The saying "Use your *chie* little by little" (*chie wa kodashi ni seyo*) suggests that wisdom is a type of knowledge better transmitted in small doses. This saying can apply to teaching, when it is important that students master a certain type of basic knowledge before being instructed in more advanced knowledge.

For implicit definitions of *chie*, we can look to the work of Masami Takahashi and Prashant Bordia, who did a cross-cultural study of wisdom using questionnaires to compare the implicit meanings of wisdom among Americans, Australians, Indians, and Japanese. The study found that being wise among Americans and Australians was most closely associated with "knowledge," while Japanese and Indian young adults mostly associated it with being "discreet" and secondarily with age and experience (Takahashi and Bordia 2000: 4). The study concluded that

> the Eastern participants identified "wise" with the "discreet" characteristic, which requires not only "knowledge" but also prudence or exercising sound judgment in a practical and emotional situation. In other words, "wise" is conceptualized in the East not as mere analytical ability but as a psychological quality that emphasizes more "direct" understanding with a great deal of emotional involvement or an effective integration of multiple aspects of human consciousness (e.g. cognition, affect, intuition, etc.). (7)

The emphasis put on "discreet" as a characteristic of wisdom shows that wisdom is associated with an emotional intelligence. To be discreet, a person must think about the concerns, preferences, and viewpoints of others, which requires emotional sensitivity. Discretion further requires a social intelligence more than intellectual knowledge. Wisdom, which has discretion as a core characteristic, is thus prosocial and requires understanding social relations.

Wisdom and Emotions in Japanese Buddhism

The eighteenth-century Japanese Zen monk Hakuin describes in the following autobiographical passage how he became enlightened:

> I picked up my begging bowl and went into the village below Iiyama Castle. I was totally absorbed in my koan – never away from it for an instant. I took up a position beside the gate of a house, my bowl in my hand, fixed in a kind of trance. From inside the house, a voice yelled out, "Get away from here! Go somewhere else!" I was so preoccupied, I didn't even notice it. This must have angered the occupant, because suddenly she appeared flourishing a broom upside down in her hands. She flew at me, flailing wildly, whacking away at my head as if she were bent on dashing my brains out. My sedge hat lay in tatters. I was knocked over and ended heels up on the ground, totally unconscious. I lay there like a dead man.
>
> ...
>
> A few people who happened to be passing by approached me in wonderment. They grabbed hold of me and hoisted me upright.
>
> "What's wrong?" "What happened?" they exclaimed.
>
> As I came to and my eyes opened, I found that the unsolvable and impenetrable koan I had been working on ... were now penetrated completely. Right to their roots. They had suddenly ceased to exist. I began clapping my hands and whooping with glee, frightening the people who had gathered round to help me.
>
> "He's lost his mind!" "A crazy monk!" they shouted, shrinking back from me apprehensively. They then turned heel and fled, without looking back. (Hakuin 1999: 33)

Hakuin's clapping of hands and whooping with glee after focusing on koan indicates that expression of emotions can accompany moments of deep insight. In the context of Hakuin's Zen Buddhist meditation, his insight was a supposed awakening to a universal truth about the nature of reality.

Among Buddhist traditions, there are a great variety of meditation practices that are seen as fostering wisdom. In North America, the type of meditation that has become most popular is "mindfulness meditation," which attempts to cultivate non-judgmental awareness in the present moment by focusing on the breath or body (Samuel 2016; Wilson 2014). Although in the popular English-language media this practice is frequently equated with "Buddhist meditation," it has never been practised by a large percentage of Buddhists nor is it the most common type of meditation throughout the Buddhist world. In East Asia, meditation more frequently involves the recitations of words than silently focusing attention on the breath with non-judgmental, present-centric awareness.

While in Buddhists texts strong emotions are sometimes seen as distracting, if not dangerous, there are various emotional states associated with wisdom. Common among these are equanimity, loving-kindness, and joy. Emotional states counter to wisdom include anger, resentment, self-importance, worry, and sloth.[1] Various meditation practices aim to purify the mind of defilements (Sanskrit: *kleśa;* Japanese: *bonnō*) that create negative emotions and to foster the acquisition of wisdom (*prajñā*), which entails seeing the world as it is in accordance with certain doctrinal claims. The most basic defilements that interfere with wisdom are greed, hatred, and ignorance. These emotions are referred to in Buddhism as the three poisons, because they are toxins in the mind. Meditation is a way to detoxify the mind.

Core to Buddhist doctrine is the idea that we suffer due to cravings for what we do not have or a desire to avoid or eradicate what we do not like. Our cravings are based on a misperception of the true nature of reality. Indicative of this delusion is the idea that we can free ourselves from suffering by satiating our desires. Intellectual knowledge about the causes of our suffering is not enough. We need to do things. The eightfold path of the Buddha's Four Noble Truths includes right thought and right understanding, which are associated with wisdom. To have right thought and understanding, the mind needs to be cultivated. A basic practice for cultivating the mind is meditation, of which there are many kinds in the history of Buddhism. Some common forms of meditation involve focusing on the breath, observing feeling, visualizing an image, or reciting certain words.

In Pure Land Buddhism, the most common form of Buddhism in Japan, the typical practice is the *nenbutsu*, which literally means mindfulness on the Buddha. It usually involves reciting the phrase "I take refuge in Amida Buddha" (*namu amida Butsu*). In Pure Land Buddhist soteriology, everyone will be saved from the realm of rebirth because Amida has vowed to bring all into his Pure Land, from where they will be able enter Nirvana. In Shin Buddhism, a popular Japanese type of Pure Land Buddhism, when we realize that we have no power to save ourselves and yet are already saved by Amida, an entrusting heart is said to develop. This entrusting heart leads to wisdom (*chie*), because it is through entrusting that people relinquish their own sense of self-power. The resignation of self-power allows them to better discern reality as it is, because it removes delusional thinking, which grows out of selfish desires. The liberation from self through faith fosters a feeling of elation. The founder of Shin Buddhism, Shinran, wrote that awakening to faith or an entrusting heart leads to great joy (*kanki*). Shin Buddhists also claim that, because Amida saves us despite our depraved state, the awakening of an entrusting heart (*shinjin*) also results in a deep sense of gratitude.

How one gets this entrusting heart, however, which is the source of wisdom in Shin, is not clear. Because of Shin institutions' emphasis on other-power, any practice that attempts to assist in acquiring this entrusting heart is viewed with suspicion. Yet, various groups of lay Shin Buddhists have developed practices they say instill this source of wisdom.

One of these groups was associated with the Taikan-an in Osaka, which in the early twentieth century promoted a self-examination practice called *mishirabe*. This practice involved people remembering the things they had done wrong as a way of getting them to see how they were in need of Amida's grace. It was from this practice that Naikan was developed by Yoshimoto Ishin in the early 1940s. Although Yoshimoto was a devout Shin Buddhist, he removed the religious elements from Naikan in the 1950s. This modification made it easier to teach Naikan at public institutions such as prisons and schools, which legally were not allowed to endorse any religion. The removal of religious language also made it easier for Naikan to enter the field of medicine. In the 1960s, some physicians started to use Naikan as a psychotherapeutic method to heal patients with psychosomatic disorders or other illnesses such as alcoholism.

Practitioners of Naikan say it is a method for self-discovery and for allowing people to see reality as it actually is. To understand how Naikan attempts to do this, we can examine one-week intensive Naikan trainings (*kenshu* 研修) as they occur at a particular Naikan training centre in Tokyo.

Intensive Naikan at a Naikan Training Centre

Throughout Japan, there are about twenty Naikan training centres that hold intensive week-long Naikan trainings. Several hospitals in Japan also run intensive Naikan sessions. During the seven-day programs, the people practising Naikan, called *naikansha*, examine their lives using three basic questions: What have I received? What have I given back? What troubles have I caused?

To get a sense of what happens during an intensive week of Naikan, we can examine a training centre located in an upscale residential neighborhood in Tokyo, where I did intensive week-long trainings on four different occasions. The training centre was established by Mr. Motoyama and is run by him and his wife. The training centre is also their home, where they raised their children. They hold week-long Naikan trainings there fifty-one weeks a year. The one week the Motoyamas take off is when the Japan Naikan Association holds its annual conference, which Mr. Motoyama attends.

The week-long training starts on Sunday afternoon between 1 and 3 p.m. Mr. Motoyama talks with clients individually as they arrive. He asks them about their interests in Naikan and has them write their name and address in a book. He tells clients that during the week they are not to talk with or engage in any way with the other clients. They should not even say "Good morning" or any other greeting if they pass each other in the hall. Mr. Motoyama receives the fee at this time of 70,000 yen (about US $650), which covers all costs for the week, including food and lodging.

The client is individually taken into a corridor separated from the rest of the home by a door and is shown his or her room by Mrs. Motoyama. The client will not leave this corridor for the entire week. On one side, there are five square tatami mat rooms about 12 feet (3.6 metres) square. On the other side are fogged windows that let light in but shut out the view of the outside world. After entering the room, Mrs. Motoyama explains how the heating and cooling systems work and that there is a security system which will activate if any doors or windows are opened during the night. She takes the *naikansha*'s valuables (for example, cell phones, wallet) and locks them in a cabinet in the room.

The *naikansha* then goes behind a screen. The screen (called a *byobu*) is about 5 feet (1.5 metres) high. It folds in half and is placed in a corner, where it forms a square space about 3 feet (1 metre) long and wide. It is in this space that the *naikansha* reflects on his or her life using the three Naikan questions.

If it is the *naikansha*'s first time at the centre, Mrs. Motoyama briefly explains how Naikan is done. The *naikansha* reflects on three questions: What have I received from a specific person at a specific time? What did I give back to that person at that time? What troubles did I cause that person at that time? She suggests that the *naikansha* start by reflecting on his or her mother when he or she was between the ages of six and eight years. So the *naikansha* starts by contemplating the following questions: What did I receive from my mother between ages six and eight? What did I give back to her during that time? And what troubles and difficulties did I cause her when I was between the ages of six and eight? To help the *naikansha* remember the questions, a sheet is pasted inside the screen with the questions written on it as well as the format for answering them during formally structured interviews, called *mensetsu*.

About ninety minutes after Mrs. Motoyama leaves the *naikansha*, Mr. Motoyama arrives to conduct the first interview. He conducts all the interviews throughout the week. He opens the sliding door to the room, enters, than slides the door closed behind him. He kneels in front of the screen, bows, opens the screen, puts palms together, and then bows again. The *naikansha* also bows to him. Then, without making eye contact, Mr. Motoyama asks: "During this time who have you been examining yourself in relation to and when?" The *naikansha* answers: "I have been examining myself in relation to my mother between ages six and eight." He or she then answers the three questions. The *naikansha* might say, for example, "When I was seven years old my mother gave me a bicycle for my birthday. She also cleaned and put a bandage on my knee when I fell on the sidewalk while playing with a friend. What I gave in return was a picture of a sunset over a mountain that I drew in school. The trouble I caused her is that I broke a picture frame when I threw a ball in the house." The interviews end with the practitioner, Mr. Motoyama, saying, without making eye contact: "Who will you examine yourself on next and during what time period?" The *naikansha* then says, for example, "I will examine myself in relation to my mother between the ages of nine and eleven." Mr. Motoyama bows, closes the screen, bows again, and then leaves.

Such interviews are held about every two hours, following the just-described format. They last between three to five minutes. Unless the *naikansha* is having trouble doing Naikan, there is no discussion between the *naikansha* and the interviewer. In general, Mr. Motoyama makes no comment. If the *naikansha*'s answers are too vague, however, he might suggest that the *naikansha* make the answers more concrete so that they can be visualized. For example, if the *naikansha* says: "What my mother gave me was cooked meals. What I gave back was that I made her laugh. And I caused her trouble by not doing what she told me," Mr. Motoyama may instruct the *naikansha* to give more specific, concrete answers that depict actual events. For example, what meal did she cook in particular for you that was special? What exactly did you do or say that made her laugh? What exactly did you do that she did not want you to do? Answers that can be seen in the mind's eye are more powerful for leaving an impression that one has not lived by his or her own power.

Naikansha at first may want to explain why they caused the trouble they did, or talk about troubles other caused them. During the first few interviews, the practitioner may allow this explanatory approach without comment if the person is answering the three questions and showing some progress to answering them directly and concretely. If the problem persists, however, the practitioner will instruct the client to just answer the three questions directly without explanation.

After the second interview on the first day, dinner is brought to the *naikansha*'s room and is eaten behind the screen. During this and subsequent meals throughout the week, recordings are played of other people's interviews. The *naikansha* is told in a list of instructions placed in the room that he or she is to listen to these interviews only as a source of reference and not to imitate them.

After dinner on the first night, Mr. Motoyama gives a lecture on Naikan, indicating how it is based more on a practice than any set of ideas. Men *naikansha* on the first floor and women *naikansha* who stay in rooms on the second floor are called together into his office. Typically there are between three and six *naikansha*. During this time, Motoyama explains how many different people come to do Naikan including businessmen, housewives, students, teachers, athletes, and actors. Some come because they have a specific problem, maybe with an addiction or maybe in a relationship with someone in their family. Others come who have no particularly problem and want to do Naikan for self-development or to help them in their professions. No matter what the reason for someone coming to a Naikan training centre, what is done is the same. He also says that our minds have a negative bias: we remember the hurt done to us more easily than the hurt we have caused. We suffer because we take things for granted and do not see reality as it actually is.

After the lecture, all return to their rooms, and about two hours later there is one more interview. Right before bedtime, Mrs. Motoyama assigns each person a cleaning task that is to be done first thing in the morning. One person is assigned cleaning the tub at one end of the hall. Another is assigned cleaning the toilet at the other end. Another may be assigned wiping down the floors.

The schedule for the next five days is as follows: Wake at 5:00 a.m. and spend the first forty-five minutes of the day cleaning and taking care of personal hygiene. At about 5:45 a.m., the *naikansha* goes behind the screen and starts Naikan. The day is punctuated by three meals taken alone behind the screen and by eight or nine interviews, one about every two hours. Except for going to the toilet or taking a bath in the afternoon, the *naikansha* spends all day, every day, behind the screen doing Naikan. There are no breaks for doing anything else. Reading, listening to a radio, texting on a phone, or anything else that would be a divergence from doing Naikan is not permitted.

Midway through the week, *naikansha* might be invited to examine their life in terms of "lying and stealing." Rather than using the three questions, they will go over periods of their life looking for instances when they stole or lied.

On the last day, during the last interview, Motoyama solicits the *naikansha*'s impressions about Naikan. Then he gives the *naikansha* some written materials and tells him or her about the importance of doing daily Naikan. There are no follow-up sessions. After the week is over, the *naikansha* typically never sees either of the Motoyamas again.

Naikan as a Path to Wisdom

Testimonials show there is a common rhythm during a week of Naikan.[2] In the beginning, *naikansha*, in social isolation and separated from diversions, soon become bored. Memories, particularly new concrete memories, are at first not easily found or fit into the questions. In addition to boredom, a resistance to Naikan often starts to develop. *Naikansha* want to explain themselves or want to relate how others have caused them trouble. The questions may seem unfair or manipulative. On the third or fourth day, boredom recedes in intensity as new memories emerge, and there is a greater sense of presence in the past. The deepest insights typically come after the third day.

Several factors help induce insights. Among these are the lack of social interaction, sensory deprivation, removal of distractions, the repeated interviews eight or nine times a day, the recordings played of other people's Naikan interviews, the prescribed ritual way in which the interviews (*mensetsu*) are conducted, and the focus on the three questions, which generate new memories that lead to new self-understandings.

Those who have given testimonials about their Naikan experiences frequently mention two insights: first, that they were selfish and did not appreciate others; second, that they were loved and supported by others much more than they thought. Their lives, they saw, were not a result of their own efforts so much as they were of the efforts of others. Although *naikansha*, when describing their experiences, rarely refer to Buddhist ideas about wisdom or use the word "*chie*," we do see evidence of how *naikansha* have insights related to social discernment and about the nature of their social realities, which are the hallmarks of wisdom in Japan.

We find in *naikansha* testimonials, for example, how their insights are understood as revealing both personal and social truths about the nature of reality and how to live. In particular, they see how they had a distorted view of their social relations, with disproportional attention being given to how they were harmed. Hence, Naikan fosters wisdom by helping practitioners be more aware in their social relations and thus more discreet.

Here are several brief examples from Naikan testimonials that show how wisdom is fostered:

1 A twenty-eight-year-old airline stewardess: "I did believe that it was my mother's fault that I developed anxiety neurosis. After my Naikan, I realized that I always received an infinite amount of love from her." Later this same woman states: "Until now, I believed *I* took the exams, and *I* passed both the physical and written exams [to become a stewardess]. After Naikan, I realized that it was my parents who prepared a supportive environment in which I could concentrate on preparing for the exams and financial support as well … I am here now thanks to other people, I am lived thanks to other people" (Ozawa-de Silva 2006: 63, 75).
2 A patient who suffered from a social anxiety disorder and did intensive Naikan in a hospital stated the following about her father: "When I realized that he supported me financially, and always helped me, tears came to my eyes. I began to feel gratitude toward him, because he understood my problems most" (Japan Naikan Medical Association et al. 2013: 179–80).
3 A twenty-five-year-old woman majoring in psychology at a university: "At the beginning, I was wondering whether I could become like other Naikan people … I doubted I could ever say thank you from the bottom of my heart without pretending. However, once I started examining myself, I was in tears with the realization of being loved at the early stage of Naikan." This same woman also said: "I realized that I didn't grow up by myself just by eating food" (Ozawa-de Silva 2006: 58–9).
4 A middle-aged male school teacher, when asked after one week of Naikan how it had changed him, said: "Up until now my way of living was extremely self centred. For example, when there was something painful or unpleasant, I would try to think of something enjoyable to forget it. As a result of this, I caused others trouble and

> pain. I had little consideration for others. After … doing Naikan I saw how foolish I was and was remorseful about the depths of the bad karma [I produced]. There were so many people I troubled. I realized how blessed I have been and how I grew due to the support of others. I have not lived by my own power but it is due to the efforts of others that I have lived" (Yoshimoto 1980: 155).

When *naikansha* have insights about their self-centredness and how they have lived through the support of others, the most common emotional responses are guilt, gratitude, awe, and joy. The guilt causes remorse that connects the *naikansha* with others, rather than giving rise to self-punishing thoughts. The *naikansha* sees how he or she has caused trouble to others and feels regret, not only for the actions that caused trouble but also for not recognizing earlier the hurt and difficulties caused. Seeing how, despite his or her acts that caused others suffering, he or she was still taken care of by them induces the emotion of gratitude.

Guilt and gratitude are complementary. The sense of remorseful guilt deepens the sense of gratitude. The more *naikansha* vividly see how others have given to them while they, through their own selfishness, caused others difficulties, the more they recognize and appreciate the kind acts of others. Once the sense of guilt and gratitude reach a certain level, *naikansha* may have a quasi-mystical experience in which they are in awe of how their life has been completely dependent on others. They awaken to how they have lived as a result of the work of others.[3] The emotional response to this experience is one of joy.

The insights about oneself and the social world in which one lives cause emotions so intense that *naikansha* often start to weep. During Naikan retreats, it is so common for people to start crying that Naikan is known as the "crying meditation" (*Naki-kan*). In a small survey conducted in 2014 with twenty-three people (eleven men and twelve women), twenty-one out of the twenty-three reported crying during their Naikan retreat.[4] The crying shows how insights stimulate an emotional response.

The intensity of the emotions demonstrated through crying also validates insights. If the insights were merely cognitive and caused little emotional response, they would be less powerful. To paraphrase Geertz's definition of religion, we might see Naikan and the crying it induces as establishing "a system of [memories] … which acts to establish powerful, pervasive and long-lasting moods and motivations in [*naikansha*] … by formulating conceptions of a general order of [their own] existence and … clothing [remembered experiences] with such an aura of factuality that … the moods and motivations seem uniquely [powerful]" (Geertz 1973: 90). In other words, the practice of Naikan leads people to see their lives in a particular way that elicits emotions, which, in turn, validate *naikansha*'s new view of their lives. This new view of their lives as being the result of the work of others rather than just themselves allows them to see their relationships in a new way.

Conclusion

The founder of Naikan, Yoshimoto Ishin, liked to quote the ancient Greek maxim "know thyself" (Yoshimoto 1996: 42). How we come to know ourselves depends on how we self-reflect on ourselves. The way Naikan leads people to know themselves is by making them more aware of how they have treated family and friends and how those intimate others have taken care of them. The wisdom acquired through Naikan, and particularly the realization that our lives are not simply the result of our own efforts, is both cognitive and emotional. It is experienced in what the Japanese call *kokoro*, which is often translated as "mind" and connotes something humans have that involves both thinking and feeling.

Unlike the mindfulness meditation popular in the United States, which focuses on present-moment awareness, often as a means of calming a person's mind, Naikan emphasizes memories of social interactions. By focusing on interactions related to receiving, giving, and causing others trouble, Naikan's three questions require *naikansha* to think beyond their own perspectives and to consider the perspectives of others. In this way, these questions make *naikansha* more sensitive to how their actions affect others and how others have benefited them. Naikan also shows them their own self-centred tendencies that can undermine their social relations. By leading *naikansha* to insights on themselves in relation to others, Naikan helps develop discretion, a core characteristic of *chie* and of the wise.

NOTES

1 On emotions in Buddhism, see Harvey 2013.

2 For Naikan testimonials in English, see Krech 2017, Reynolds 1989, and Ozawa-de Silva 2006. For a collection of Naikan testimonials in Japanese, see Yoshimoto 1980.

3 The common Japanese word for this experience is *ikasareteiru*, which is often translated literally as "to be lived." The idea fits in with the larger Pure Land Buddhist idea of other power.

4 See the study titled "Shūchū Naikan ni oite nagasareru namida no shinri rinshōgakuteki rikai no kokoromi" 集中内観において流される涙の心理臨床学的理解の試み (A Clinical Psychological Attempt to Understand the Tears that Flow during Intensive Naikan), http://yamato-mahoroba.sakura.ne.jp/blog/2015/01/post-288.html (accessed 18 November 2019).

REFERENCES

Barth, Fredrick. 2002. "An Anthropology of Knowledge." *Current Anthropology* 43: 1–18.

Geertz, Clifford. 1973. *The Interpretation of Cultures.* New York: Basic Books.

Hakuin. 1999. *Wild Ivy: The Spiritual Autobiography of Zen Master Hakuin.* Translated by Norman Waddell. Boston: Shambhala.

Harvey, Peter. 2013. "Emotions in Buddhism." In *Emotions and Religious Dynamics*, edited by Douglas Davies and Nathaniel Warne, 47–62. Surrey: Ashgate.

Japan Naikan Medical Association and Japan Naikan Association, eds. 2013. *Naikan Therapy: Techniques and Principles for Use in Clinical Practice.* Fukuoka: Daido Gakkan.

Krech, Gregg. 2017. *Question Your Life: Naikan Self-Reflection and the Transformation of Our Stories.* Monkton, VT: ToDo Institute.

Lebra, Takie Sugiyama. 1976. *Japanese Patterns of Behaviour.* Honolulu: University of Hawai'i Press.

Ozawa-de Silva, Chikako. 2006. *Psychotherapy and Religion in Japan: The Japanese Introspection Practice of Naikan.* New York: Routledge.

– 2015. "Mindfulness of the Kindness of Others: The Contemplative Practice of Naikan in Cultural Context." *Transcultural Psychiatry* 52 (4): 524–42.

Reynolds, David. 1983. *Naikan Psychotherapy: Meditation for Self-Development.* Chicago: University of Chicago Press.

– 1989. *Flowing Bridges, Quiet Waters: Japanese Psychotherapies, Morita and Naikan.* Albany: SUNY Press.

Samuel, Geoffrey. 2016. "Mindfulness within the Full Range of Buddhist and Asian Meditative Practices." In *Handbook of Mindfulness: Culture, Context, and Social Engagement*, edited by Ronald Purser, David Forbes, and Adam Burke, 47–62. Cham, CH: Springer.

Takahashi, Masami, and Prashant Bordia. 2000. "The Concept of Wisdom: A Cross-Cultural Comparison." *International Journal of Psychology* 35 (1): 1–9.

Walsh, Roger. 2015. "What Is Wisdom? Cross-Cultural and Cross-Disciplinary Syntheses." *Review of General Psychology* 19: 278–93.
Wilson, Jeff. 2014. *Mindful America: The Mutual Transformation of Buddhist Meditation and American Culture.* Oxford: Oxford University Press.
Yoshimoto, Ishin. 1996. *Naikan he no shōtai: Aijō no saihakken to jiko dōsatsu no susume.* Osaka: Tokiwa Shobō.
–, ed. 1980. *Naikan no taiken.* Nara: Naikan Kenshujo.

4 Navigating Wisdom and Time: Reflections on Aging and Eldercare

PHILIP Y. KAO

Wisdom is often thought to be the product of experience, the outcome of a seasoned and full life. Therefore, we typically think of the elderly as embodying wisdom. People around the world often look to their elders for wise counsel on a wide range of matters. But what can we say about this tenuous relationship between aging and wisdom? Are the old necessarily wise? Moreover, how is wisdom related to the aging process? If wisdom is not acquired innately but rather through particular pathways, relationships, and associations, what can we learn about wisdom's forms and circulations throughout the life course? Ursula Staudinger, one of the original researchers associated with the Berlin Wisdom Paradigm project, states that the early motivation for the project's research arose from the desire to locate a positive attribute to aging (Staudinger et al. 1998; Baltes and Staudinger 2000). In other words, could wisdom be "a characteristic, ability, or skill that may improve, as we grow older" (Boulware 2015: n.p.)?

Even the aging seek wisdom from time to time. There are a plethora of wisdom guidelines and self-help aphorisms for both the elderly and their caregivers, including such advice as (1) be thankful for what you have/count your blessings; (2) let go of the trivial and insignificant/don't sweat the small stuff; (3) accept change; (4) be open to the unknown and uncertainty; (5) see and find beauty in old age; and so on. What is the evidence for wisdom in older adults? Moreover, how does wisdom appear (or not) in places like long-term care facilities where people deal simultaneously with life's existential and pragmatic issues? What follows is an attempt to address these questions as well as to explore the temporal attributes of time in the context of aging and caregiving. Rather than focusing on wisdom as an integrated set of psychological functions to be performed for better or worse, this chapter seeks to situate the ontology of wisdom at the nexus of philosophies of time and personhood.

Clarifying our own thinking on aging and wisdom will do much to correct pernicious ageist conceptions, especially those underlying our fixation with maintaining some idealized notion of independence, biomedical solutions to "aging," and doubling down on institutionalizing care even when it does not work. This chapter argues that a re-evaluation of practical wisdom, which contains philosophical and abstract conceptualizations of time and ontology, is needed. What would wisdom look like if we changed our orientation from psychological functioning and performance to something more phenomenological and open-ended? In other words, can phronesis be recast in the context of aging as a particular meditation on personhood and time that extends beyond simply enhancing our psychological capacity in late life? Wisdom cannot be made into a set of procedures or "best practices" but, rather, emerges once people begin to discern how differing experiences of time constitute and historicize personhood and well-being.

There is a tendency to equate wisdom with old age; this association requires further critical analysis. Does the data and current gerontological research support this "conventional wisdom"? Life experience can contribute to the construction of wisdom, especially in contexts where elders are valued for their cultural and symbolic roles. For instance, among the Bambara of Mali, the elderly have prestige and power on account of age. Leopold Rosenmayr (1988) argues that wisdom in the cultural context of the Bambara can only be understood in relation to that society's notions of maturity. In other words, seniority functions as an organizing principle throughout various age sets, myths, and rituals. He goes on to say: "The 'wisdom' of the old was the product – not the source – of their prestige and power" (37). But, more often than not, wisdom is simply viewed as a folk idiom, a by-product of old age, and something to look forward to later after having conquered life's trials and tribulations. Whether wisdom is forged in the existential fire or not, the aging process, and particularly the experiences and exigencies of the "old-old," are testing grounds for wisdom. The social, cognitive, and psychological changes that occur in late life are shaped by a life course endowed with lessons and opportunities regarding moral skill and practical wisdom. Furthermore, wisdom is often required to navigate the changing tides and processes associated with such phenomena as disability, loss, and cognitive aging. For the individual, the exercise and practice of wisdom in old age can lead that person to reduce stress, achieve life satisfaction, and produce a sense of positive psychology, nobility, honesty, and naturalness.

Surviving into late life is not necessarily proof of wisdom or "wise living." Longevity and quality of life both matter. Locating and operationalizing wisdom in the context of aging and public health interventions takes on a compound set of issues, requiring not just an interdisciplinary understanding of health and senescence but also a dynamic relationship with the institutions and policies that structure and address ageism and demography. Therefore, the intersection of wisdom and aging is not simply a depot station on a one-way street; it is a process that engages the world through various theories, values, and technological innovations. At stake for society is the risk of losing the ability to provide venues that enable wisdom to flourish and to be tapped into as a set of knowledge motivating critical reflection and adaptability. Given the shortening time span of information and the frenetic pace and volume of data gathering, the growing dependence on technology and fast(er) decisions means that our patience and reception to wisdom, whatever the definition, is not always grasped.

Wisdom and Aging: Correlations, Aspects, and Attributes

One of the challenges in researching wisdom, both from a basic and an applied standpoint, is the lack of a fixed or even common definition. Like scientific definitions of culture and life, wisdom is a process that is arguably a predominantly human trait, functioning at a metalevel of sorts. Wisdom consists of particular metacognitive functions, such as the wisdom of emotions as moral and navigational resources, as well as of metabiological aspects – for example, the interactive and technological ways humans shape their ecologies and vice versa. Definitions of wisdom in the context of aging must relate to the aging process and the circumstances of the "old-old," who face morbidity and the nearness of death. Furthermore, the creative, synergistic, and interactive melding together of the highest qualities of the mind can occur during the second half of life. This process reflects a developmental intelligence, which is beautifully captured by Gene Cohen in the figure of an eye as a seat of wisdom and awareness (Miller, Cohen, and Barker 2016). For Cohen, developmental intelligence constitutes the highest level of maturity pertaining to some of the major qualities of the mind, and it is also one of the positive outcomes of aging. By conjuring up the analogy of the mind's eye, we can see how the maturation of skills such as cognition, emotional intelligence, life experience, consciousness (spirituality), judgment, and social intelligence reveals a form of wisdom as developmental intelligence. For Cohen, developmental intelligence is a synergy of all these maturing skills, and when integrated with aging and life experience, the mind reveals a manifestation that is greater than simply the sum of its functional qualities and components.

Dilip Jeste suggests that personality, behavioural attributes, and psychosocial functioning plays a significant role in our understanding of wisdom and its neurobiology (Jeste et al. 2010). For Thomas Meeks and Dilip Jeste, there is often an inverse relationship between physical disability and life satisfaction for aging persons across time. Epistemic humility, self-reflection/understanding, emotional regulation, prosocial behaviour, good listening, and value relativism are some of the characteristics that may help older individuals realize satisfaction. However, these attributes are more than just signs/components of wisdom. Rather, they are fluid determinants of wisdom (Meeks and Jeste 2009). If we take Jeste's suggestion that there is a putative neurocircuitry of wisdom, then investigating accidents involving trauma areas to the brain or diseases affecting particular regions of the brain, such as frontal-temporal dementia, could lead to discovering how judgment, personality, and components of wisdom connect with parts of the brain including the amygdala (older evolutionary part of the brain) and the prefrontal cortex (newer evolutionary part of the brain). Injuries to these parts of the brain may affect the expression/understanding of emotions and the logic and mechanics of short-term memory required for making utilitarian choices. Significant changes in personality accompanied loss of wise decisions/behaviour in the famous case of Phineas Gage's gruesome accident.[1] On another note, Jeste draws attention to the grandmother hypothesis, which posits an explanation regarding our life extension well beyond the moment of infertility (Jeste and Oswald 2014). Scientists have recently discovered that humans have many more specific variants of genes *CD33* and *APOE*[2] than do chimpanzees, suggesting that such variants might have evolved to preserve wise grandparents by delaying their cognitive decline and thus "rewarding" their role as transmitters of practical wisdom and culture to future generations.

A commonly held notion depicts aging as a journey consisting of acquiring life experiences, which results in the individual obtaining life perspective and the status of a "wise elder." It is not just coincidence that many of our ideals and representations of wisdom find expression in the wise old sage archetype. In many ways, longevity becomes proof of the existence and embodiment of wisdom in mind, body, and soul. As mentioned earlier, cognitive aging can bring about valued skills and thought structures that are more nuanced and "deeper" than, for example, the mere ability to perform quick mathematical calculations. Research is still underway exploring the cognitive evidence for wisdom appreciation and practice in the context of aging. Surviving into old age and having more experiences can lead to refined and "battle-tested" cognitive templates. There are also metacognitive and emotional aspects of wisdom. Navigating feelings, regulating emotions, and being able to detach oneself from the immediacy of particular fight or flight drives enables a greater usage of self-reflection and an ability to experience life events as a series of life lessons and schemas.

Reversing the arrow, we also recognize that wisdom is not necessarily a by-product of aging, but we note that wisdom promotes healthy aging and longevity. For Jacqui Smith (2015), cognitive aging is multidirectional. Knowledge stabilizes and plateaus more or less as people age, but other functions such as reaction time decrease. The multidirectional nature of this process suggests that wisdom might account for these divergences and that people can never be wise all the time. Jacqui Smith and Lindsay Ryan propose looking at psychic vitality as an indicator of the issues the "old-old" face (Smith and Ryan 2015). If wisdom entails making better decisions and knowing how to continue living longer and healthier lives, then threats to wisdom appear when psychic vitality is challenged by health issues such as hearing and vision loss. Focusing on shortening the frame that the "old-old" spend in morbid time, Smith says that setting the conditions for maintaining psychic vitality is a constitutive requirement for the flourishing and usage of wisdom in the lives of the elderly. Psychic vitality is linked to adaptive capacity, maintenance of health, and risk management. Rather than thinking about the role of wisdom in adulthood, Smith suggests, we should look at the role wisdom plays for people eighty-five years and older. As we live to a greater age, Smith says, wisdom is required to anticipate and master the uncertainties of living longer. For example, does living longer mean that we are not only postponing but elongating the period of declining psychological vitality, deterioration, and multimorbidity?

Jacqui Smith, Dana Kotter-Grühn, and colleagues offer a new way to investigate the process of and changes during aging by taking measurements and conducting surveys, not as a function of time but as cognitive and psychological states moving backward from death as a starting index (Kotter-Grühn et al. 2009). In this way, these researchers are able to discern from the Berlin Aging Study (BASE) that the rate of change closer to death may be more pronounced in some areas than in others. For example, one BASE phase found that neuroticism (feelings of anxiety and unease) stabilize with age, but increase closer to death. Additionally, the sense of self-mastery and control decreases with age and the closer the individual is to death. Feelings of loneliness increase with age, but increase drastically towards the end of life. Self-assessments regarding the aging process, subjective well-being, and "how young people feel" all exhibit different trajectories. Interestingly, as people get closer to death, the younger they feel; in other words, measures of subjective age increase dramatically. There is evidence that people past ninety years of age and closer to death recount feeling like they are still seventy and "young at heart." All in all, Smith contends, there is still a lot we don't know about the aging process for the "old-old." The fragility or robustness of psychic vitality plays a key part in determining the quality of life as a person nears death, whether that is at eighty-five, ninety-five, or one hundred and five years of age.[3] More research is needed to determine how to optimize psychological aging and maintain psychic vitality, but investigators understand already that the older individual will need to devote a lot of time and personal effort to the task and that targeting just one functional domain may not be enough.

Wisdom and Time

Caregiving for the elderly is charged with mixed emotions, but it also opens up pathways for wisdom. For one thing, caregiving means participating in aging as part of life's process. Needless to say, aging is not easy, and a fair amount of cognitive and emotional work is required in order to maintain a sense of poise and perspective. Not only does aging remind us of our shared mortality, but it also invites caregivers to act on empathy. The vulnerability inherent to our corporeal existence (Harrison 2008) and our encounter with death through another person is one of the fundamental and psychodynamic characteristics of caregiving. Caregiving is an interactive field of relations where wisdom is not operationalized as an individual set of skills and techniques but instead is constructed intersubjectively. Emmanuel Levinas (1998) reminds us that death is not an abstract alterity but, rather, is interpersonal. For Levinas, "it does not make sense to talk about a completely individual self, out of relations to others. The self is only conceivable as a self in relation to and distinguished by its proximity to others" (Domrzalski 2010: n.p.). Through acts of caregiving and the encounter with mortality and vulnerability, a new connection with someone and an awareness of the transformative nature of interhuman life takes hold. Here, wisdom or, rather, our mindfulness about the human condition is experienced.

Whether care is provided in the familiar surroundings of an individual's own home or in the context of the long-term care facility, care is a task heavy with burden and anxiety. Long-term care facility residents and staff in places like continuing care retirement communities (CCRCs) wrestle with issues of aging, personhood, care, and uncertainty every day. Within this context, wisdom is taken to be knowledge about what to do in unforeseen circumstances, how to make better decisions, and, more generally, how to relate to mortality and time – all in a bid to age more "successfully." There are the usual complaints that facilities are short on staff and that the greying of society will continue to strain the economy. In addition to these public concerns, those on the ground, closer to the practice of caregiving, stress that an overall change is needed in the social attitude and orientation towards caregiving and the aging process.

Nursing home reforms have drawn much of their inspiration from earlier anti-institutional movements in the hopes of rescuing the "individual" from the total institution. In some North American retirement communities, the need for "person-centred" care has taken centre stage. One such model is an international non-profit organization called the Eden Alternative (2014). Concerned with improving the nature of care and living in places such as assisted living facilities for the elderly, "the Eden Alternative focuses on creating Elder-centered communities – wherever Elders live – that thrive on close and continuing relationships, meaningful interactions, opportunities to give as well as receive, and a rich and diverse daily life. Elder-centered communities are places where treatment is the servant of genuine human caring, Elders are the daily decision-makers, and where wise leaders grow other leaders" (2). Furthermore, the organization's definition of an "elder" is precisely someone who, by virtue of life experience, is here to teach us how to live.

This shift in focus is as much about customer service as it is about marketing. By paying lip service to the need for engaging with elderly residents in a way that dignifies them and takes notional account of their food preferences, hobbies, and biographical sketches, long-term facility managers and residents' family members can stop worrying. While most of the changes in long-term care facilities have focused on employing more recreational staff to help residents pass time as hurriedly as possible, managers and policymakers are still working towards empowering the residents, making them the decision-makers. What follows will be a philosophical discussion of time in order to show that the experience of time itself as a resource and value is often ignored by modern caregiving practices. It is within this ritualized context that we can sense the haunting lack of wisdom and the flattening and deception of time. In order to save ourselves from eternal shipwreck, what might it mean to reformulate our commitment to others and ourselves beyond the obscurity of Levinasian conceptions of intersubjective time?

It may very well be true that no other species in the animal kingdom infantilizes its elders. Humans are social and live and experience life with others from different backgrounds and generations. Care is part of this social story; it is the way in which humans confront the experience of time. For Nouwen and Gaffney (1974), real care is a confrontation involving care for all ages, because people participate in the same process of aging. Even though I find such universalisms suspect, I do believe that what is at stake is our experience of time and how this experience takes on (or does not take on) a particular form through caregiving. Caregiving may contain our temporal impulses, but it can also release us into the greater exigency of experiential learning and being. Therefore, let me posit conceptually that caregiving is not just a moral concern for some kind of well-being, but should also be a commitment to the living as an ontological necessity. As a result, being critically aware of our homemade philosophies of time will ensure whether or not our elders – through certain acts of caregiving – are being cared for or becoming alienated from the experience of experience itself. In this sense, wisdom is made manifest as a human project, designed to transcend human nature without denying it and thus reclaim what the Spanish philosopher Ortega y Gasset (2004: 757) regards as our human condition: we are shipwrecked and can rely on nothing more or less than our circumstances.

Normative conceptualizations of the life journey portray the life course as a series of stages, invoking from birth to death an unwinding from progression to regression. Put another way, a gross characterization of human development proposes that the formative years are focused on "becoming." This phase is followed by maturity, with all the trappings of the "stable" self. What follows finally is the process of "unbecoming"; fighting against loss (and the clock) are the tests that wait for us at death's doorstop. Behind this construction lies a relationship to time that ends up being conflictual. "Successful aging" becomes an anxiety-producing race against time. Underlying our discernment of wisdom is yet another ineffable, namely the nature of time and our relationship to it. Therefore, it makes sense to explore the temporal aspects of wisdom. How many times have we come across gnomic statements associating wisdom and proper timing? The key here is not only knowing what to do in a challenging situation but also when to do it. Birren and Fisher (1990) argue that time is relevant and plays a role in the context of wisdom. They maintain: "The demand on the decision maker is to have an orientation in time that examines the past for relevant knowledge, experience, and precedent; that examines the present context of the problem to be solved; and that projects into the future the long-range effects" (322). Wisdom has temporal components, certain attributes that influence how it comes into being and is socialized. For example, wisdom is often associated with a timeless quality. It can draw strength and insight from the past as well as predict particular elements of the future. In many cultural traditions, especially religious ones, wisdom as a practical guided understanding of the metaphysical can only happen as a result of ruptures in time. Thus, mythic and sacred times are pathways for illuminating the ineffable. Persons who attune to various experiences and forms of time open themselves up to the possibility of ritual power, healing, and even profound revelations. What will be elucidated in the following section is how narration, as a wise meta-practice, can induce particular temporal arrangements to address the "existential crises" that aging residents silently face in long-term care facilities.

It will be useful to venture into a more focused discussion of time and look at how certain philosophical approaches to time can help us re-examine caregiving practices and regimes. It seems that the issue of philosophical time is rarely articulated or apprehended in a long-term care facility. Yet, time and the temporal nature of human experience, and how this experience itself is lived and felt by older and aging residents, seems to receive very little direct attention. It is often said that old age is a foreign country, especially for young people who often fumble to access its customs, language, and ethos. Part of the problem, especially in the Western context of a long-term care facility, lies with the fact that our everyday metaphysics presupposes persons live through time rather than in time. Do human lives take place through or in time? Is there any difference? The philosopher Henri Bergson (1949) argues for a philosophy of mobility, of becoming and change, enabling time to be rethought independently of any spatial presupposition. Bergson points out that science treats time as a succession of states unfolding before a pre-existing space. When we count the number of things like sheep or houses over a landscape, or the number of years someone has lived, we are dealing with a pre-imagined horizon of space. But what is this space?

Suzanne Guerlac contends that Bergson shows us "we count in space, not in time. The concept of number implies juxtaposition in space. In order for the numbers to grow as I advance in my counting, I have to hold onto the successive images or representation of the units I have already counted, and therefore I juxtapose them with each of the new units I evoke in my mind. The juxtaposition occurs in space. Even when we think we are counting in time, we are actually representing units in space" (Guerlac 2006: 61). For Bergson, this approach to time is what he refers to as real duration. Bergson's philosophy attempts to recast our relationship with ourselves, not in some kind of attunement of ourselves to an external world unfolding in space but in terms of an intuition of ourselves, in freedom, by taking ourselves up in real duration. Bergson argues that measuring time using the intellect, and therefore not grasping it by entering into the reality of time *in time* via intuition, is responsible for much of our philosophical blunderings. Herbert Wildon Carr (1912) also sympathizes with Bergson's philosophy when he says: "It is this unreal time that we have in mind when we speak of our fleeting existence and think of the things that outlast us; it gives meaning to such expressions as eternal youth. Life seems made up of definite states ... which we pass through, and which we imagine have a period of stability and then change. But the change is continuous throughout each state, and the states are a merely external view of life. It is our body that enables us to take this view. Our body is an object in space, and we consequently regard it in this external way" (18). Furthermore, Carr emphasizes that, for Bergson, "our life is true duration. It is a time flow that is not measured by some standard in relation to which it may be faster or slower. It is itself absolute, a flowing that never ceases, never repeats itself, an always present, changing, becoming, now" (19).

If we take Bergson with a pinch of salt, we come to realize that life framed in this philosophical and metaphysical way does not lend itself to scientific analysis. Yet, where science fails and philosophy perseveres, there may still be something to rescue for our anthropological purposes: the notion that some human realities may not be penetrated by ethnography alone, no matter how reflexive our methods. In the language anthropologists are more accustomed to, persons are historical subjects. We do not inhabit time; instead, time inhabits us. This concept is more than just a snapshot or ethno-theory of personhood; what we are dealing with is a conception of time that is fleeting, continuous, and singular in its occurrence – so much so that persons are much more than just the sum of their histories. Rather than some fuzzy and abstract philosophical notion of time that inheres in the world, this conception of time means that, when we try to analyse and study aging as a social and temporal process, we must be aware of our spatial presumptions of reality. Further, when we set old age and aging within the framework of a life course, we are dealing in abstractions and symbols that are not just culturally variable. Hence, vivisecting life in this way may blind us from seeing how a life is lived, making such dichotomies as inside/outside, self/other, and mind/body irrelevant. This idea is probably Bergson's contribution to an anthropology of time: rather than remaining hung-up on distinctions between different orderings of time (for example, A-series versus B-series), he sees the past carried along through the present to the future, continuously. The present announces what follows and what is contained preceding it. Therefore, life is a ceaseless becoming and not simply a succession of unrelated slices of time. Consequently, memory for Bergson is the site of consciousness. A temporal synthesis is required to actualize mobility as action and not as a thing to be represented on an immobile canvas of space. Along these lines, Guerlac (2006: 68) says: "This synthesis requires memory. But the point Bergson wants to stress here is that memory does not act like a slide projector, which displays past moments in distinct isolation from one another. It is cinematic. It performs an operation of temporal synthesis. The problem with scientific discourse is that it slices up time and movement into isolated positions, the way a slide projector does. Science eliminates features of experience. It ignores duration, the qualitative element of time, and mobility, the qualitative element of movement."

Given these distinctions, trying to suggest that the experience of time and life is qualitatively differently for an older person is for Bergson a nonstarter. It is a syntax error produced by our bastardization of time. Old persons are old in our governing cultural framework because they have traversed more distance, hence space, from a beginning point, which even they cannot remember. Yet, there is a legacy of ourselves; we are not born every day again in some chaotic fashion. For Bergson, "inner duration is the continuous life of a memory which prolongs the past into the present, the present either containing within it in a distinct form the ceaselessly growing image of the past, or, more probably, showing by its continual change of quality the heavier and still heavier load we drag behind us as we grow older. Without this survival of the past into the present there would be no duration, but only instantaneity" (Bergson 1949: 40). The concept of personhood is not afforded some greater heuristic or existential insight by studying "older" persons. In fact, old age and aging are ontologized as matter and memory, so much so that person-centred caregiving becomes nonsensical. Old age is much more than discourse; it acts as evidence for us that time exists and that we are all waiting for and wading in time. As residents come to inhabit time in the spatial organization of a nursing home, for example, we see that they are not treated as persons in time but as sites of caregiving where persons wage war against time.

Conclusion: The Ontology of Wisdom in Narration

In "The Narrative Quality of Experience," Stephen Crites (1971) offers another useful phenomenological understanding of time. Crites argues that "the formal quality of experience through time is inherently narrative" (292). In order to set up his argument, Crites suggests that action is altogether temporal and that human action, which is subject to being experienced and produced by a conscious agent, has a unity of form through time. Like the specious present, which can encapsulate the duration of a sentence beyond the mere succession of separate words, walking across the room and gesturing towards an approaching grandchild is for Crites the unity of form through time that can be appropriately called style. Crites goes on to say: "If style is the form of conscious movement, music is that form purified" (293). By treating style in this way, with its inherent musicality, Crites then offers the following relation: "Narrative quality is to experience as musical style is to action" (292). Seeing narrative as a cultural form capable of generating experience and meaning, and of expressing a phenomenological coherence through time, Crites argues for the primacy of the narrative structure in everyday personal and social life. Without getting sidetracked into a discussion about his notions of mundane and sacred stories, we note that stories are not simply arbitrary or whimsical fictions. The narrative forms themselves are fundamental to the way humans inhabit time. The sacred story forms our consciousness and "projects a total world horizon, and therefore informs the intentions by which actions are projected into that world" (296).

Crites (1971) introduces another dimension in the drama and asserts: "Between sacred story and the mundane stories there is a mediating form: the form of the experiencing consciousness itself" (297). Whether or not we buy into Crites's version of consciousness, what we are working with, it seems, is not just how consciousness mediates dialectically between the sacred and the mundane but also how the form of human experiencing is narrative. For Crites, "the stories give qualitative substance to the form of experience because it is itself an incipient story" (297). In summary, Crites showcases how the primary ways and forms of experience are narrative. Because we are temporal beings, time can be understood as the way we reconcile the tensed modalities of the past, present, and future – in the present. This distinction between the past, present, and future lends itself to a tension in human life so that experience is always unfolding. We may recollect the past in a variety of ways, but the successive nature of temporality means that "forms," like consciousness, are taken up and understood by us in temporal ways, providing the dramatic tension in human life. For Crites, the mundane and sacred stories are necessary for the expression of the tensed modalities of time and have their own sense of meaning and coherence. We can see how personal identity depends on a continuity of experience through time. But, underscoring all, "narrative alone can contain the full temporality of experience in a unity of form" (303). The narrative quality of experience thus grips the conscious present in a moment of existential predicament between a past remembered and a future anticipated but still undetermined. Crites draws our attention to this critical modality, which "gives the story a dramatic character as a whole. And since action and experience join precisely at this decisive and critical juncture in the drama, the whole drama vibrates with the musicality of personal style" (303).

Although the narrative is a cultural form that expresses, reflects, and encapsulates our existence as temporal creatures, Crites (1971) warns that the (post)modern condition is a new form of consciousness, trying to break the sense of narrative time. He cites abstraction and contraction as two examples of strategies that are intended to arrest experience, giving it a new atemporal coherence. The abstraction Crites talks about is reminiscent of the Frankfurt School critique of instrumental rationality and the technocrats' usage of population statistics. Contraction, on the other hand, seeks "the particular image isolated from the image stream ... isolated sensation, feeling, the flash of the overpowering moment in which the temporal context of that moment is eclipsed and past and future are deliberatively blocked out of consciousness" (309). These (post)modern strategies announce an alienation from the narrative form. Furthermore, the post-Cartesian mind and body have given over to a particular dualism, namely that the mind abstracts from experience what it deems necessary and existential, and the body becomes the locus of feelings – the contraction of an embodiment so that our cyborg selves help us to mediate between what is real and what is phantom. Crites describes the threat to personhood, but not in those exact words, in the following: "Both mind and body are reifications of particular functions that have been wrenched from the concrete temporality of the conscious self. The self is not a composite of mind and body. The self in its concreteness is indivisible, temporal, and whole, as it is revealed to be in the narrative quality of its experience. Neither disembodied minds nor mindless bodies can appear in stories. There the self is given whole" (309).

Narrativity has its limitations, though. Galen Strawson (2004) famously argues against narrativity by deconstructing both psychological and ontological accounts of narrativity as well as ethical ones. For Strawson, the diachronic view of the self and self-experience take it to be natural that an individual considers the self as something in the past that will be there in the future through some continuity. Meanwhile, the episodic view does not figure the person as a "self" that existed in the past and will be there in the future. These temporal styles of being are not entirely mutually exclusive; there are several possible configurations with episodic modes trying on particular stories and frameworks from time to time. What is troubling for Strawson is the inherent association that "the aspiration to explicit Narrative self-articulation is natural for [everyone]" (447), especially if they are seeking out a fully meaningful and well-lived life. Yes, we can construct and revise the stories we tell when self-reflecting upon ourselves; this form-finding can be useful, and we are much more than the narratives we construct with and for others. But still, the narrative quality of experience has significance, especially for human existence in times where aging narratives can be hijacked by particular regimes of biomedical care, surveillance, and ageism. Hanna Meretoja (2014) purports that the three-dimensional "interconnections between the ontological, epistemological and ethical dimensions of the relation between narrative and human existence" (89) often get entangled in ways that reify particular presuppositions such as what human existence is, in itself, really about. What is useful to take away from Meretoja in light of Strawson is that "we should be attentive to the difference between experience and narrative … that narrative interpretations of experience have a constitutive role in our existence" (105). In other words, as John Christman (2004) succinctly points out, "what the condition of narrativity amounts to, then, is the more basic requirement that the person must be able to look upon the factors and events of her life with a certain interpretative reflection, whether or not those factors and events have any particular narrative unity in a traditional sense" (695). For residents in a long-term facility, providing the opportunity to recall and celebrate personal memories is crucial. These "super memories" are instrumental as anchors for grounding self-interpretation, whether or not they lend themselves to sequencing. Moreover, Christman argues for the condition of narrativity as the capacity for social-mediated self-reflection, since no one is an island. Here, narrativity embeds empathic forms of knowledge and prosocial commitments. Christman reminds us that "what we are left with is that selves are individuals who reflect on experiences and events in a way that gives meaning to them. But more must be said, for clearly many of the things that I reflect upon and can make sense of include the acts and events of others that are external to my 'self'" (707).

More than metaphysics is at stake in this bifurcation of experience against the narrative form. It is not just that telling stories is therapeutic in the usual way narrative strategies are employed in the context of gerontological discourse. Through the anti-narrative nature of caregiving practices, which attend to the body in its instantaneous form without entering into the world of time with others through the narrative form that structures human consciousness and social experience, people are left alienated not only from their experience of aging but from life's dramatic tension and musicality altogether. I do not have an exact prescription here, but I do want to suggest that Crites's argument for the narrative form is inherently an argument about our existential nature in time. For the purposes of caregiving and aging, there seems to be very little in the way we approach time in places like the nursing home. This absence is not because the nursing home is a secular institution with death denial as one of its services, but rather because caregiving seems to have separated temporality into a spatial arrangement so that persons can age in place according to institutional routines, procedures, transitions, and transfers.

One of the ways places like the nursing home can come to grips with the philosophies of time discussed in this paper is to situate caregiving within an experiential narrative, where the future is embraced and acknowledged with multiple scenarios. For researchers interested in ritual time, Renée Rose Shield's (1988) ethnography, hauntingly entitled *Uneasy Endings*, provides a useful case study of how nursing home residents are trapped liminally within an institution. In her study, the residents do not bond with each other or their caregivers. Because there are no new roles for the residents to undertake, and a lack of communitas, the rite of passage is incomplete, and residents are left in limbo, jettisoned from time's river. However, if we look to rectify the situation and focus on how caregiving practices can offer conceptions of time that lessen the anxiety society feels towards its elderly and the prospects of aging, the experience of aging will take on a whole new meaning. Living in time, as Bergson suggests, allows us to respect movement as a metaphysical property and unity through which meanings resonate historically and ontologically. Aging is fundamentally about how we situate ourselves to one another in and through time. Therefore, caregiving is one of life's experiences. A phenomenology of caregiving sensitive to time suggests that we understand backward and live forward. Care is also social and intersubjective. It is not something someone does for another or simply the result of pathology or an instrument of palliation. To summarize, I am arguing that caregiving should be critically reflective of the ways its various practices and regimes measure and hide time. An attention to Bergsonian time, in addition to allowing for more authentic and emergent narrative qualities of aging to be performed, can alleviate much of the anxiety and alienation surrounding residents in long-term care facilities.

Providing care for an elderly person is different from providing care for a baby. People often equate the two, citing overlapping types of dependency, but there are significant physical and ontological differences. Older persons have larger bodies; their skin has a different texture and elasticity. The elderly have also lived longer; their experiences are the extended products of a particular temporal trajectory, which babies are just coming to terms with. Put another way, the wisdom that needs to be operationalized is a holistic perspective of human development, which enables us to recognize that the elderly continue to learn as part ontogeny. Christina Toren proposes that, in regards to ontogeny, "making sense of the world is for any one of us [young or old] a material, self-organizing, historically structured, intersubjective process that at once transforms new experience in the course of its assimilation (to this extent conserving what I know) and transforms my existing structures of knowing in the course of their accommodation to new experience (to this extent changing what I know)" (Toren 2012: 65). From this vantage point, we approach the person as a historical system, engaging with others and the world. Beyond developmental biology and models of the body and senescence, recognizing Toren's model of autopoesis as microhistorical – an ongoing dynamic-systems engagement with others in making sense of the world intersubjectively – implies that the past continues to bear upon the present (Toren 2007).

To conclude, a subtle but personal account with a friend, whom I will call Dr. Z, points towards wisdom in our approach to aging and caregiving. I once confessed to Dr. Z that dying was something I had not yet resolved and that I was perhaps obsessing over it in an unhealthy way. Dr. Z said: "There is nothing to stress about. You like music right?" I nodded in complicit agreement. To which he replied: "Think about your favourite piece or song. It has a beginning, a middle, and an end." Reflecting on what he said led me to realize that he was talking about more than just the inherent time span of a life course. There was wisdom in his statement. Wisdom is there all the time.

NOTES

1 Phineas Gage was an American railroad worker who suffered a traumatic injury when an iron stake was struck through his brain's left frontal lobe. He survived, but his personality and behaviour following the accident had changed drastically as a result.

2 "The apolipoprotein E (*APOE*) gene on chromosome 19q13.32 was the first, and remains the strongest, genetic risk factor for Alzheimer's disease (AD). Additional signals associated with AD have been located in chromosome 19, including *ABCA7* (19p13.3) and *CD33* (19q13.41)" (Moreno-Grau et al. 2018).

3 Taken from the University of Pittsburgh's 2015 Jonas Salk Symposium on Wisdom and Aging.

REFERENCES

Baltes, Paul B., and Ursula M. Staudinger. 2000. "Wisdom: A Metaheuristic (Pragmatic) to Orchestrate Mind and Virtue toward Excellence." *American Psychologist* 55 (1): 122–36. https://www.mpib-berlin.mpg.de/volltexte/institut/dok/full/Baltes/wisdomam/index.htm.

Bergson, Henri. 1949. *An Introduction to Metaphysics.* Translated by T.E. Hulme, with an introduction by Thomas A. Goudge. New York: Liberal Arts Press.

Birren, James E., and Laurel M. Fisher. 1990. "The Elements of Wisdom: Overview and Integration." In *Wisdom: Its Nature, Origins, and Development,* edited by Robert J. Sternberg, 317–32. New York: Cambridge University Press.

Boulware, Jean Matelski. 2015. "Conversations on Wisdom: Ursula M. Staudinger." Center for Practical Wisdom at the University of Chicago. https://wisdomcenter.uchicago.edu/news/discussions/conversations-wisdom-ursula-m-staudinger.

Carr, Herbert Wildon. 1912. *Henri Bergson: The Philosophy of Change.* London: T.C. & E.C. Jack.

Christman, John. 2004. "Narrative Unity as a Condition of Personhood." *Metaphilosophy* 35 (5): 695–713. https://doi.org/10.1111/j.1467-9973.2004.00345.x.

Crites, Stephen. 1971. "The Narrative Quality of Experience." *Journal of the American Academy of Religion* 39 (3): 291–311. https://doi.org/10.1093/jaarel/XXXIX.3.291.

Domrzalski, Ruth. 2010. "Suffering, Relatedness and Transformation: Levinas and Relational Psychodynamic Theory." *Advocates' Forum.* https://ssa.uchicago.edu/suffering-relatedness-and-transformation-levinas-and-relational-psychodynamic-theory.

Eden Alternative. 2014. "It Can Be Different" (brochure). https://www.edenalt.org/wp-content/uploads/2014/02/Eden_Overview_092613LR.pdf.

Guerlac, Suzanne. 2006. *Thinking in Time: An Introduction to Henri Bergson.* Ithaca, NY: Cornell University Press.

Harrison, Paul. 2008. "Corporeal Remains: Vulnerability, Proximity, and Living On after the End of the World." *Environment and Planning A: Economy and Space* 40 (2): 423–45. https://doi.org/10.1068/a391.

Jeste, Dilip V., Monika Ardelt, Dan Blazer, Helena C. Kraemer, George Vaillant, and Thomas W. Meeks. 2010. "Expert Consensus on Characteristics of Wisdom: A Delphi Method Study." *The Gerontologist* 50 (5): 668–80. https://doi.org/10.1093/geront/gnq022.

Jeste, Dilip V., and Andrew J. Oswald. 2014. "Individual and Societal Wisdom: Explaining the Paradox of Human Aging and High Well-Being." *Psychiatry* 77 (4): 317–30. https://doi.org/10.1521/psyc.2014.77.4.317.

Kotter-Grühn, Dana, Anna Kleinspehn-Ammerlahn, Denis Gerstorf, and Jacqui Smith. 2009. "Self-Perceptions of Aging Predict Mortality and Change with Approaching Death: 16-Year Longitudinal Results from the Berlin Aging Study." *Psychology and Aging* 24 (3): 654–67. https://doi.org/10.1093/geronb/gbt005.

Levinas, Emmanuel. 1998. "From the One to the Other: Transcendence and Time." In *Entre Nous: Essays on Thinking-of-the-Other*, translated by Michael B. Smith and Barbara Harshav, 133–53. New York: Columbia University Press.

Meeks, Thomas W., and Dilip V. Jeste. 2009. "The Neurobiology of Wisdom: A Literature Overview." *Archives of General Psychiatry* 66 (4): 355–65. https://doi.org/10.1001/archgenpsychiatry.2009.8.

Meretoja, Hanna. 2014. "Narrative and Human Existence: Ontology, Epistemology, and Ethics." *New Literary History* 45 (1): 89–109. https://doi.org/10.1353/nlh.2014.0001.

Miller, Wendy L., and Gene D. Cohen, with Teresa H. Barker. 2016. *Sky above Clouds: Finding Our Way through Creativity, Aging, and Illness*. New York: Oxford University Press.

Moreno-Grau, Sonia, Isabel Hernández, Stefanie Heilmann-Heimbach, Susana Ruiz, Maitée Rosende-Roca, Ana Mauleón, Liliana Vargas, et al. 2018. "Genome-wide Significant Risk Factors on Chromosome 19 and the *APOE* Locus." *Oncotarget* 9 (37): 24590–600. https://doi.org/10.18632/oncotarget.25083.

Nouwen, Henri J.M., and Walter J. Gaffney. 1974. *Aging: The Fulfilment of Life*. New York: Doubleday.

Ortega y Gasset, José. 2004. *Obras Completas*, Vol. 1: *1902–1915*. Madrid: Taurus/Fundación José Ortega y Gasset.

Rosenmayr, Leopold. 1988. "More than Wisdom: A Field Study of the Old in an African Village." *Journal of Cross-Cultural Gerontology* 3 (1): 21–40. http://dx.doi.org/10.1007/BF00116958.

Shield, Renée Rose. 1988. *Uneasy Endings: Daily Life in an American Nursing Home*. Ithaca, NY: Cornell University Press.

Smith, Jacqui. 2015. "Applying Wisdom to Life in Old Age." Presentation given at the 2015 Jonas Salk Symposium on Wisdom and Aging, University of Pittsburgh, 7 December. https://www.publichealth.pitt.edu/salk2015.

Smith, Jacqui, and Lindsay H. Ryan. 2015. "Psychological Vitality in the Oldest Old." In *The Handbook of the Psychology of Aging*, 8th ed., edited by K. Warner Schaie and Sherry L. Willis, 303–19. Amsterdam: Elsevier.

Staudinger, Ursula M., Anna G. Maciel, Jacqui Smith, and Paul B. Baltes. 1998. "What Predicts Wisdom-Related Performance? A First Look at Personality, Intelligence, and Facilitative Experiential Contexts." *European Journal of Personality* 12 (1): 1–17.

Strawson, Galen. 2004. "Against Narrativity." *Ratio* 17 (4): 428–52. https://doi.org/10.1111/j.1467-9329.2004.00264.x.

Toren, Christina. 2007. "An Anthropology of Human Development: What Difference Does It Make?" In *Human Development in the Twenty-First Century: Visionary Ideas from Systems Scientists*, edited by Alan Fogel, Barbara J. King, and Stuart G. Shanker, 104–11. Cambridge: Cambridge University Press.

– 2012. "Imagining the World That Warrants Our Imagination: The Revelation of Ontogeny." *The Cambridge Journal of Anthropology* 30 (1): 64–79. https://doi.org/10.3167/ca.2012.300107.

PART THREE

Transmitting Wisdom

5 Yoga and Wisdom: Reflections on the Body at the Intersection of Epistemology and Ontology

JOSEPH S. ALTER

Introduction

In simple terms, the practice of yoga is thought to produce wisdom – deep, transcendent self-knowledge and an understanding of universal truth and cosmic ontology. Ian Whicher points out:

> The "heavy" authority given to the *guru* or "weighty one" places the preceptor at the hub of the entire initiatory and pedagogical structure of Yoga. The Upaniṣads have preserved examples of some of the more profound teacher/disciple relationships, in which the pinnacle of spiritual wisdom, not merely intellectual knowledge, was pursued. Having experienced directly the scriptural revelation, the enlightened adept is thus deemed fit to prepare others for self-realization. Hence the *Śiva-Saṃhitā* declares "[Only] knowledge imparted by way of the teacher's mouth is productive; otherwise it is fruitless, weak and leads to much suffering." (Whicher 1998: 35)

From a standpoint based on the authority of knowledge that reflects cumulative human experience in the world – that is, from an academic perspective – gurus embody profound contradictions involving the power of wisdom, transcendental consciousness, and words, spoken and written, that cross a threshold of stipulated, discrete realities to articulate wisdom, knowledge, and experience. It is, of course, possible to resolve the contradiction by claiming that the guru's wisdom transcends manifest knowledge, in the sense that individual self-consciousness is identical to consciousness of the transcendent self once one has achieved enlightenment. Wisdom manifest in the realization of enlightenment in these terms is often spoken of as "liberation," a word that suggests a world of experience inherently constraining and limiting, if not also a form of bondage and subservience.

Apart from philosophical arguments that might be put forward to challenge this view, my concern is with the problem of language in relation to claims of embodied wisdom and the way in which the use of language to communicate wisdom necessarily produces knowledge that is grounded in the *social* reality of semiosis. The concern here is not with the meaning of what is said – either material or immaterial – but with the fact that language, either spoken or written, relates to a reality that is irreducible to anything other than semiotics. As theorized by Charles Sanders Peirce, semiotics is dynamically triadic involving three elements: a representamen, an interpretant, and an object (Hoopes 2014; see also Sebeok 2001). An object, such as "enlightenment" – either embodied or disembodied – can only have meaning as an idea that is a function of the communicative and therefore social logic of semiosis. In other words, wisdom's ineffability, which derives in different ways from the stipulation of dualist and non-dualistic ontologies, is a function of reality constructed by language on the basis of knowledge in a world constituted of triadic signs.

What follows, therefore, are some critical reflections on a profound tension or paradox in the yogic means by which the cultural idea of embodied wisdom, encompassing language, is produced. This paradox is reflected in the way wisdom can only ever be a manifestation of the material dynamics in human consciousness, even though wisdom ostensibly produces profound insight that transcends the problem and limitations of materiality in the world (see Larson 2013; Whicher 1998; White 1996). The paradox is not unique to yoga. But the tension between wisdom and knowledge can be seen in various aspects of practice precisely because yoga engages the problem of materiality directly and systematically (Arnau 2013; Sharma 2011; White 2012). In *Roots of Yoga*, James Mallinson and Mark Singleton have provided a detailed overview of this and other core ideas, highlighting different interpretations of practice articulated in a broad range of largely pre-modern texts.

> In the context of the dualistic, Sāṃkhya-oriented *Pātañjalayogaśāstra*, *jīvanmukti* [liberation while living] is also a difficult and contradictory notion … In the *Pātañjalayogaśāstra* the commentary [indicates with reference to *samādhi*] that the wise man is liberated while living (II.I.4). However, the continued presence of the *jīvanmukta*'s body in the liberated state is philosophically problematic on account of the two stages of *samādhi* (with and without cognition, 9.I.3), and because the modifications must be entirely abolished before the highest wisdom manifests – facts which did

> not escape the commentators, and which ultimately made living liberation an unsustainable notion with Pātañjala yoga. (Mallinson and Singleton 2017: 399)

Beyond the problem of the body, however, motivation to reflect on the paradox stems from the way yoga and wisdom are increasingly disconnected from one another in the context of modernity, even though modern practitioners at various levels of experience seek to embody an ideal, unproblematic synthesis of yoga and wisdom and to profit from variously persuasive performances of idealized embodiment (Alter 2008). To be sure, the point is not at all that modernity has produced the paradox, which is, I will argue, a structural feature in the relationship between yogic epistemology and *sāṃkhyan* ontology (see Alter 2006). Nevertheless, modernity has certainly made it possible to capitalize on forms of deep deception that are attendant on the practice of yoga and the fetishization of gnostic, transcendent wisdom (Singleton and Goldberg 2014; Singleton and Byrne 2008). On the one hand, monetized individuality and self-branding has made it possible to control and effectively trademark claims to wisdom. On the other hand, deep alienation, as a function of neoliberal globalization, produces a "consumer demographic" very receptive to these claims, eager to engage in forms of practice that are at once physical and metaphysical. Those who persuasively claim to embody wisdom in the context of modernity – almost always charismatically, both in person in real time and via social media – can become very powerful in complex ways that are closely linked to the very idea of timeless, transcendent yoga.

From a sociological standpoint, yoga must be understood in the same way as religion, namely as a cultural articulation of meaning based on the fetishization of social relationships (Alter 2004, 2006). Whereas in religion the relationships are inherently sociological, albeit involving both human and non-human entities, in yoga the relationships that underlay the fetishization of enlightenment are broadly social, but necessarily ecological rather than anthropocentric. Thus, self-knowledge is congruent with transcendent insight such that ecological and environmental diversity at all levels ultimately resolves into the singularity of undifferentiated cosmic universality. Just as the fetishization of god in religion reflects the ontology of human social relations, as these relations constitute belief, so the fetishization of ultimate truth – and an ineffable awareness of truth in terms of wisdom – reflects an ontology of ecology that is essentialized in claims to an embodied experience of transcendent truth. Religion and yoga are not the same, but they are the same in that they are not simply cultural constructions of reality; they reflect elementary forms of social and ecological fetishization in human consciousness. Deeply vested collective investment in the suspension of disbelief – and the embodied manipulation of individual belief – is what makes religion and yoga powerful, both in their incipient forms and in modern and postmodern permutations.

Wisdom is, of course, the idealization of an idea about the relationship among general knowledge, truth, and self-awareness. It is a cultural phenomenon. As such, what counts as wisdom is variable depending on context, even though in many contexts the terms and conditions of wisdom are thought to be universal. Context-specific cultural construction further complicates distinctions among wisdom, knowledge, and perception, and differences between public knowledge as a function of communication and wisdom based on self-reflection. Wisdom most certainly has a social foundation in the sense that a person must be recognized as wise by someone else. No matter how reflexive or introspective, wisdom does not exist in isolation from a community, and, in some sense, consensus is the foundation upon which wisdom is culturally constructed. Consensus is an unconscious, functional prerequisite for language rather than a conscious articulation of strategic, negotiated compromise on definitive meaning. This idea follows from Willard V. Quine's (1960) indeterminacy of translation thesis.

Yet, wisdom is embodied and articulated through the medium of a person or a select group of people – judges, elders, teachers, counsellors, advisors – sometimes as a feature of institutionalized religious belief, but certainly not directly or always. In fact, the disarticulation of humanistic wisdom from divine insight based on self-determination is axiomatic of the Enlightenment and has become an institutionalized feature of modernity. The fetishization of wisdom tends both towards its apparent, transcultural, abstract universality – the domain of philosophy – and towards embodiment rather than towards belief in objectified things that represent divinity. When the embodiment of wisdom is linked to a metaphysical ideal such as transcendent consciousness or self-realization, embodiment brings into sharp focus the social self of the person who is self-aware. Therefore, a person thought to be wise stands in an awkward relationship between charismatic self-essentialization, enlightened self-perception, and the social reality of public, cultural knowledge based on language.

Because wisdom is as deeply fetishized as religion, it is important to engage in critical self-reflection in order to make a small contribution to knowledge that works, sociologically and historically, against the humanistic conceit of embodied wisdom. By "small contribution," I have in mind something more than false modesty or contrived humility.

What follows is a small contribution in the simple sense that a public archive full of similarly small contributions to knowledge – books, essays, chapters, reflections, notes; all the stuff of academia – ultimately displaces the relativism of enlightened profundity by much more than just the sheer weight of a mountain of words. It produces a history of understanding based on critical insight that is multidimensional, transcendent, democratic, and discernable rather than ineffably magnanimous. I do not mean to say that sage wisdom should be dismissed as irrelevant or intrinsically problematic, much less as inherently deceptive. However, from an academic perspective, the seductive ineffability of profound, embodied wisdom must always be translated into disembodied knowledge before it can be taken seriously to determine its social significance.

It is especially for this reason that ethnography in general and ethnographic examples in particular are problematic. The heaviness of the guru is a sign of fetishized wisdom based on the gravitas of enlightened perception, which is antithetical to the project of building knowledge based on relentless critique of the very idea of enlightened perception. Bodies, especially heavy ones that are ostensibly detached from the world, get in the way of understanding wisdom from the standpoint of a sociology of knowledge that semiotically links meaning to society at large. Archives inherently transcend space and time – representing collective consciousness through enumeration – whereas this quality is not a characteristic either of gods or of godmen, except in the singularity of the human imagination.

Sāṃkhyan Ontology

Sāṃkhya is a philosophy based on ontological dualism articulated in a body of third- or fourth-century literature found in southern Asia (Larson 1979; Larson and Bhattacharya 1987). As articulated in the *Sāṃkhyakārikā*, the universe is composed of two distinct realities: consciousness and matter, *puruṣa* and *prakṛti*. As a dualist tradition, the intellectual history of *sāṃkhya* philosophy has inspired significant intellectual debate, since *advaita* non-dualism is characteristic of most other systems of orthodox thought. Early arguments for archaic, pre-Vedic provenance for dualism, as well as for *sāṃkhya*'s relatively more recent anti-Brahmanical orientation, are now less convincing than arguments for the realization that the history of philosophy in South Asia contains as many possible differences in perspective as does reasoning elsewhere in the world (White 2006).

Although *sāṃkhyan* ontology is most directly relevant to understanding the paradox of embodied wisdom, the problem hinges, in part, on the fact that the stipulated epistemological procedures in *sāṃkhya* are resolutely rational, focusing technically on *pratyakṣa* (perception), *anumāṇa* (inference), and *āptavacana* or *āgama* (testimony) based on experience and discriminating knowledge. The logic of *āptavacana* is anchored in a semiotic appreciation of the power of words in relation to the enumerative structure of the philosophical system as a whole and the way in which words facilitate a rational delineation and definition of the *tattva* (principles) that constitute reality (see Lucyszyna 2016). In other words, *sāṃkhyan* epistemology is anchored in logic, as logic is a function of *buddhi* (intellect). *Buddhi* is a material expression of *prakṛti* (Fitzgerald 2017a, 2017b). But *buddhi* in *sāṃkhyan* conceptualization produces knowledge based on reason, as distinct from other forms of knowledge that are similarly material but ineffably anchored in mysticism and gnostic insight or the word of god (see Shokhin 1994). A fundamental problem is that *sāṃkhyan* philosophy struggles with having to use words to describe an ontology that transcends language but nevertheless takes shape in the body of enlightened souls.

Sāṃkhya is significantly different from Cartesian dualism in the sense that *puruṣa* and *prakṛti* encompass and define the nature of human experience, including the mind and consciousness (Burte 2015; Jacobsen 1999, 2007). The mind derives from dualism; it does not structure duality in terms of a distinction between mind and body. As such, *sāṃkhya* is not based on the distinctively anthropocentric assumptions of humanism, but on what might be called deep skepticism concerning human experience in relation to reality (see Jacobsen 1995). Significantly, however, *sāṃkhya* is fundamentally atheistic, based on the rational argument that god cannot exist as an independent, causal agent of change in a universe where everything that exists – including god – must be a function of change, which is a function of the relationship between transcendent, pure consciousness and primordial matter (see Jacobsen 2012). God is simply the expression of an idea within the larger framework of *avidya*, generalized ignorance (Alter 2006, 2012). Ignorance, a consequence of creation, is the fundamental problem thought to be overcome by means of *pramāṇa* epistemology.

Ignorance manifest in the *prakṛtic* body can be enumerated and delineated such that the material structure of ignorance in *sāṃkhyan* physiology suggests an epistemology of knowledge. The disequilibrium of the three *guṇa* that results from the convergence of *puruṣa* and *prakṛti* can be understood on a hierarchical scale that ranges from the subtlest manifestation of flawed materiality in consciousness to the grossest manifestation of imbalance in the physical body. As we will see, within the logic of fetishized dualism, it is possible to "work the body" against the flow of ignorance so as to achieve almost perfect equilibrium such that the relative purity of flawed *prakṛtic* consciousness reflects the transcendent reality of *puruṣa*. Fundamentally, however, increased knowledge does not resolve the problem of ignorance that defines human experience.

The problematic question is thus raised: how it is possible to postulate the existence of, and come to know something about, transcendent consciousness, which exists apart from the means that must be used to know it, especially if the means by which to know anything is necessarily an expression of ignorance? As a philosophy of delineation and enumeration, *sāṃkhya* necessarily postulates the existence of *puruṣa*, and, on this level, a purely rational, strong sociological argument would hold that *puruṣa* is the expression of radical idealism based on alienation – alienation that stems from the human inability to reconcile mortality, and the inevitability of death, with consciousness as a function of social reality. In other words, *puruṣa* is a fetish, an idealized projection. Within the framework of ontological dualism, it cannot be known directly by means of *pramāṇa*.

An interpretation of Ian Whicher's perspective on this question is especially germane. In a detailed study that problematizes distinctions between epistemology and ontology in the context of *sāṃkhyan* dualism, Whicher (1998) points out that perception is superior to inference and testimony, since perception produces insight on *viśeṣa*, the "particularities" of an object, whereas inference and testimony produce insight on *sāmānya*, the "generalities" of knowledge that are at a remove from the object itself (see also White 2011). "Words themselves are incapable of producing knowledge of particulars" (Whicher 1998: 145). As explained by Vyasa in his commentary on relevant passages in the *Yoga Sūtra*, "valid testimony cannot communicate the particular ... [b]ecause the particular does not have the conventional association with a word" (quoted in Whicher 1998: 146).

It is critically important to keep in mind here that particularities cannot be expressed in words, because words that produce knowledge in the form of generalities are, in essence, literal articulations of the material nature of subtle consciousness. In semiotic terms, all three dimensions of the word as a sign have a material aspect within the framework of *sāṃkhyan* conceptualization. Paradoxically, therefore, a word such as *viśeṣa* represents the endlessly recursive problem – the logic of cosmic ignorance, one might say – of trying to represent that which cannot be represented. For some, this paradox opens that door to what they think is enlightenment. But the paradox also stipulates the foundation for a critical sociology of knowledge that extends to the environment. Regardless, it can only be what we think it is as articulated in words.

More so than other philosophical systems of thought, *sāṃkhya* recognizes the logical problem of stipulating ontology within a framework of epistemological skepticism concerning the nature of reality. The problem is further complicated by what might be called "idealistic materialism" (Anthony 2016). The most refined articulation of knowledge is necessarily an expression of ignorance, thereby suggesting that transcendental consciousness must be achieved by means of embodied experience rather than by means of rational enumeration. Ostensibly, yoga is the means to this end, albeit in terms that valorize the reflexivity of isolated embodied experience as against knowledge based on relational, collective sociality. Wisdom, which is ineffable in any case, becomes all the more ineffable in the fetishized domain of embodied experience. As the adept comes to represent single-pointed enlightenment, both the body and wisdom appear to be objects with intrinsic meaning and transcendent significance rather than objects that can only be meaningful within the structure of a triadic sign.

Yoga Epistemology

In many ways, practising yoga is a metaphysiological process that "denumerates" *sāṃkhyan* rational enumeration, working embodied experience against the flow of ignorance that devolves from primordial misperception in human consciousness (see, for example, Couture 2017; Larson 2012; Larson and Bhattacharya 2008). As discussed by Mallinson and Singleton (2017), this process is reflected in the way in which the word "yoga" itself refers both to means and end, practice and goal, epistemology and ontology (4–6). To understand this concept, it is first necessary to delineate the structure of *sāṃkhya*n physiology.

Sāṃkhyan physiology is a delineation of embodied experience in relation to a hierarchical conceptualization of nature ranging from the subtlest to the grossest manifestations of perceived reality in the domain of visible, sensory perception (see Samuel and Johnston 2013; Larson and Bhattacharya 1987). In its primordial state, *prakṛti* is composed of three *guṇa*: *sattva, rajas,* and *tamas*. The *guṇa* are agentive properties of matter that are latent, balanced, and immobile in their primordial state. For reasons that do not easily fit into the logic of *sāṃkhyan* duality (see Whicher 1998: 59), *puruṣa* and *prakṛti* somehow converge, destabilizing the *guṇa*. Reality as sensed and experienced is the result of this "con-fusion," mapping out microcosmically in the domain of perception, sensation, and consciousness. The first, and most subtle, manifestation of devolved *prakṛti* is intelligence and the principle of discrimination (*buddhi*), followed by self-consciousness (*ahamkara*). Further delineation results from the integrated imbalance of the *guṇa* in unmanifest self-consciousness, producing five cognitive senses (hearing, touching, seeing, tasting, and smelling) and five instruments of perception (speaking, holding, moving, procreating, and eliminating). Together the senses and the instruments of perception derive from the mind, as the mind relates to the five relatively subtle aspects (*tanmatra*) of the five gross elements (*bhuta*): ether, air, fire, water, and earth.

Here the materialist structure of the subtle body is immediately apparent, as is the focus on elementary aspects of cognition that establish a structure for intellectual thought. The *sāṃkhyan* map of the conscious body provides a sensory framework for understanding the most basic aspects of perception, as perception is the foundation of reasoning and discernment.

With regard to the problem of embodied wisdom, it is important to consider how language fits into the structure of the subtle body, especially since testimony, as one aspect of *sāṃkhyan* epistemology, is defined explicitly in terms of sound, speech, and words. Given the hierarchical structure of *sāṃkhyan* physiology, it is not surprising that speech is considered the grossest manifestation of sound, although the sound of the letters in the Sanskrit alphabet – not words, but letters – are a degree subtler than spoken words. In some sense, language is a gross corruption of the subtlest sound conceptually associated with transcendence, the sacred syllable *om* being a relatively subtle but still fundamentally corrupt articulation of the supreme sound, which is cognate with *puruṣa*.

With regard to the fact that speech is inherently gross, it is not surprising that yoga epistemology is not problematized in terms of language. Sound is very important, as are esoteric mantras communicated secretly by a guru to a disciple (see Mallinson and Singleton 2017: 259–64), but the meaning of the words that constitute a mantra are, in some sense, irrelevant. Mantras most certainly do not add up to produce an extensive archive! They are meaningless with regard to the development of public knowledge, an attribute that helps to explain the logic of secrecy in the literature on yoga, which is, quite obviously, encoded in words, both written and spoken. In what appears to be a profound contradiction, yogic texts explain various techniques and then admonish readers to keep what they have learned absolutely secret. In terms of the development of public knowledge, this incongruity makes no sense. In terms of yoga epistemology, however, secrecy is a process whereby insight is embodied by transforming the gross sound of words into relatively more subtle self-understanding as a reflexive cognitive process rather than one that is structured in terms of communication. In some ways, the close connection between the recitation of a mantra and breath control illustrates the dynamic link between sound, consciousness, and the material nature of subtle reality. Both in terms of structure and function, secrecy in general, but internalized sign-sound secrecy, seeks to work the body against language and semiosis more broadly.

Beyond the materiality of language and sound, however, yoga epistemology can be understood with reference to *ashtanga* as delineated in the *Yoga Sūtra* (Whicher 1998). The so-called eight limbs of yoga as outlined by the sage Pātañjali, in what has come to be regarded as a canonical text (see White 2014), defines a structure of practice extending from moral observances, self-discipline, postures, and breath control to control of the senses, concentration, meditation, and the embodied enstasy of *samādhi*. *Samādhi*, as we will see later, is where the powerful, authoritative wisdom of embodied self-realization within a *sāṃkhyan* framework takes on problematic significance in contexts where wisdom that derives from the experience of knowledge is learned, shared, and communicated by means of language. In any case, and regardless of the extent to which the eight limbs are conceptualized as a sequence of progressive steps or aspects of self-discipline, the logic expressed in the practice of yoga is progressive purification that produces ethereal immortality once the body is no longer subject to change as a function of time. Among other things, the perfected practice of yoga is manifest in a body that is self-contained to the extent that nothing flows in or out, not even the relatively subtle element air, much less semen and other material things that reflect the gross problem of death and decay, birth and rebirth.

Yoga epistemology is, in many ways, a case in which communication based on language is antithetical to the development of experience based on hygienic forms of self-discipline that extend from relatively gross physiology – colonic purgation, nasal hydration, vomitation – into the domain of embodied ethics and morality, and on to control of the senses, thought, and cognition. Forms of concentration and meditation are, in terms of *sāṃkhyan* physiology, means by which to purify the mind of the accretions produced by consciousness and thinking, which are subtle derivatives of *prakṛti*. In this sense, enemas, meditation, and mindfulness are all of a piece.

Yoga epistemology is embodied precisely because the problem to be resolved through the practice of yoga is the material structure of ignorance that is manifest in creation. Yoga makes use of the body to reverse the logic of creation, overcoming ignorance by transcending consciousness rather than by producing knowledge. Among other things, what is important about this idea is that wisdom is thought to derive from a process that is intimately physiological rather than intellectually didactic. Experience based on deep reflection produces wisdom that is cosmological precisely because it transcends the sociological dynamics that are integral to the production of knowledge and public culture more generally.

Gurus, Embodied Wisdom, and the Weight of Language

In an insightful, penetrating, and multilayered essay, David Gordon White (1984) explains why gurus are heavy. In doing so, he draws explicitly on philology and etymology – the word "guru" signifying weight and weightiness on many different registers of meaning – but more broadly on the intricate layers of symbolic correspondence across domains of mythology, cosmology, medical physiology, and soteriology. Underlying his argument is a recognition that symbolic correspondences – and signs more generally – transcend distinctions between practices such as yoga, alchemy, and tantra and are deeply imbedded in Saivite literature. Gurus are wise, because gurus are heavy. And here is why gurus are heavy:

> The processes involved in the transmutation of the body are identical to those of metals. The body is "pierced" by the ingested, perfected mercury, which causes it to rid itself – through sweat, urine, feces, etc. – of that which is *sthula* [gross] in it, such that only the *sūkṣmā* [subtle] remains. As *sthula* "envelopes" are successively stripped away, the body, like the metallic stages, becomes denser, more powerful, shining and immortal. The body becomes perfected (*kaya siddha*), as hard as a diamond (*vajra*), impenetrable and all penetrating. It shines and smells like *hataka* gold. The hair becomes as black antimony, and the face and form of the man become those of a beautiful adolescent just entering into maturity. He becomes eternally young and unsusceptible to disease or injury. He is possessed of all of the *siddhis* [supernatural powers] which include invisibility (*anjana*), the ability to fly (*khecara*), to make things appear or disappear at will, to make his body infinitely small (*anima*), great (*mahima*), light (*laghima*), heavy (*garima*), the ability to attain all of his desires, to control

> others' minds, and numerous others, ranging from the sublime to the pornographic. (White 1984: 57)

In a book entitled *The Alchemical Body*, White (1996) elaborates on the multiple levels of symbolic correspondence that support his argument, providing insight on logic that confounds binary distinctions between materialism and idealism. Among other things, his analysis is profoundly synthetic and systematic without becoming overburdened with the dead weight of reductive essentialism. Not all gurus are the same, but the concept of a guru who embodies wisdom – one who transcends the snare of ignorance – is deeply woven into the fabric of thought and the practice of philosophy in southern Asia.

White's analysis, which is deeply intellectual and critically analytic, reminds us of the power of language and the weight of words. On one level, this idea is not surprising. However, in a context where symbolic correspondences cross the spectrum, turning gross elements into pure gold, it is critically important to remember that words are signs that signify correspondences which constitute reality by means of representation. Words are not the thing they represent; they capture it – they do not make it real as a tangible, corporeal thing unto itself. Worth their weight in gold as knowledge, words are worked by language against the very idea that truth is somehow ineffable and yet, at the same time, incarnate as wisdom.

One of the most common, evocative, and persuasive tropes in the modern literature on yoga is the idea of gaining insight on the wisdom of ultimate truth by going in search of a reclusive, mystical, enlightened sage living in the remote Himalayas. Having achieved *samādhi*, a sage embodies wisdom that is otherwise ineffable. And yet, the search for a truly enlightened sage reflects an epistemology at odds with the logic of yoga. Wisdom is undermined by what will invariably be experienced as knowledge, which is why – at least in large part – the trope itself is virtually immortal, living on and on, being reborn again and again, in the quest narrative of earnest seekers of truth.

The trope of the reclusive sage is also extremely powerful in the politics of knowledge associated with claims of speaking wisdom to truth that transcends language. Almost all of the men who identify themselves as speaking with authority on the practice of yoga base their claim – either directly or indirectly, implicitly or explicitly – on a narrative in which they have assimilated the mystical wisdom of a Himalayan master. Through austere practice, guided self-discipline, and deep meditation at the master's feet, their experience culminates in a single, condensed, powerful act of elementary communication whereby the enlightened sage whispers a secret mantra or *dhāraṇī* in the adept disciple's ear.

Mantras and *dhāraṇī* stand in a peculiar relationship to language and, in an important way, are conceptualized as a form of communication that transcends – or seeks to transcend – duality. Mircea Eliade's (1970) discussion is worth quoting at some length:

> For the ascetics, yogins, the contemplatives, *dhāraṇīs* become instruments of concentration … In some instances, we divine the meaning of mutilated words … but the majority of them are bizarre and unintelligible phonemes … [T]hese sounds revealed their message only during meditation. For the uninitiated the *dhāraṇīs* remained unintelligible; their meaning did not belong to rational language, to the language that serves to communicate ordinary experiences … [T]hese are experiences, then, that are in some measure bound up with the discovery of language and that, by this ecstatic return to a primordial situation, shatter diurnal consciousness. *All of the tantric yogin's effort is expended upon reawakening this primordial consciousness and rediscovering the state of completeness that preceded language and consciousness of time …*
>
> *Dhāraṇīs,* like *mantras,* are learned from "the master's mouth" (*guruvaktratah*); they are, then, something quite different from the phonemes that make up secular language or that can be learned from books – they have to be "received." But once received from the master's mouth, *mantras* have unlimited powers …
>
> The unlimited efficacy of *mantras* is owing to the fact that they are (or at least, if recited, can become) the objects they represent. (212–15; emphasis added)

It is striking that the articulation of the mantra, both in the logic of yoga epistemology as well as in powerful search narratives, betrays an acknowledgement of the flaw in a dualist ontology that can only ever be reflected as an idea in human consciousness. Regardless of the extent to which the secret mantra is a sound, a set of phonemes, a word, or a set of words, the fact that the secret is communicated from a master to a disciple introduces semiotics – the sign of which has three dimensions – into the domain of *prakṛtic* ignorance that is human experience. Of course, from the standpoint of a sociology of knowledge, everything about yoga is inherently semiotic, including inference as such. But the mantra betrays the way in which the power of signs in general and language in particular challenges the logic of *sāṃkhyan* dualism and the epistemology of yoga from the standpoint of enlightenment: an inference that necessarily devolves from the limits of comprehension rather than from suffering and the pain of death. The arbitrary meaninglessness of sounds in the form of mantras and *dhāraṇīs* is a profound reminder of the magical arbitrariness of words themselves in relation to the objects they represent. And, therefore, this meaninglessness is a reminder of the concrete reality of knowledge that is based on an understanding of how words work – semiotically – apart from the substance of things and ideas they seem to denote in a world of direct experience.

On one level, this reminder is nothing more than to acknowledge that, for wisdom to be embodied, it must be articulated in language. Language defines an elementary form of human sociality and opens the door – so to speak – to an appreciation of the cosmic reality of biosemiosis, the elementary form of life as an ecological principle. The mystical sage lost to the world in the Himalayas, whose single-pointed concentration reflects an ideal of perfected isolation (see Kye 2018), becomes, in a sense, the antithesis of reality manifest in life and the semiotic relations that constitute lived experience in the world (Burley 2004). Put another way, one might say that only those of us who are not enlightened seek wisdom in a form that transcends language and the signs of life that we can hear, touch, see, taste, and smell all around us.

Skepticism concerning the definitive power of inference within the structure of *sāṃkhyan* dualism need not be defined in terms of Cartesian duality and the power of deductive reason based on a history of ideas rooted in the European Enlightenment. Nor is it particularly useful to base a critique of *sāṃkhya* on the so-called naïve materialism of *Cārvāka* philosophy, which holds that direct perception of things in the world is the only means by which to ascertain fundamental reality (see Bhattacharya 2012). Skepticism emerges from the simple fact that language, as a semiotic system, locates meaning in the structure of signs and in the social fact of communication, even when – or especially when – language is used to articulate the possibility of an idea that transcends experience, as in the idea of enlightenment. Whether or not intended as such, the designation *cārvāka* draws attention to the power of the mouth, one possible etymology of the word suggesting that ancient materialist philosophers "chewed the self" and another suggesting that proponents used the power of well-chosen, "agreeable words" to cast doubt on the logic of both *sāṃkhyan* dualism and the non-duality of Vedic beliefs and practices.

The power manifest in language to produce meaningful skepticism about the nature of ultimate reality is more easily appreciated outside the framework of Cartesian dualism wherein language is a function of mind apart from body. Language can only have become a feature of the mind, and the means by which to communicate ideas, if the first principle of language, as a semiotic system, is recognized to be acts of communication that entail the interpretation of signs. Thus, language is based on the material reality of social relations – bodies in contact through semiosis involving, at a minimum, sense perception. Although language is grounded in the material substance of bodies in the world, *sāṃkhya* does not confront the logical problem that everything known – including inferences about enlightenment and the delineation of sounds from words – is necessarily a product of the social reality of semiotic relations in this form. No matter how ineffable it appears to be, the idea of enlightenment is brought down to earth – the grossest of elements – by means of language, effecting, thereby, a socio-semiotic translation of metaphysical wisdom into concrete knowledge.

For whatever its value as a theoretical and philosophical argument, the point here is important in terms that are clearly manifest in *Cārvāka* materialism, however naïve it can be said to be. Embodied wisdom, in any form, but especially as manifest in the modern form of so-called godmen, is antithetical to the production of collective knowledge based on discussion, debate, disagreement, compromise, and consensus. Whatever else it may have achieved – purportedly such things as hedonistic self-indulgence – *Cārvāka* atheism, deployed in the domain of *sāṃkhyan* dualism, suggests a powerful critique of the delineation of wisdom from knowledge in relation to human experience, pointedly casting doubt, based on worldly experience and word-of-mouth communication, on the idea that enlightenment – a powerful, esoteric, and fundamentally exclusive claim to transcendent self-knowledge – can be embodied by a mortal soul.

But language does not, in any sense, silence claims to wisdom, either by those inspired by gross self-interest or those motivated by the interest of the common good. Language simply translates the conceit of wisdom into public knowledge within a framework of common, collective interest.

Conclusion

The idea of embodied wisdom is not new, nor is the problem of language as a flawed medium that must be used to communicate the possibility of transcendent enlightenment. As I have argued here, the paradox of representation and embodiment is built into the structure of *sāṃkhyan* subtle materialism and the physiological practice of yoga. As David White (2009) has argued, the power associated with yoga makes it possible for an adept practitioner to either transcend the snare of ignorance or take full advantage of it in ways that invite opprobrium.

Compounded by a number of features, including an ethic of self-serving individuality, the slippage between epistemology and ontology makes it possible for contemporary gurus to claim power on the basis of enlightenment and to control the means by which these claims are persuasively communicated to the public at large.

It is therefore important to delineate a form of practice involving yoga that is unique in the context of modernity, involving the convergence of embodiment and language in ways that challenge the pretense of wisdom in terms of the praxis of education.

Without suggesting that they are paragons of virtue, or that they are completely unique, or that they have completely resolved the paradox outlined earlier, it is useful to consider the way in which Swami Kuvalayananda on the one hand and Swami Sivananda on the other both advocated for the rigorous, embodied practice of yoga and produced massive archives of knowledge about the integrity of practice (Alter 2004, 2007; Strauss 2002, 2005). Not only did they write about yoga, as others have done, but they also published intensively and extensively on a very large scale. The point here is not that they were the first to do so, since yoga was subject to orientalist critique and textual commentary throughout the nineteenth century. But, in the nationalist context of the twentieth-century yoga renaissance, they translated wisdom into knowledge to produce an axiology of praxis based on public education.

Sivananda and Kuvalayananda's contributions to the development of modern postural yoga are well known, with Sivananda being more spiritually oriented within the framework of the Divine Life Society and Kuvalayananda being explicitly concerned with science, physical education, and the medical application of yogic techniques at his research centre, Kaivalyadhama. However, both men established institutions through conscious effort and a calculated realization that publishing books, journals, pamphlets, and reports about yoga in conjunction with translating, commenting on, and reprinting classic texts was an essential and necessary component of modern, embodied practice. They both also collected large bodies of literature on the history of philosophy – both Eastern and Western – so as to render knowledge about wisdom, and its relationship to the practice of yoga, less and less arcane.

To a degree, the impress to write, publish, and teach, while admonishing students to practice and learn so as to gain understanding through experience, can be understood as a perennial modern response structured by the primordial paradox of *sāṃkhyan* dualism and by the social ontology of semiotic reality that supports language. It was also explicitly designed, as a feature of the modern yoga renaissance, to work against what was regarded as highly problematic articulations of esotericism and magic. Never completely or consistently, both Sivananda and Kuvalayananda nevertheless worked explicitly to break down the mystique of ineffable wisdom they otherwise embodied as self-identified swamis – and that many other modern sages have continued to affect and exploit in various ways – by connecting the materialism of the body to the substance of words in the construction of a disembodied public archive of philosophical knowledge.

REFERENCES

Alter, Joseph S. 2004. *Yoga in Modern India: The Body between Science and Philosophy*. Princeton, NJ: Princeton University Press.

– 2006. "Yoga and Fetishism: Reflections on Marxist Social Theory." *Journal of the Royal Anthropological Institute* 12 (4): 763–83.

– 2007. "Yoga and Physical Education: Swami Kuvalayananda's Nationalist Project." *Asian Medicine: Tradition and Modernity* 3: 20–36.

– 2008. "Yoga *Shivir:* Performativity and the Study of Modern Yoga." In Singleton and Byrne, *Yoga in the Modern World*, 36–48.

– 2012. "Sacrifice, the Body, and Yoga: Theoretical Entailments of Embodiment in *Hathayoga*." *South Asia-Journal of South Asian Studies* 35 (2): 408–33.

Anthony, Biju. 2016. "Is Samkhya a Form of Idealism? An Exploration into Classical Samkhya." *Journal of Indian Council of Philosophical Research* 33 (1): 151–64.

Arnau, Juan. 2013. "Consciousness and Matter, a Complex Relationship: The Case of Samkhya." *Pensamiento* 69 (261): 753–68.

Bhattacharya, Ramkrishna. 2012. "Svabhavavada and the Carvaka/Lokayata: A Historical Overview." *Journal of Indian Philosophy* 40 (6): 593–614.

Burley, Mikel. 2004. "'Aloneness' and the Problem of Realism in Classical Samkhya and Yoga." *Asian Philosophy* 14 (3): 223–38.

Burte, Dattatreya P. 2015. "'Nature' and 'Elementary Nature' in Phenomenology and Samkhya." *Journal of Indian Council of Philosophical Research* 32 (1): 31–43.

Couture, André. 2017. "Samkhya and Yoga: Towards an Integrative Approach." *Journal of Indian Philosophy* 45 (4): 733–48.

Eliade, Mircea. 1970. *Yoga: Immortality and Freedom*. Princeton, NJ: Princeton University Press.

Fitzgerald, James L. 2017a. "The Buddhi in Early Epic Adhyatma Discourse (the Dialog of Manu and Brahaspati)." *Journal of Indian Philosophy* 45 (4): 767–816.

– 2017b. "A Semantic Profile of Early Sanskrit 'Buddhi.'" *Journal of Indian Philosophy* 45 (4): 669–709.

Hoopes, James, ed. 2014. *Peirce on Signs: Writings on Semiotic by Charles Sanders Peirce*. Chapel Hill: University of North Carolina Press.

Jacobsen, Knut A. 1995. "The Anthropocentric Bias in Mircea Eliade's Interpretation of the Samkhya and the Samkhya-Yoga Systems of Religious Thought." *Religion* 25 (3): 213–25.

– 1999. *Prakrti in Samkhya Yoga*. New York: Peter Lang.

– 2007. "The Meaning of Prakrti in the 'Yogasutra' and 'Vyasabhasya' (Ultimate Principle)." *Asian Philosophy* 17 (1): 1–16.

– 2012. "Songs of the Highest God (Isvara) of Samkhya-Yoga." In White, *Yoga in Practice*, 325–36.

Kye, Mi-Ryang. 2018. "Pratyahara Practices in Tantra." *Journal of Yoga Studies* 19: 11–45.

Larson, Gerald James. 1979. *Classical Samkhya: An Interpretation of Its History and Meaning*. Delhi: Motilal Banarsidass.

– 2012. "Patanjala Yoga in Practice." In White, *Yoga in Practice*, 73–96.

– 2013. "Materialism, Dualism, and the Philosophy of Yoga." *International Journal of Hindu Studies* 17 (2): 181–219.

Larson, Gerald James, and Ram Shankar Bhattacharya. 1987. *Samkhya: A Dualist Tradition in Indian Philosophy*. Delhi: Motilal Banarsidass.

– 2008. *Yoga: India's Philosophy of Meditation*. vol. 12. Delhi: Motilal Banarsidass.

Lucyszyna, Ołena. 2016. "Classical Samkhya on the Relationship between a Word and Its Meaning." *Journal of Indian Philosophy* 44 (2): 303–23.

Mallinson, James, and Mark Singleton. 2017. *Roots of Yoga*. New York: Penguin.

Quine, Willard Van Orman. 1960. *Word and Object*. Cambridge, MA: MIT Press.

Samuel, Geoffrey, and Jay Johnston. 2013. *Religion and the Subtle Body in Asia and the West: Between Mind and Body*. New York: Routledge.

Sebeok, Thomas A. 2001. *Signs: An Introduction to Semiotics*. Toronto: University of Toronto Press.

Sharma, Ramesh Kumar. 2011. "Embodiment, Subjectivity, and Disembodied Existence." *Philosophy East and West* 61 (1): 1–37.

Shokhin, V.K. 1994. "Samkhya-Yoga and the Tradition of Gnosticism." *Voprosy Filosofii* 7–8: 188–207.

Singleton, Mark, and Jean Byrne, eds. 2008. *Yoga in the Modern World: Contemporary Perspectives*. London: Routledge.

Singleton, Mark, and Ellen Goldberg, eds. 2014. *Gurus of Modern Yoga*. New York: Oxford University Press.

Strauss, Sarah. 2002. "The Master's Narrative: Swami Sivananda and the Transnational Production of Yoga." *Journal of Folklore Research* 39 (2–3): 217–41.

– 2005. *Positioning Yoga: Balancing Acts across Cultures*. Oxford: Berg.
Whicher, Ian. 1998. *The Integrity of the Yoga Darśana*. Albany: SUNY.
White, David Gordon. 1984. "Why Gurus Are Heavy." *Numen* 31: 40–73.
– 1996. *The Alchemical Body: Siddha Traditions in Medieval India*. Chicago, IL: University of Chicago Press.
– 2006. "Digging Wells While Houses Burn? Writing Histories of Hinduism in a Time of Identity Politics." *History and Theory* 45 (4): 104–31.
– 2009. *Sinister Yogis*. Chicago, IL: University of Chicago Press.
– 2011. "Yogic Perception, Meditation and Altered States of Consciousness." *Indo-Iranian Journal* 54 (1): 61–6.
– 2012. *Yoga in Practice*. Princeton, NJ: Princeton University Press.
– 2014. *The Yoga Sutra of Patanjali: A Biography*. Princeton, NJ: Princeton University Press.

6 Social Construction of Wisdom in Institutions

CHARLOTTE LINDE

This chapter will analyse wisdom, not as a trait intrinsic to individuals but as the result of relations between individuals and institutions in specific contexts constructed by mutual negotiation, both explicit and implicit. As a proxy for the difficult question of how to define wisdom, my focus will be on the social identification of people who count as wise within an institutional context: people who are thought to be worth consulting on either technical/instrumental issues or issues of how to live well, both within that particular institutional context and more generally. The chapter will look at three domains: a major American insurance company, a Buddhist meditation centre, and Silicon Valley.

Note that the words "wise" or "wisdom" are not generally used as a description of people in any of these three domains. Rather, there are a variety of ways that certain people are proposed and taken as good examples for others within a given institution. This study, then, examines the social production and negotiation of exemplary people, allowing us a window into the social processes by which people are recognized and proposed as worth emulating.

Exemplars have been used as a concept in a number of works on the nature of wisdom within both psychology and philosophy. Within psychological studies of wisdom, exemplars are used as a way to probe subjects' beliefs about wisdom (see Staudinger and Glück 2011 for a review). Typically, subjects in such studies are offered lists of current and historical figures who might be considered wise and asked to rank them, or subjects are asked to give their own examples of people whom they consider to be wise. A typical listing of such exemplars includes Gandhi, Jesus Christ, Abraham Lincoln, Martin Luther King, Winston Churchill, Thomas Jefferson, Socrates, Albert Einstein, and Socrates (Weststrate, Ferrari, and Ardelt 2016).

In the field of philosophy, Zagzebski (2017) uses exemplars as an elementary term in her attempt to derive a theory of ethics based on the observation that people recognize virtue through their admiration for individuals whom they regard as models of lived virtue. Zagzebski uses as exemplars historical figures such as Jesus, Confucius, Socrates, and Saint Francis. Additionally, she includes less well-known heroes such as Holocaust rescuers and caregivers for the severely mentally disabled. However, in both the psychological and philosophical studies, the exemplars are taken as a given. There is no discussion of the social processes by which stories of potential exemplars are preserved and transmitted.

Such use of exemplars focuses on the individual, beginning with someone hearing and being moved by a story of an exemplar, but it leaves out the cultural processes that create and propose exemplars. The people moved by the stories of Jesus, Confucius, Socrates, or Saint Francis have not met or observed them as living people. Similarly, the current or recent public figures such as Gandhi or Martin Luther King Jr. are not personally known to the subjects in the psychological studies. It took, and continues to take, many complex social processes for the stories about these figures to be made available for use as exemplars within given social contexts. One view of this current study might be that it shows the mechanisms by which such examples are created and spotlighted on centre stage.

In contrast to these Western studies of exemplars, Humphrey (1997) offers an ethnographic account of Mongolian use of exemplars, which differs considerably. Here, the use of exemplars is an explicit, named, and discussed social practice. People choose their own exemplars for various admired qualities and for different reasons at different times. This process is one example of the production of exemplars: the production of agreement on who counts as wise, whereby people are taken to be good examples for others because of certain desirable traits.

Within the social contexts examined in this chapter, wisdom is the social trait studied and discussed. However, there are many other possible exemplary traits. There can be exemplars of talent or genius in many different fields, for example, socially produced exemplars of personal qualities such as coolness, even exemplars of celebrity: people who are famous for being famous. There can also be socially produced exemplars of negative traits: the black sheep of the family, the class dunce. However, this chapter will not examine these negative exemplars.

Additionally, exemplars in a given social context may exhibit a kind of ordinary success that anyone can hope to achieve, given hard work and ordinary good luck. Or, they may exemplify extraordinary virtues and success: to be admired by others but not taken as an example of a possible personal path to success.

In this study, I describe the production of exemplars in three fields, and then discuss whether or not each type should be considered an exemplar of wisdom. One of the major discoveries of this research has been finding commonalities across domains in the social structures that produce exemplars – something that groups and institutions do as part of the ways they maintain themselves.

How People Are Produced as Exemplars

The major way an individual becomes known as a possible exemplar within an institution is by representatives of the institution spotlighting the individual through various means: structural positions, circulation of stories, and formal and informal metrics of success. It is then up to the members of that institution whether they choose to emulate, ignore, or criticize such an exemplar. This nomination process differs from a nomination for positions of direct managerial authority. Rather, these nominations are proposals for moral authority: admire and emulate this person.

Structural Positions

Promotions and titles indicate positional authority within an institution. Some of these carry practical consequences, such as promotion to higher levels of management. While a person in a management position has authority over subordinates, it is up to the subordinates to decide whether that person has the moral authority of being a good manager and whether his or her career strategies should be emulated.

Other titles are purely symbolic: for example, a manager at the National Aeronautics and Space Administration (NASA) being given an award for "Meritorious Civilian Service." This title indicates upper management's esteem of the person, but entails no additional responsibilities or authority (although there may be a monetary award involved). At a commercial firm, someone who has been awarded the "Sales Person of the Month" award might get a parking space with a sign for that month, but no more permanent change in responsibilities or rewards.

Narratives: Stories of the Worthy

Within institutions, stories circulate about individuals. Some of these are informal, oral stories told by individuals about other individuals. These are, in effect, the elementary units of the creation and maintenance of reputation. Other stories have a more public character: stories told at an award ceremony, profiles of an individual in the company magazine, or short biographical statements on a website. The use of stories plays a powerful role in creating exemplars. Stories demonstrate the nature of exemplary people and how they act within a particular institution or community.

In addition, within given institutions there may be central narratives of exemplary characters, usually the founder(s), which demonstrate the virtues and career paths expected of other, more local exemplars. Thus, these founders' narratives provide the structure of what an exemplary person looks like within the institution and suggest virtues and trajectories for members.

Occasions for Spotlighting People as Worthy of Emulation and Consultation

Many institutions have occasions that are used, among other functions, to indicate potential exemplars: meetings of various kinds that include awards, award ceremonies, promotion announcements, and other such events. All these occasions provide an opportunity for telling the relevant stories about proposed exemplars to a wide audience within the institution.

Metrics

Specific domains have their own metrics for ordinary and extraordinary success. Some are explicit and official: in the American university system, the tenure clock gives someone seven years to achieve tenure (on average, depending on the university); in various law or consulting firms, there will be a specified number of years to achieve partner status. Other such metrics in other fields are observational and informal: "A physicist who has not made the great discovery by forty is not likely to win the Nobel Prize."

Such metrics provide an abstract form of exemplary success. Without reference to specific stories of particular successful careers, they offer numerical specifications of what counts as success in a given domain.

Institutions Studied

The data for this study come from a three-year team ethnography of an insurance company (Linde 2009), membership in a Tibetan Buddhist meditation organization, and participant observation of NASA and Silicon Valley technology firms.

One important finding of this study is that the domains of the insurance company and the meditation centre are structurally similar in how they use exemplars. In both cases, people are presented by the central organization as good examples within the context of the institution, and there are similar ways in which these potential exemplars are accepted or ignored by the people to whom they are proposed.

The Silicon Valley study shows some of the same practices for spotlighting the worthy, within a larger and more loosely connected institution. However, this domain also raises the issue of what these exemplars are exemplary of: whether the concept of "wisdom" is relevant in an environment that values rapid and "disruptive" technological change, as opposed to the value of the past in understanding the present.

I will discuss the insurance company in greatest detail, as it is the domain that I have analysed most closely. I will use the examples of the meditation centre and Silicon Valley as contrast cases to show similarities, differences, and areas for further analysis.

Case 1: Insurance Company

The first data source for this study is a major American insurance company, which I will call MidWest Insurance, an established firm that has been in business since the 1920s. While I was a researcher at the Institute for Research on Learning, my colleagues and I carried out a three-year ethnographic study in the mid-1990s, including observations of the training and work of insurance sales agents and their offices, ongoing training programs, sales conventions, regional meetings, special task forces, and corporate meetings. This work was originally commissioned by MidWest to answer questions about agents' sales practices and the company's new training program for agents.

Typically, job tenure at most insurance companies is very short, and turnover is very high for both sales agents and operations staff. However, at MidWest, most agents stay until they retire, and turnover for operations staff is also extremely low relative to the rest of the industry.[1] One reason for this long tenure is that sales agents are independent contractors, not employees. Without describing all the legal and contractual issues of the independent contractor status, we can say that the closest analogue to the relationship of the agents to MidWest Insurance is the relationship of a franchise owner to the parent company. The comparison is not exact, but the main points hold: agents rent or buy their own premises, hire and train their own staff, but sell only MidWest products, with restrictions on how and to whom they may sell. Because agents own their own agencies, they are not entirely dependent on management for their financial success; they are personally responsible for much (though not all) of their business development. This structure means that MidWest agents describe themselves as business owners and entrepreneurs.[2] The independent contractor status, as well as the details of the contract, also means that managers must persuade rather than require agents to make certain business decisions, specifically a concentration on life insurance sales in addition to the easier task of selling automobile and home insurance.

Within the insurance company, proposed examples modelling how to have a good career are found both in insurance sales and management. Managers are implicitly proposed as people worth listening to by virtue of their position. In particular, all managers had a background in sales before entering management, which is viewed as a warrant for their ability to give advice on sales.

Specific sales agents are chosen by management to be spotlighted. These are agents at every career stage: put together, they present a composite example of how to act at each stage of an exemplary career. Typically, agents who are doing what management wants are highlighted, including those who excel at life insurance sales and, observed towards the end of our study, those who have developed successful business processes in their offices, allowing them to spend more time on life insurance sales, which typically take much more time than automobile or home owners' insurance.

EVENTS FOR HIGHLIGHTING PEOPLE TO EMULATE

Sales agents who are proposed as worthy of emulation are spotlighted at regional or national conventions as the recipients of awards. A few may be featured in the internal company magazine. Some may be asked by management to give talks or lead classes at regional or national gatherings.

Other agents can choose whether or not they attend regional or national meetings or talks and classes. Thus, agents decide whether they are present at these events honouring agents and presenting exemplars. In general, agents do not explicitly critique or reject exemplars whom they do not personally admire. Rather, they ignore them or, at most, label such presentations "boring." Thus, the agents who have chosen to be present at such events are self-selected as an audience potentially receptive to such models of how they themselves might manage their careers.

STRUCTURAL POSITIONS

In many institutions, structural positions within the institution indicate authority and success. Thus, in an institution with a tree-structured hierarchy, positions in line management are less elevated than those in middle management. Positions in the "C suite" – chief executive officer, chief financial officer, chief operations officer – have more authority than those below them and are considered to be at the top of the ladder of success. However, MidWest Insurance has a more complex structure of authority, since sales agents are not employees but independent contractors with a considerable amount of personal control over the ways they run their businesses.

All sales managers are expected to begin their careers as sales agents. Fairly early in their career, agents who have done well in building their business may be invited to move into management, which is, to some extent, an endorsement by the existing managers of that person's career to date.

This proposed change is not necessarily viewed as a desirable move or, indeed, as a real promotion by sales agents. Many agents decide that they can make more money by continuing as a sales agent and consider transferring to management a move for the unambitious. Entrepreneurship is very highly valued by agents: in this context, it means not relying on a salary but, rather, being in control of their compensation through their own business and sales efforts.

For managers, their time as a sales agent serves as a minimum validation of their ability to give advice and instruction on how to build a sales agency. Higher-level managers have access to communication with a larger group of agents, but, again, it is the agents' choice whether or not to respect and listen to them. It was clear that certain members of upper management were highly respected, while others were criticized or, more politely, ignored.

STORIES

Within MidWest Insurance, stories are a particularly important way of nominating exemplars and indicating in what ways they should be taken as exemplary. (Note that, among American corporations, MidWest is a particularly narrative-rich environment, deploying stories in many ways as teaching materials and indications of how to behave.) In particular, MidWest uses the story of the founder as the prime exemplar. In the following section, we will explore the difference between a deceased exemplar and exemplars who are alive, visible, and available for consultation.

FOUNDER'S STORY

The story of the founder of MidWest presents the primary exemplar, the most cited example of what the ideal agent should be like and what it means to be "really MidWest." Stories about the founder are still frequently told at MidWest, more than seventy years after the founding of the company, as examples of how to behave; the founder's virtues are taken as the most important virtues for agents; and we heard agents criticizing the current management by showing that they were failing to live up to the example of the founder.

The founder, always referred to by name as Mr. McBee, or T.D. McBee, is used within MidWest to tell the story of the first part of MidWest's history. An authorized history of the company, written in the mid-1950s, is still easily available. This history is framed as the story of Mr. McBee; the course of the company's first twenty-five years is told as being the events of Mr. McBee's life or the result of his decisions. This personal framing of the company's history permits the story of the founder to be used by others as a model for a life in a way that an impersonal account of a corporate history would not.

Mr. McBee's story is told as the story of humble but principled beginnings, leading to a triumphant climb to commercial success. The story includes the following characteristics of the founder and the company:

- *The American rural and small-town origins of the founder and the company, which still shape the company's values.* Here is a particular instance of the common American claim about the virtues of the farm over the wicked city, which goes back at least to Thomas Jefferson, if not earlier.
- *The distinct vision by a charismatic founder with a gift for salesmanship of the kind of insurance company he wished to found.* The vision began with the idea that farmers of good moral character (and he considered that farmers were likely to be of better character than dwellers in wicked cities) should be charged lower rates for auto insurance, since they ran lower risks than drivers in the city. It also included a distinctive model for the relationship between the company and its sales agents.
- *The development of the company from a local organization selling auto insurance to an international full-service company offering fire, life, and health insurance.* This development is presented as an ever-growing commercial and ethical success. Although the story is sometimes invoked to make the point that the company has previously faced and overcome hard times, the details of those hard times are not specified. It is the upward trajectory that matters.
- *The frequently repeated claim that the company is a family and holds family values.* This claim is more substantive than the usual corporate trope of the XYZCo family of valued employees. Many employees and agents at MidWest have family members

> who currently work for the company or who did so in the past, and the five presidents of the company have come from two families.

PARADIGMATIC STORY: COMPOSITE EXEMPLARS OF ORDINARY SUCCESS

Stories of individuals with a typically successful career can be used as teaching tools to show what kind of career is possible and what aspects of others' lives to emulate. I call these "paradigmatic narratives." (Someone's story can also be used to illustrate a bad example, a paradigm of what not to do. However, we observed little or no such use of bad examples at MidWest.)

I define the paradigmatic narrative as a representation of the ideal life course within an institution, including its stages, preferred time for attaining each stage, preferred age at beginning and end, possible options, and so on.[3] Readers may be most familiar with the paradigm for an academic career: the move from graduate student to tenure-track position to promotion and tenure with status in a department. Not every graduate student achieves this career, and many may add steps, such as postdoctoral fellowships and lateral moves into administration and other positions, or may take unusually long or short periods for each stage. However, the pattern is clear, even if individual instantiations differ (see Traweek [1988] for an example). For the professorate, this career trajectory is institutionally reified, with each stage achieved through institutional decision, contracts, titles, and changes in responsibilities. By contrast, the career of a sales agent at MidWest has only one named and institutionally reified stage: the move from trainee agent to independent contractor, who has the legal right to write insurance contracts on behalf of the company. However, there are recognized stages of an agent's career, which form an important part of the social practice of the company. These stages are identified and conveyed by narratives, told both by the agent in question and by others.

The paradigmatic narrative is not the story of one person; it is a composite of local examples illustrating aspects of the ideal career trajectory. It can also be distinguished from a myth or folktale, because the full paradigmatic narrative is never told on any given occasion. Rather, pieces of it are told as possibilities. Thus, a manager recruiting a possible new agent might cite the beginning part of the story: "You'll work hard for the first seven years or so, and then you can start to reap the rewards. You can invest and then rest. Look at the kind of business Bob built. He had to work hard at the beginning, but now he can take off every Wednesday to play golf." Additional stages are described, in the form of narratives of the careers of others, as they become relevant for a particular individual. The paradigmatic narrative represents an ideal trajectory – in this case, during our fieldwork in the late 1990s, we heard stories narrating the trajectory of an ideal agent's career from the 1960s through the 1990s. It was an ideal of ordinary success, representing a career that many agents were able to accomplish, the sequence that a hardworking and ordinarily competent agent could expect if he had no unusual reverses.[4] It was an implicit social contract, though not a legal one.

The paradigmatic narrative is a way in which some people's stories are told as exemplary. Not all careers fit the paradigm, and not all stories form part of the paradigmatic narrative. Thus, when a manager tells a story about George, it may only be understood as a story about George and his idiosyncrasies. But when he tells a story about old Bob down the street, it is to be understood as an instance that approximates the ideal agent career, which the hearer can understand as a model for himself. Similarly, agents tell their own stories as instances of the paradigm or as conscious deviations from it. As Goffman (1981) has pointed out, it is the task of a narrator to justify the apparent egotism of telling a personal story by making it the story of Everyman, a tale of what any reasonable person would do in similar circumstances. The paradigmatic narrative represents the work of an entire institution to create such relevance for particular narratives as forming part of the story of Everyagent.

The paradigmatic narrative is closely related to the promotion and reward structure of the organization. MidWest honours agents by publicly presenting awards at regional and national meetings, by profiling them in a monthly magazine, and by asking them to teach other agents, serve on task forces, and so on. These honoured agents generally have careers matching the paradigmatic narratives, and their careers are narrated at such events.

Certain types of occasion are conducive to the telling of narratives that form part of the paradigmatic narrative. Instances of the paradigmatic narrative are very likely to be heard on formal, ceremonial occasions. Part of the reward ceremonies at conventions and meetings involves a senior manager narrating the story of the agent being honoured. Another important occasion for telling these stories is during conversations about recruitment: a manager shows a potential candidate what an agent's career could look like.

PARADIGMATIC NARRATIVE AS METRIC

The paradigmatic narrative was not just told to agents; it was also used by them to define their own progress and success. The narrative allows agents to measure whether they are on track or not and indicates how they should feel about where they are. It suggests what kinds of work and rewards may be expected at different points in a career. Importantly, it also suggests possible responses to demands from management. An agent may decide whether a particular demand is reasonable, given his stage of development. For example, agents have no problem with a manager asking a second-year agent to stay evenings and weekends to make cold calls (an unsolicited call to a potential client who has had no prior contact with the caller). However, the same demand made of a fifteen-year agent, even one who has been quite unsuccessful, violates the paradigmatic narrative and the sense of the ideal career. In discussing their professional history, agents will mark stages of their careers by how many evenings they had to work and when they could start to take afternoons off to play golf.

In addition to the use of paradigmatic narratives to establish career stages, there are also specific metrics that represent awards for sales success. Within MidWest, these metrics as a category are referred to as "pins, points and plaques." These metrics are a recognition system for success. In general, this system is symbolic: there are few tangible bonuses or other major material rewards. However, the symbolic rewards are extremely significant to those agents who choose to participate in the system. (Not all agents do participate, which complicates the meaning of such rewards.)

Within a district, agents' rankings in sales for given periods are made available to the agents. This list was quite consequential to the agents. Their district ranking had no financial consequences beyond the intrinsic consequence of having sold however many policies they had sold. However, their relative ranking was significant to many (though not all) agents. Agents would scan the rankings to see their standing relative to their peers, make bets with friends on who would rank higher, and have bets proposed by managers on whether they could raise their rankings.

Additionally, there are national awards, such as Millionaires' Club and President's Club, which mark various forms of sales success throughout the company. Winners of these awards are spotlighted at national conventions and congratulated by the president of the company. The plaques for these awards are usually displayed prominently in the agents' offices.

In general, these visible rankings and prizes reward sales success, which is part of what constitutes the ideal career for the exemplary agents. However, such awards are partial, spotlighting specific successes, and are intended to be motivational – indications of targets to strive for. The ideal career is broader, including both an ongoing pattern of sales successes and desired ways of shaping general business practice and office management.

ARE THE PROPOSED EXEMPLARS ACCEPTED?

As already discussed, agents who have succeeded in building a good business in ways approved by managers are proposed as examples to be admired, emulated, and consulted. But whether these proposed exemplars are actually admired, followed, or consulted is not only determined by the actions of management. The other agents choose whether or not to admire these proposed exemplars, attend their talks, take their classes, or consult them. Additionally, some agents who are not officially proposed as exemplars are admired and consulted by other agents who know them.

As mentioned earlier, the politeness norms of MidWest are such that we did not hear direct rejections of people nominated as exemplars. Agents who might have disagreed politely ignored or deflected the proposed exemplar. When we asked them what they thought of a given presentation, the closest that they would come to criticism was that it was "boring."

Perhaps the most important finding about the use of exemplars is the following insight: exemplars are not solely created by a top-down decision. Management can extol the exemplary nature of a given person or propose a composite narrative of an exemplary career. But the individual members themselves decide whether they do, in fact, admire and use this particular example.

Case 2: Meditation Centre

Let us now turn to a very different organization, which has similar mechanisms for the creation of exemplars in a very different area of human activity. I am a member of a Tibetan Buddhist group, which is currently headed by a Tibetan teacher, the son of the deceased founder. These two teachers are the source for the teachings given within the 200 centres in 50 countries that comprise the organization. While the current head of the organization gives the most advanced teachings, the initial and intermediate teachings are given by selected students, who are trained and authorized to give individual meditation instruction and lead group classes at various levels. These teachers are explicitly identified to the members as to their level of authorization, though many members do not fully understand the system of levels, as it does not match anything in their prior experience. (Nor, indeed, is it derived from Tibetan models: giving teaching credentials to relatively young members was not part of the traditional Tibetan monastic model.)

The system of training and authorization is quite complex, as is the sequence of trainings proposed to members. While the teachings themselves are traditionally Tibetan Buddhist, the system of teacher training and delivery of the teachings owes more to Western educational models of management and certification. In the 1970s, the early period of the organization, it was sometimes nicknamed the "Buddhist IBM," a joke or criticism or sometimes a boast, both within and outside the organization. (I would note that other Buddhist organizations in the West, such as Zen groups with origins in Japan, China, or Korea, and Southeast Asian Vipassana groups are also experimenting with nontraditional methods of teacher training and structures for offering teachings on meditation.) In all of these organizations, the traditional Asian authority structures centred on monks and monastic organizations. While there has been some transfer of Buddhist monasticism to the West, it forms a small part of the organizations and teaching activities of Western Buddhism. Therefore, new or borrowed systems are in the early stages of development.

As was the case in the insurance company, the organization proposes the teachers as people to learn from. However, the students choose whose classes to take and which teachers to work with individually, based on their sense of who is admirable, as well as whom they find personally compatible. Additionally, the local administrators choose which one of a number of teachers to invite to teach a given program. Thus, certain people credentialed at a given level will be eagerly requested, while others may be politely ignored. Similarly, there are people who are esteemed for their presence and advice in ways unrelated to their level of teaching credentials.

This mismatch between credentials and actual wisdom is not a phenomenon unique to this organization. There are traditional stories in a number of Buddhist traditions in which a humble and uneducated person is shown to be wiser than a widely famed teacher or monk. For example, Schireson (2009) offers traditional Japanese Zen stories of tea ladies and old peasant women defeating Zen masters in Dharma combat, in which an intense verbal exchange takes place challenging one or both of the parties to demonstrate their deepest understanding of the Buddhist teachings.

The main structural difference between exemplars in the insurance company and exemplars in the meditation centres, of course, is that the meditation centres offer instruction in what is explicitly understood as a wisdom tradition. Thus, the question of whether the teachers are wise is a reasonable inquiry on the part of new and ongoing students. By contrast, the exemplars proposed by the insurance company are sales agents who have created a good business in ways that the company would like other agents to emulate. But the agents may ignore these suggested ways of running their business while continuing to run a successful insurance sales office.

The question of the spiritual attainment of the teachers manifests in a variety of ways in a meditation centre. Newcomers to the organization may have been attracted to the centre by reading or viewing teachings by the current or founding teacher. Or they may have decided to try to learn to meditate in a situation where meditation instruction is free. Thus, if they do not think that the main teacher is worth listening to, or that meditation is worth doing, they are deciding in effect that wisdom is not to be found in this place and do not even show up. Those who do come to the centre will often ask the person giving initial meditation instruction or an open house talk how long they have been meditating and what effect it has had on their lives. These questions place the instructor in a complex situation: the instructor wishes to speak for the efficacy of meditation and the teachings of this tradition, yet the speech norms of this group (like those of almost all spiritual groups) forbid a speaker to claim possession of wisdom. It is a challenging exercise in spiritual politeness for a teacher to engage in conversation with a newcomer and be asked, "Are you enlightened?"

Other people may have decided to investigate the value of meditation not necessarily as part of a wisdom tradition, but through reading scientific studies or because of a recommendation from their physician, therapist, Alcoholics Anonymous sponsor, yoga teacher, and so on. They have the same question: do the people they see at the meditation centre, particularly the ones that offer teachings, demonstrate the qualities that the newcomers hope to attain.

HOW EXEMPLARS ARE PRESENTED

As I have already mentioned, the exemplars are proposed by the central organization and, ultimately, by the main teacher, based in part on recommendations by local leaders. Let us now look at the same mechanisms of structural position, stories, and metrics that we considered for the insurance company.

STRUCTURAL POSITIONS

In contrast to the insurance company, the exemplars in the meditation centre have quite explicit, named structural positions. The common factor of these positions is authority to teach at given levels within a training program that is quite complex and explicitly structured.

Some of these positions have titles that are used during a program: director or assistant director of the program. Other, more permanent positions have titles that can be used as terms of address at any time.

However, as mentioned earlier, the definition and scope of these positions is not necessarily known to students, particularly to new students. All they see is the literal position of the person at the head of the room, with others orienting to them as the main speaker.

STORIES

Unlike the insurance company, this meditation tradition does not rely heavily on narratives. Although the Buddhist tradition contains many stories, the focus of how the tradition is transmitted is through training in practices rather than through participation in narratives.

At the level of the local centres, the use of narratives about proposed exemplars is quite limited. Short written biographies of teachers will be included in announcements of particular programs. Typically, the biographies mention when the teacher met the main teacher, how long they have been meditating, and perhaps a short mention of their professional history or other interests.

Teachers will use stories of their own experiences, or their experiences with the main teachers, as examples within their teaching. However, these stories are not used by others as warrants for why the person should be considered exemplary.

METRICS

The meditation centre does not use specific metrics in the presentation of potential exemplars. There is, however, one implicit metric contained within the complex sequence of teachings: which levels of training has the potential exemplar completed. This qualification is public knowledge, although it is more meaningful to mid- and long-term members than it is to newcomers and beginners.

Case 3: Silicon Valley

This section on exemplars in technology development industries is based on my experience of thirty-five years of participant observation living and working in Silicon Valley, including thirteen years as a social scientist in the advanced computer science division at the NASA Ames Research Center.

WHY "SILICON VALLEY"?

"Silicon Valley" is an ethno-identifier for the interrelated high-tech industries located in the San Francisco area of California. Wikipedia describes it this way:

> Silicon Valley is a region in the southern part of the San Francisco Bay Area of Northern California that serves as a global center for high technology, innovation, and social media. It corresponds roughly to the geographical Santa Clara Valley, although its boundaries have increased in recent decades. San Jose is the Valley's largest city ... The word "silicon" in the name originally referred to the large number of innovators and manufacturers in the region specialising in silicon-based MOS transistors and integrated circuit chips. The area is now home to many of the world's largest high-tech corporations, including the headquarters of more than 30 businesses in the Fortune 1000, and thousands of startup companies. (Wikipedia 2019)

There are several excellent ethnographies of Silicon Valley as an actual place: *Cultures@Silicon Valley* (English-Lueck 2017), *Desi Land: Teen Culture, Class and Success in Silicon Valley* (Shankar 2008), and the Silicon Valley Cultures Project (2019). In this chapter, I discuss Silicon Valley more as an imagined community roughly located in the San Francisco Bay area.

I speak of Silicon Valley rather than specific technology companies and organizations for a number of reasons. The companies that comprise Silicon Valley share many cultural similarities, and there is a great deal of movement of people between companies and complex relations between established corporations, start-ups, universities, venture capital firms, and other organizations. Many genealogical charts attempt to show the movement of individuals and groups of people as they move from one firm to found another. At an individual, more personal level, people move between companies in a similarly complex pattern.

As a result of this kind of movement, a key factor that characterizes Silicon Valley as an institution is that, for many of the people who work in this sector, their primary reference group is not their current employer but, rather, their current and former colleagues in their technical subsector who know their work, their classmates, and others not necessarily employed in the same organization. This network makes sense, since job movement in Silicon Valley is so frequent and so common that it is rare for people to think of themselves as lifetime or long-term employees of a given company. And, it is well known that many people move from one employer to another not singly, but in groups. One company may acquire another, which includes its employees. An employer may hire an entire team at one time. Or one person may be hired and then bring over other colleagues to the new employer. (I know many people with multi-decade careers in Silicon Valley who have never gotten a technical job any other way. I myself worked for twenty-six years at two positions to which I was introduced by people with whom I had previously worked or by former classmates from my graduate program.)

STRUCTURAL POSITIONS

As with the other two institutions discussed, one way that exemplars are proposed in the world of technology development is their appointment to specific structural positions. Within corporate structures of large, established technical firms, the standard path for career advancement is to go from individual team member to various levels and types of management: team leader, project manager, division manager, and so on. People in these positions can serve as exemplars. However, in many firms it is recognized that there are people who are technically excellent, innovative, and valuable, but not good candidates for management positions.

Some firms have established positions for the most distinguished of such people, with titles such as technical fellow, distinguished engineer, senior engineer, and the like, which recognize their scientific or technical ability over the course of a career. Holders of such positions consult on matters of technical and scientific strategy.

Senior scientists and technology developers also have opportunities to serve as technical advisors to venture capital and angel investor firms. The identity of these technical advisors may be publically highlighted to take advantage of their reputation. Their advice, obviously, is not. Such positions propose exemplars of scientific and technical prowess in a different authority structure than the standard corporate organization chart.

It should be noted that this discussion of corporate structural positions holds for established organizations. The organization and meaning of structural positions in the world of start-ups is considerably more fluid. However, even there, an increasingly formalized set of legal and organizational stages and roles exist.

STORIES

Oral stories establishing an individual's reputation are particularly important in the world of technology development because of the structure of secrecy, confidentiality, and information flow. In the academic world, if we consider a person's reputation within a given scholarly field, much of the knowledge of what he or she has done is a matter of public record. While the person's colleagues within a subfield may have personal knowledge of that person's most recent, unpublished research and what the person is like as a co-worker, a great deal of public knowledge is available to those to whom it might be relevant, such as hiring and tenure committees. Such knowledge includes a list of publications, number of publications, rank of journals in which the person published, citation indices, student rankings of teaching, and other such information.

By contrast, information about what technical workers have done may be documented within a given corporation but not available outside (with the exception of names on patent applications or patent grants), although it may be public knowledge which firms the person has worked at. But the person's co-workers, past and current, know what that person has worked on, what his or her contribution was, and what kind of colleague he or she was. Thus, the accounts of a person's colleagues are essential in establishing the story of who the person is. Good and bad examples are established in this reputational system.

In addition to the oral reputation system, there is also a more public mechanism for the presentation of potential exemplars from among technology firm founders and leaders. The business and general media present a steady stream of hagiographic programs, articles, and books about technology firm founders and leaders. Deceased or retired examples include Steve Jobs, co-founder of Apple, and Bill Gates, co-founder of Microsoft. More recent widely cited entrepreneurs include Elon Musk, founder of Zip2, SpaceX, and Tesla; and Mark Zuckerberg, co-founder of Facebook.

There are certain standard story types into which many such stories fit. Perhaps the oldest Silicon Valley story is that of major innovation coming from small beginnings: "Two guys in a garage" stories, which go back to the story of the founding of Hewlett-Packard. Another story type is the "skunkworks" story: the story of hidden technical development in the face of ridicule or opposition within an organization. A very common story form is the hero story: the single driven genius who creates an innovative product or company. These heroes are the subjects of biographies/hagiographies offered in books and articles. These are usually the stories of corporate founders or current CEOs. Specialist magazines and journals may spotlight less highly placed innovators. (Next time you fly, check the business section of the airport bookstore to get a sense of how widespread this genre is.)

The following is an example of a reference to a well-known story of a genius founder used as an example by a currently embattled corporate founder:

> Uber's search for a new CEO is full of Machiavellian drama.
>
> The company's former chief executive, Travis Kalanick, may have stepped down from the top position, but he's angling for a glorious return, according to a report in Recode.
>
> Kalanick reportedly told several people at the company that he was "Steve Jobs-ing it," a reference to the cofounder of Apple who was fired from the company but later returned and turned it into the world's most valuable firm. (Ghosh 2017)

To some extent, the production of these stories is not specific to Silicon Valley as an institution or a community The stories form part of the larger production process of celebrity, which includes business, political, and entertainment celebrity.

METRICS

Let us now consider metrics of success in Silicon Valley. First, of course, is money, both in absolute dollars and in market share. Terms such as "unicorn" for a start-up valued at a billion dollars or more indicate success for a start-up.

There are also ethno-metrics for the money gained by individuals for their participation in a start-up. These form part of stories that individuals tell about their experience in start-ups and can be used to indicate whether the person felt that experience was worth doing or not.

Success metrics for a start-up include such comparisons as "My college roommate made N billions on his start-up; I only made N millions on mine." This type of metric shows a use of money as a way of keeping score in a game with known and imagined opponents.

There are also smaller scale and more common success metrics, based on the practical consequences of a person's participation in a start-up, such as

- enough money to retire on;
- enough money for a house or a down payment on a house (in the notoriously high-priced real estate market of Silicon Valley); and
- enough money to buy an impressive car.

Another metric has to do with the number of successes, expressed as the proverb "Once is lucky, twice is smart." Success in Silicon Valley start-ups are known to involve luck and accidents of timing, as well as the creativity, brilliance, and other such qualities that are seen as characteristics of exemplars. Succeeding twice or three times by founding different enterprises is taken to indicate that the individual is indeed smart, talented, a genius, and not merely someone who was in the right place at the right time.

Exemplars and Wisdom

Let us now turn to the relationship between exemplars and wisdom. Exemplars can be proposed for many types of qualities. We must now consider seriously whether wisdom (whatever that is) is one of these qualities.

As previously mentioned, there are exemplars of many qualities. People can be admired for their talent, their genius, or their celebrity. In order to relate a system for proposing exemplars to wisdom, those exemplars must contain some aspect of moral or ethical meaning. Also, the proposed exemplar must be one that it is possible to learn from, to emulate. An athlete may be admired for spectacular performance, breaking a world record, or moving from behind to victory in whatever sport. But most people will not be physically able to emulate such feats. Such athletes cannot serve directly as exemplars, although they might inspire someone else to emulate the discipline and effort that made their achievements possible.

Additionally, there is the question of the possible relationship between the proposed exemplar and the community to whom that exemplar is proposed. One type of exemplar represents qualities that an ordinary person might admire but not emulate because they are too far removed from ordinary possibility. Like athletic feats, extraordinary heroism or unimaginable generosity would fall into this category. Another type is the ordinary exemplar: someone whose achievements are within the imagined reach of an ordinary person, given reasonable amounts of effort and absence of bad luck.

A more subtle issue is the nature of the traits of the exemplar that the community is expected to emulate. For example, the founder of MidWest Insurance is proposed as an exemplar, and agents within the company are encouraged to emulate his virtues and his entrepreneurial spirit. However, they are not encouraged to follow his example in founding their own insurance company (see Martin et al. 1983 for the classic formulation of this "founder's paradox").

This pattern is common to the ways in which religious exemplars are proposed. For founders of a religion or a religious group, their teachings are to be believed and their virtues are to be emulated. However, their actions are not to be emulated to the extent of trying to start a new religion.

Big Wisdom and Little Wisdom: Operationalizing Wisdom

When the topic of wisdom is raised, people usually think first of what we might call "big wisdom," the kind of wisdom that tries to answer questions such as "What is the meaning of life?" But there is also practical wisdom – the practical question of how to bring wisdom to bear on particular circumstances. This type of wisdom is what Aristotle identified as *phronesis*, practical wisdom. It does not ask questions like "What is justice?" Rather, it asks questions like "What is a just solution for how to dispose of the land that Granny left jointly to me and my cousins if I want to be fair in this inheritance dispute?"

Within philosophy, this area is called "virtue ethics," the investigation of particular virtues, what they look like, and how people might be trained to manifest such virtues in their behaviour. Such theories are based on examples or cases: thus, they necessarily require exemplars. (Other forms of ethics, not relevant to this discussion, are "deontic ethics" and "consequentialist ethics," which make ethical arguments either from first principles or from the consequences of actions.)

Relation of These Exemplars to Wisdom

Let us now ask whether the exemplars in the three domains discussed are examples of wisdom, pseudo-wisdom, or some other valuable qualities.

One immediate issue that arises in considering whether these cases exemplify wisdom is that two of the three domains are commercial: they involve various forms of commerce and making money. It is a frequent belief in discussions of wisdom that wisdom and profit are incompatible: one cannot serve both Athena and Mammon.[5] An exquisitely detailed history of this argument is given in *The Price of Truth: Gift, Money and Philosophy* by Marcel Hénaff (2010).

I believe that this objection does not hold within a discussion of practical wisdom. Money may be excluded from considerations of ultimate wisdom, though, in my opinion, even here there are serious arguments to be made against this decision. But, in the area of the practical action, issues of money and profit arise very frequently. At least some of the communities in which these issues arise appear to think that examples of fairness and benevolent dealing can be found, recommended, and admired.

Exemplars in the Insurance Company

Let us now examine this question in the case of the proposed exemplars in the insurance company. Of what are they examples? Does being an exemplary insurance agent have anything to do with wisdom?

Let us begin with the ethical component of insurance sales as the management and many of the sales agents of MidWest understand it. In their view, providing clients with appropriate types and levels of insurance coverage allows them to manage and mitigate their risks and is thus a beneficial action beyond a simple sales transaction. While some forms of insurance are legally or financially mandatory, such as automobile insurance (required by government motor vehicle departments) and homeowners' insurance (not legally required but mandated by banks for issuing a mortgage), life insurance is not mandatory. The management of MidWest at the time of this study were particularly focused on increasing life insurance sales. From a business point of view, they emphasized life insurance sales because agents' sales levels of life insurance lagged behind their automobile and homeowners' insurance sales. Past experience showed that the greater the number of different insurance products a client bought from one company, the better the chance that the customer would remain with that company, rather than frequently shopping around for cheaper policies.

That experience is the commercial argument for life insurance sales. The moral argument concerns risk management. At least some managers and sales agents see their moral value as helping clients to manage life risks. Many managers and agents had personal experience of the value of life insurance: they told stories of family breadwinners who held life insurance policies, which saved their families on the breadwinner's death; and tales of families financially ruined because the breadwinner had lacked life insurance. The point of these stories was that purchase of life insurance was a moral duty for an adult with family responsibilities. And it was a moral duty for a sales agent to persuade clients to purchase life insurance, even though selling it took longer and was more difficult than selling other lines of insurance.

Managers and agents were also concerned with the ethical and practical issues raised by the details of individual policies of all types: How much insurance did the client really need? What was a level of cost that the client could manage long term? How could the client's desire for a low monthly payment be balanced with a policy whose deductible would not be financially devastating for the client in the case of a claim? Exemplary agents took these questions very seriously in trying to craft a policy for an individual client.

The first time I, as an ethnographer, sat in on a meeting of an agent and client to review the client's levels of insurance coverage, I was amazed when the agent suggested that the client lower the levels of coverage on his automobile insurance because he had an old car whose replacement cost would not justify high insurance premiums. My first thought was surprise that a sales agent would voluntarily suggest lowering the amount of insurance and thus the amount of his own yearly commission. My second thought was, "Wow, if I were the client, I'd be his for life." My final realization was that the agent was making exactly the same calculation in his business practice: foregoing short-term gain for long-term client retention. This experience was an instance of the general belief at MidWest that ethical behaviour benefited everyone: agents and clients were not in a zero sum game with one another.

I would agree with this analysis, with the reservation that it depends on time scale: how long is long term? And yet, more long term for the company as a whole, are the actuarial calculations that underlie the structure of these policies accurate? We will return to the crucial issue of time scale in the discussion of wisdom in the Silicon Valley world of technology development.

SO IS THIS WISDOM?

Do these proposed insurance exemplars exemplify wisdom? Indeed, can we talk about wisdom and commerce in the same breath, or the same example?

If we take as exemplars of wisdom Buddha, Confucius, Jesus, and Socrates, the answer appears to be no. The insurance company exemplars do not concern themselves with the ultimate questions of the meaning of human existence. However, if we allow questions of practical wisdom, questions of how to lead a moral and effective life in particular situations, then we can see these exemplars as exhibiting wise approaches to how to run an insurance office.

Within the insurance company, the word "wisdom" was not typically used to describe this level of behaviour. The word used in discussion was "character." In the old system of recruitment, potential new agents were recruited by district managers. (This practice was changing as we began the study to a more corporate style of recruiting among existing employees.) District managers told stories about recruiting candidate agents at their church or from sales or service people in other businesses whose conduct impressed them. This method was explicitly described as recruiting for character: the belief was that sales skills can be taught, but character cannot.

Finally, these people are presented as exemplars of ordinary success. They are not extraordinary moral heroes. They achieved their positions through effort, good judgment, moral choices, and an absence of bad circumstances. Thus, they are presented as representing what any insurance agent could achieve if he were to attempt it. This presentation of ordinary success is somewhat incomplete, because it lacks discussion of the ways in which times and circumstances have changed. The earliest exemplars built their businesses at a time when their wives could be expected to work in the office at least until a secretary could be hired. These exemplars also began their careers at a time when the competition was the agents of other insurance companies or independent brokers. It looks back to a time before the repeal of legislation prohibiting banks from selling insurance and before internet-based insurance companies.

Exemplars in the Meditation Centre

Let us now consider the exemplars proposed within the meditation centres and their relation to wisdom.

HOW EXEMPLARS ARE PROPOSED

First, a broad range of potential exemplars can be found within this system. The most prominent exemplars are the founding teacher and his son, the current head of the organization and main teacher. And the historical Buddha, Shakyamuni Buddha, stands as the ultimate exemplar within this system, as well as many other great teachers in the Indian and Tibetan traditions. (As a side issue, it should be noted that the historical Buddha as exemplar is used quite differently in traditional Asian discussions from the way it is used in current Western discussions. Further research is underway on this difference.)

Within the meditation centres, certain students are trained and credentialed to teach and to supervise teaching at various levels. They are often nominated locally and approved by the head teacher. This system is not transparent to new students. It is clear that there are people at local and regional centres who appear to have some level of authority, but exactly what these levels are and how people are chosen is unclear. There is not an explicit relation presented between teaching authority and spiritual development or wisdom. That is, certain people are given teaching authority: these people are often understood to be proposed as exemplars, but that role and its limits are not explicitly stated.

HOW THEY ARE RECEIVED

Students at the meditation centres form their own judgments about these potential exemplars. It is their choice to admire them or not, emulate them or not. While I have heard occasional criticism of some possible exemplars, a more likely rejection is silence. For example: "We could invite A, B, or C to teach [a specific program]." "Oh, I'd love to work with A or C."

There are also some long-time students who do not have the highest levels of teaching authorization but are locally admired and taken as good examples, both of life wisdom and as teachers. Such students are described by the unofficial title of "senior teachers."

SO IS THIS WISDOM?

Unlike the insurance company, these meditation centres could be said to be in the wisdom business. Buddhism, and specifically Buddhist meditation, is widely considered to be a wisdom tradition.

The granting of teaching authorizations at various levels, though, is organized first around teaching and administrative skill, as well as on speaking ability and the ability to connect with others. These criteria may overlap to a greater or lesser degree with self-cultivation and the ability to live wisely (to outer appearances).

The question of whether these people are proposed as ordinary or extraordinary exemplars is somewhat ambiguous, both within this particular Buddhist community and within Buddhism generally. The historical Buddha presented his achievement as one of waking up, and frequently stated that it was within the capacity of all human beings. At the same time, the followers of the Buddha, both in his lifetime and after, through reverence, tended to elevate him to a status above, or far, far above, that of an ordinary person, someone who had achieved a state unreachable to others. This same reverential elevation has happened to many other exemplars within Buddhist history.

Within the meditation centre, students are not told how to regard the potential exemplars, but it is not uncommon for them to feel that the achievements of even those local exemplars whom they admire are beyond their own capacities. Why people are attracted to, or even prefer, examples of behaviour or capacity that are unimaginably far from anything they themselves could aspire to remains a topic for a different investigation.

The issue of wisdom and its relation to exemplars in the meditation centre has taken on a new dimension since the initial writing of this chapter. Recently, instances of sexual harm by the main teacher as well as a number of the senior teachers have come to light. This disclosure can be seen as another instance of the uncovering of sexual harm and the issue of power dynamics prompted by the #MeToo movement, as occurrences have happened in various institutions: politics, the arts, sports, businesses, and particularly in many religious groups.

Understanding the relation of the social negotiation of exemplary people to the overt and the hidden dynamics of power relations and their misuse is a crucially important topic, which is currently being worked on in many institutions and disciplines, both theoretically and practically. Discussing this widespread investigation does not lie within the scope of this chapter. It is, however, important to state that it is ongoing. See (Gayley 2018) for a preliminary analysis of the traditional Tibetan approach to the issue.

Exemplars in Silicon Valley

Exemplars in Silicon Valley are created by somewhat different processes than the exemplars in the insurance company and the meditation centre. Both the insurance company and the meditation centre are institutions with a formal authority structure, which at least partially defines members' standing within the institution. This structure allows for mechanisms to propose exemplars to a known audience from a given pool of possibilities. As already discussed, "Silicon Valley" as an institution is more informal and diffuse. It consists of many existing corporations, start-up companies, private and public funding mechanisms, social networks, and forms of publicity and reputation generation and maintenance. Thus, there are exemplars proposed within companies, as well as those proposed by the external press, and the externally proposed exemplars have a wider potential audience. Additionally, there are technology awards such as the Marconi Prize and the Turing Award. And there are the mechanisms of reputation within informal social networks and communities of practice.

WHAT ARE THEY EXAMPLES OF?

In general, these exemplars are taken to exhibit technical brilliance, creativity, or scientific genius. Secondary characteristics may include determination, perseverance, and intense energy and focus. Unlike the exemplars at the insurance company or the meditation centre, these are extraordinary examples: not everyone has that kind of brilliance or talent. Their accomplishments cannot serve as a blueprint for many others, although their determination and work can be taken as inspirational.

As we consider whether these people can be considered exemplars of wisdom, we must raise the question of whether there is a moral component to their achievements. In general, within this community, technical and scientific development is taken as an unquestioned good. The assumptions are that technology development is a benefit to humanity, that new and "disruptive" technologies are valuable in preventing stagnation, and that the direction of change can be assumed to be an upward arc of progress. However, it seems that these questions must be considered case by case, rather than acceding to a general belief that all innovation is beneficial. (As I wrote this essay, the news was full of investigations of possible Russian use of Facebook to influence the 2016 presidential election. "Move Fast and Break Things," Facebook's former motto, no longer seems adequate as a statement of values.)

HOW THEY ARE RECEIVED

It is hard to know how these proposed exemplars are received by the audiences of the various media that offer them. It is easy to ignore news stories and hero profiles of people who seem to have no relevance to one's own life. I have heard insiders in Silicon Valley make occasional complaints about the exclusivity of the exemplar process. For example, they complain that Steve Jobs is given all the credit for founding Apple, while his co-founder, Steve Wozniak, is erased from the record. But these are critiques about the historical accuracy of the identity of an exemplar, not critiques of the idea of exemplars in general or of the value of a particular contribution.

Within this community, there is a broader question to be asked: Is the entire idea of exemplars relevant to a community that valorizes innovation and disruption? That is, do the present and the future have anything to learn from the past? There is an issue of time scale here. It takes time for the values and problems of a given technology to become apparent. Both insurance as an industry and religion as an institution can look to the past to guide future action. But the rhetoric of technology development appears to look only forward. The much discussed desire for innovation and "disruptive technologies" is an example of such rhetoric. This desire is not just to sell more goods and services, to claim a larger share of a given market, but rather a desire to create new types of goods and services, and thus whole new markets. The question is therefore raised of whether there can be a place for wise elders in fields in which technical skills and knowledge rapidly become outmoded.

In fact, even in these fields, there is recognition of higher-level abilities such as technical judgment about large-scale decisions of investment and corporate direction. It is at this level that elders are consulted, through mechanisms such as advisory positions in venture capital firms and internal and external consultation to corporations on long-term technology strategy decisions.

What Have We Learned about Wisdom?

This chapter began with the question of whether studying exemplars can form a proxy for approaching the study of wisdom. Keith Basso (1996) so beautifully argued that wisdom sits in places. Here, I argue that wisdom also moves in stories. It is exemplified in stories and the protagonists of particular stories. It is the movement of such stories, their proposal, and their uptake (or not) that create the meaning of practical wisdom within given communities.

NOTES

I would first like to express my thanks to Joseph Alter and Philip Kao for inviting me to the Anthropology of Wisdom workshop at the University of Pittsburgh, which was the occasion for the first version of this chapter. I am grateful for a deeply stimulating opportunity for thought and conversation, and for their creative reading of my ethnography of insurance, suggesting to me that I had been, without realizing it, working on the topic of wisdom in the world. I am grateful to all my colleagues on the insurance project, in particular Christopher Darrouzet and Elizabeth Bishop, and to the Institute for Research on Learning for hosting it. More recently, I have benefited from many conversations with friends and colleagues, including Geoffrey Bowker, Albert Chu, William J. Clancey, Whitfield Diffie, Jan English-Lueck, the late Mary Fischer, Judith Mipaas Hibbard, Ray McDermott, Eugene Miya, Ida Oberman, Livia Polanyi, and Robert Warnock. I continue to learn about wisdom in theory and practice from and with my Buddhist teachers and friends.

1 By contrast, Leidner (1993: 95) gives an account of a life insurance company specializing in door-to-door sales, citing its extremely low retention rate of 5 per cent to 7 per cent over five years and an industry average of 18 per cent.
2 It is worth asking what it means to be an entrepreneur under these conditions. Leidner (1993) has studied the work of members of direct sales organizations (DSOs), such as Mary Kay Cosmetics and Amway, who, like MidWest agents, describe themselves as entrepreneurs. (It is important

to note, though, that MidWest agents, unlike DSO members, do bear the costs and risk of starting a business such as renting an office, hiring staff, and so on.) Leidner argues: "Most [economists] ... see innovation as essential. Entrepreneurs do something different that has economic consequences: they invent a product, refine a production process, develop a new marketing scheme. Some others believe that risk bearing is critical to entrepreneurship. An entrepreneur puts money on the line.

"By even a generous interpretation of economists' definitions, distributors are not entrepreneurs. They perform highly routinized selling and recruiting behaviors. Innovation is neither necessary nor welcome. Financial risk is purposely kept low ... Distributors risk only the absence of a paycheck, and while that may be personally risky, it is not of the same order as putting one's savings at risk. What distributors do is not entrepreneurial to any economically significant degree.

"Entrepreneurship, however, is more than a type of economic action. It is a powerful social ideal that came about with the emergence of capitalism ... Direct selling organizations emphasize less what distributors do than who they are as being entrepreneurial ... For example, they remind distributors that real entrepreneurs persevere even in the face of difficulty, and that booking more parties during a slump is a sign of the entrepreneurial spirit.

"More than anything, though, within the industry entrepreneurialism represents the strength of character to avoid the security of wage or salaried labor. [Direct sales organizations] take their single most significant liability – the absence of a paycheck – and interpret it as an advantage. Direct selling entrepreneurs are willing to risk their financial security on their own ability to sell the DSOs' products" (163–4).

3 The notion of the "paradigmatic narrative" shares some territory with notions such as "life stage" and "role." The key difference for this study is that the paradigmatic narrative is a linguistic unit, rather than a psychological or sociological one. It is composed of actual narratives and the practices by which they are told. By contrast, role and life stage are abstractions primarily expressed by expectations and beliefs; the means by which these are constructed in practice is theoretically secondary.

4 I use the male pronoun "he" intentionally. At the time of our study, the mid-1990s, the paradigmatic narrative was definitely a story of male success, usually aided by the efforts of a supportive wife. Management was struggling with how to present an equivalent trajectory for the newly hired female agents.

5 I am grateful to the late Steven Collins for pointing out this objection during our extremely fruitful Anthropology of Wisdom Workshop at the University of Pittsburgh in 2013. His argument was that both the Buddha and Socrates, unquestioned exemplars of wisdom, said that wisdom and

the desire for money were contradictory; therefore, insurance sales agents and technology developers could not be examples of wisdom, since they were motivated by profit.

REFERENCES

Basso, Keith. 1996. *Wisdom Sits in Places: Landscape and Language among the Western Apache.* Albuquerque: University of New Mexico Press.

English-Lueck, J.A. 2017. *Cultures@Silicon Valley.* 2nd ed. Stanford, CA: Stanford University Press.

Gayley, Holly. 2018. "Revisiting the 'Secret Consort' (*gsang yum*) in Tibetan Buddhism." *Religions 9 (6)*: 179. https://doi.org/10.3390/rel9060179.

Ghosh, Shona. 2017. "Travis Kalanick Is Telling People He Will Pull a Steve Jobs and Return as Uber's CEO." *Business Insider,* 31 July. https://www.businessinsider.com/uber-ex-ceo-travis-kalanick-steve-jobs-ing-search-replacement-report-2017-7.

Goffman, Erving. (1981). *Forms of Talk.* Philadelphia, PA: University of Pennsylvania Press.

Hénaff, Marcel. 2010. *The Price of Truth: Gift, Money and Philosophy.* Translated by Jean-Louis Morhande. Stanford, CA: Stanford University Press.

Humphrey, Caroline. 1997. "Exemplars and Rules: Aspects of the Discourse of Moralities in Mongolia." In *The Ethnography of Moralities,* edited by Signe Howell, 25–47. London: Routledge.

Leidner, Robin. 1993. *Fast Food, Fast Talk: Service Work and the Routinization of Everyday Life.* Berkeley, CA: University of California Press.

Linde, Charlotte. 2009. *Working the Past: Narrative and Institutional Memory.* New York: Oxford University Press.

Martin, Joanne, Martha S. Feldman, Mary Jo Hatch, and Sim Sitkin. 1983. "The Uniqueness Paradox in Organizational Stories." *Administrative Science Quarterly* 28 (3): 438–53. https://doi.org/10.2307/2392251.

Schireson, Grace. 2009. *Zen Women: Beyond Tea Ladies, Iron Maidens, and Macho Masters.* Boston, MA: Wisdom Publications.

Shankar, Shalini. 2008. *Desi Land: Teen Culture, Class and Success in Silicon Valley.* Durham, NC: Duke University Press.

Silicon Valley Cultures Project (website). 2019. Edited by Charles Darrah, J.A. English-Lueck, and James M. Freeman. http://svcp.org/.

Staudinger, Ursula M., and Judith Glück. 2011. "Practical Wisdom Research: Commonalities and Differences in a Growing Field." *Annual Review of Psychology* 62 (1): 215–41. https://doi.org/10.1146/annurev.psych.121208.131659.

Traweek, Sharon. 1988. *Beamtimes and Lifetimes: The World of High Energy Physicists.* Cambridge, MA: Harvard University Press.

Weststrate, Nic M., Michel Ferrari, and Monika Ardelt. 2016. "The Many Faces of Wisdom: An Investigation of Cultural Historical Wisdom Exemplars Reveals Practical, Philosophical, and Benevolent Prototypes." *Personality and Psychology Bulletin* 42 (5): 662–76. https://doi.org/10.1177/0146167216638075.

Wikipedia. 2019. "Silicon Valley." *Wikipedia.org*. Accessed 4 December 2019. http://en.wikipedia.org/wiki/Silicon_Valley.

Zagzebski, Linda. 2017. *Exemplarist Moral Theory*. New York: Oxford University Press.

PART FOUR

Narrating Wisdom

7 Of Uncertainty, Sophiology, and Governance: Zen and the Art of Scenario Planning

JAMES D. FAUBION

On its website, the Brefi Group, a consulting agency, characterizes scenario planning emphatically as not being about "predicting the future":

> Scenario planning exercises involve identifying trends and exploring the implications of projecting them forward – probably as high, medium and low forecasts. These can include political, economic, social and technological. As different trends are chosen and different combinations of forecast levels are combined, a whole spectrum of possibilities can be identified.
>
> Well known examples include the end of the Berlin Wall, OPEC oil price rises, bombs and terrorist attacks. Asking the great What if? Identifying risk. (Brefi Group 2018)

They're keeping it simple. They want customers; they want "to help." I suspect they're doing quite well. But the practice of scenario planning has not been restricted to the business sector. Since the end of the Second World War and still today, scenario planning has been a central dimension of military strategy in the United States and Europe. Israel is not alone in recently carrying out theatrical scenario exercises that have culminated in putting into place concrete technologies intended as prospective responses to perceived and articulated threats (Samimian-Darash 2013, 2016). Since the later 1970s, scenario planning has become an increasingly common item in the portfolios of many of the non-governmental organizations (NGOs) devoted to socioeconomic development. More broadly, it has become increasingly central to policy formation among the polities of Asia as well as those of South America, North America, and Europe (Chletsos and Agrafiotis 2014: 26–7). Of particular note is its centrality to FORESIGHT, a program established by the European Union in 2000 and still ongoing. As a review of the first Greek exercise in FORESIGHT will amply illustrate, scenario planning might also sometimes go nowhere. Such are the variable fortunes of what David Guston (2014) would have us think of as "anticipatory governance."

But first things first: The French economist and oil executive Pierre Wack (1922–97) is typically credited with being the specific founder of corporate scenario planning. His interventions date from the beginning of the 1970s, when the board of Royal Dutch Shell, dissatisfied with its less than lustrous performance, hired him to advise their managers on matters of anticipatory strategy. He did not work alone: Edward Newland, who is also regarded as a pioneer in corporate scenario planning, was always at his side. Wack was nevertheless the chief of operations. He insisted on paying assiduous attention to the recent past and present outlay of political economy, micro-scalar and macro-scalar. He sought to "see" what might lie in the offing – but without any pretension of being able to engage in prediction (Selin 2007: 38). Instead, he crafted stories that he and his colleagues deemed worthy of consideration – and one of those stories proved to be very close to the factual mark. Targeting the increasing volatility of the political relations among the oil-producing and oil-consuming countries in the aftermath of the 1967 Yom Kippur War, Wack fashioned an account of an impending crisis very close in its basic parameters to the 1973 Arab embargo on the export of petroleum to the West. The managers at Shell heeded his vision, and were far better prepared for the crisis than any of their major competitors (see Mason 2019). Other corporate managers elsewhere of course took notice – and the snowball began. No doubt hyperbolically and offering no numbers, whether for the United States or abroad, a journalist for *Forbes* declared in 2009 that "almost no business operates without some form of scenario planning" (Niles 2009). That said, professionalization has become global. The first advanced degree program in scenario planning was established at the University of Houston in 1975, but programs have since been established across Europe, in the Middle East, Latin America, and South and East Asia (Global Foresight n.d.). Wack's precedent is perhaps most pronounced at the Oxford Scenarios Programme, housed in the Saïd Business School (2019).

Wack is often deemed the guru of scenario planning. That's not at all surprising. Well before his work at Shell, he was known as a devoted reader of the Russian-born mystic and composer George Gurdjieff. He sat at the feet of Swami Prajnanananda. He regularly spent his summers at Theravada retreats in Burma. He sprinkled his conversations and writings with easterly apothegms. He was fond of invoking *Zen in the Art of Archery* (Herrigel 1953). Not least because of its subsequent influence, Wack's particular methodology warrants examination in its own right. I turn to that examination in due course, but two preliminary tasks intervene. The first is an inevitably brief synopsis of the genealogy of Wackean scenario planning, the historical depth of which precedes – perhaps overlong precedes – that of Wack's own career. The second is a similarly brief survey of the intellectual ecology with which Wack's presumptions and principles are roughly coincident. Both investigations yield strange bedfellows, but neither, I think, yields anything that might strictly be called an "epistemology," a term inescapably entangled with the theorization of knowledge as "justified true belief" (Ichikawa and Steup 2018: sec. 1). Instead, they yield what I'll term a "sophiology," borrowing from the ancient Greek σοφία, a term that comprehends what in English can be rendered diversely as skill, cleverness, intelligence, judgment, learning, and, not least, "wisdom."

I do not coin the term "sophiology." It stems from the Hellenistic deification of practical or transcendent intelligence as the goddess Sophia, still registered in the perdurance of the designation of what remains the most spectacular architectural legacy of the early Byzantine Empire: the Hagia Sophia cathedral in what is now Istanbul. "Sophiology" (or "sophianism" or "sophism") is also a term operative in a heretical Russian Orthodox movement dedicated to the rendering of Sophia as the divine essence, manifest in our daily dealings as a combination of transcendent enlightenment and practical virtuosity. Such sophiological virtuosos as Wack might cleave to the definition of their enterprise (if not in so many words) as at once transcendental and practical, and so be it. Anthropologists must always acknowledge the conceptions and commitments of their subjects. Analytically, however, anthropologists have the privilege of and duty to be vulgarians. They dig their hands into the sociocultural topsoil and undersoil alike – or at least they should. Professional theologians, philosophers, and philosophes typically take the high ground. My use of "sophiology" registers an excavation from practice to a theory – should one even call it such – that distinctively occupies a characterological, logical, and emotional place between the philosophical high ground and the sociologist's and anthropologist's fiddling with the undersoil.

The Lineaments of Sophiology: From the Hunt to the Clinic

Digging into the undersoil: The ultimate sources of Wack's interventions perhaps take us back to the very beginnings of wisdom. Carlo Ginzburg's (1989) "Clues" implies as much. In "Clues," Ginzburg unearths the roots of the "evidential paradigm" that he thinks to be the generative matrix of modern historiographical research. He opens his essay with a discussion of the principles that guided the late nineteenth-century scholar Giovanni Morelli in his efforts to distinguish original from counterfeit works of art. Contrary to most of his contemporaries, Morelli did not look to broad strokes. Instead, he focused on "the most trivial details" of a work, "which would have been influenced least by the mannerisms" of an artist's school: "earlobes, fingernails, shapes of fingers and toes" (97). Morelli was derided as a "positivist," but he was also proceeding in much the same manner as one of the most celebrated of his fictional contemporaries: Sherlock Holmes. He was doing detective work, discerning the true from the counterfeit "on the basis of evidence that is imperceptible to most people," just as Holmes would concentrate on "footprints, cigarette ashes and the like" in tracking the perpetrator of a crime (98).

Ginzburg (1989) argues that the evidential paradigm coalesces in the later nineteenth century and serves as the matrix not merely of historiography and criminology but also of psychoanalysis and cultural anthropology. He finds its original figure, however, well before the alienist, the archivist, or the fieldworker. His figure is instead Homo venatus, man the hunter, who "in the course of countless chases" acquires the skills that allow him to "reconstruct the shapes and movements of his invisible prey from tracks on the ground, broken branches, excrement, tufts of hair, entangled feathers, stagnating odors" (102). As a prelude to his success, the hunter is of necessity a man of considerable experience, who comes at length to acquire the skill to "sniff out, record, interpret, and classify such infinitesimal traces as trails of spittle" and "to execute complex mental operations with lightning speed" (102). Ginzburg turns illustratively to an "oriental fable" of three brothers who manage to draw on "apparently insignificant data" in reconstructing the precise features of a missing animal (103). They produce "a narrative sequence, which could be expressed most simply as 'someone passed this way'" (103). How could they know so much? The first answer: they must have stolen the animal. In the end, their innocence prevails. Only a Ginzburg could continue as daringly:

> Perhaps the actual idea of narration (as distinct from charms, exorcisms, or invocation) ... originated in a hunting society, relating the experience of deciphering tracks. This obviously indemonstrable hypothesis nevertheless seems to be reinforced by the fact that the rhetorical figures on which the language of venatic deduction still rests today – the part in relation to the whole, the effect in relation to the cause – are traceable to

> the narrative axis of symmetry, with the rigorous exclusion of metaphor. The hunter would have been the first to "tell a story" because he alone was able to read, in the silent, nearly imperceptible tracks left by his prey, a coherent sequence of events. (103)

Homo venatus: he's the prototype of the Zen archer as much as he is of many other figures of embodied intuition, among whom the divide between the oriental and the occidental is at best superficial. He's not a spinner of fish-tales. He is instead a conjectural narrativist, and the validation of his conjectures subject more to vindication than verification.

Ginzburg visits a substantial army of prototypes and exemplars of the evidential paradigm on his way to the nineteenth century, but, after the hunter, he grants special privilege to another venerable figure who once again thwarts any temptation to draw a great divide between the East and the West – or, for that matter, between men and women. It's the figure of the doctor, whose locus classicus Ginzburg draws from the Hippocratic corpus and whose march he follows (breathlessly) from that point forward. He or she is a figure whom we might meet hypostasized in what we're now often asked to identify as our "primary care physician." It's not the figure of the medical researcher who is a functionary of big science, orchestrating the design of inquiries into the etiology of diseases and the effectiveness of treatments for which blind control and statistically significant variations of outcome are the gold standard. It's instead the figure of the diagnostician, who attends carefully to each patient and what is ultimately the irreducible particularity of his or her affliction.

Ginzburg rides the prevailing breezes in sailing from the Hippocratic corpus to the modern medical diagnostician without much tacking. Michel Foucault (1973) is more assiduous in registering the significant shifts in the ontological comprehension of disease that separate the doctors of the eighteenth century from their counterparts in the nineteenth century. Both Ginzburg and Foucault nevertheless arrive at the same point. Both highlight that, in the nineteenth century, medicine – very much in the manner of a police enterprise – becomes an enterprise of the experiential address of the familiar but also always potentially unique manifestations of "the case." Ginzburg and Foucault differ in many of their judgments of just what a case ontologically and epistemologically might be, but they agree on this much: the etiology of any case is always and only manifest through its symptoms; if exhibiting systematicity, symptoms might always vary from one case to the next; and symptoms typical of one disease might instead be the manifestations of another or the indication of two or more. Syphilis, the "Great Pretender," is even today one of the most diagnostically cloudy of afflictions, not least because it often doesn't manifest itself with symptomatological consistency in its early stages (Dr. Sandra Barton, personal communication). The specific genetic signature of the spirochete responsible for the disease wasn't definitively identified until 1997. After that, one can perhaps speak of the reduction of a case to its source, a syndrome to its definitive cause. Yet, even in medicine, such reductions are far from thoroughgoing – and it very much remains to be seen if they ever will be. Until then, the successful treatment of a great many cases will always be more of a matter of vindication than verification (see Rabinow and Stavrianakis 2014). The case-based physician attends to the inevitably recent past of the patient he or she treats. It's the present illness that counts. It's always medium range – or short range, depending on the metrics of proximity one adopts – prognostications that justify the clinician's interventions (or lack of). Medicine, as in other case-based practices – those of historiography, cultural anthropology, and scenario planning included – permit of prognosis. In all such disciplines, however, prognosis is always tentative, and all the more tentative as the intimacies of the present give way to the increasing indefiniteness of the future. Any Wackean sophiology demurs to the same constraint. The farther one deviates from the evidence yielded by the past, the less uncertain one's diagnosis of the past or, prospectively, of the future can be. The more one's prognostics divagate into a "theoretical" future, increasingly floating free into it might count as "providence," the less plausible they become. In short: time is of the essence, and time is rather shorter than longer.

The Nineteenth Century in the Twentieth (and Beyond): Statistics, Systems, and Reflexive Modernization

The nineteenth century is a very long century, and in many respects it is still with us. Historiographical research cleaving to the evidential paradigm is alive and well. The star of psychoanalysis may have declined in Western Europe and the United States, but it remains high on the horizon of many other parts of the world (it shines particularly brightly in Argentina). Humanistic psychology, other "softer" modes of talk therapy, and even the more hard-nosed "cognitive behavioural therapy" that up-to-date Euro-American professionals now embrace nevertheless conserve the evidential methods of Freud himself. Interpretive anthropology now is not what it used to be, but the relation between its present and its past century is a relation of family resemblance, not of radical rupture.

By contrast, sociology, political science, experimental psychology, experimental medicine – all of these disciplines have increasingly rejected a case-based ontology and epistemology of inquiry in favour of the modern expression of Baconianism, which is manifest in the project of abstracting the more general properties of any given phenomenon from the contextual constraints of its manifestation. Induction is its logical means. Statistical representation is its end. It's consequently a project that seeks to emulate – even as it always falls short of – the lawful loftiness of the most formal of the natural sciences and of the pure mathesis to which they aspire. It doesn't escape the imperium of the evidential paradigm; it rather seeks as far as possible to put it under erasure.

A similar ambition marks the more hypothetico-deductive, neo-Cartesian approaches to the analysis of processes subhuman, human, and suprahuman that coalesce during and after the Second World War. Pivotal to the victory of the Allies, they are not of a single piece, but they jointly rest on the schematization of processual recursivity and (so) on the "decidability" or "determinability" of processual series or pathways. They are constitutive of our "digital era" (Boyer 2013). Cybernetic, information-theoretic, game-theoretic, system-theoretic, they all influence scenario planning as it has been and continues to be practised. Of special relevance to the genealogy of that practice is the work of Herman Kahn, one of the original functionaries at the Rand Institute and later the founder of the Hudson Institute (Ghamari-Tabrizi 2005). Kahn was devoted to the construction of scenarios – but a construction under the sway of the formalized principles of game theory (von Neumann and Morgenstern 1944) and of the cybernetically attuned systems theory (see Shannon 1948a, 1948b) of which he was himself a champion. Kahn's (1960) most famous (or notorious) work is *On Thermonuclear War*, a Clauswitzean account of a battle between the Soviet Union and the United States whose outcome was anything but mutually assured destruction. Quite on the contrary, Kahn's stories of battle had the United States decidedly and determinately winning in the end (if with quite a lot of destruction along the way).

Kahn (1984) titled another of his essays *Thinking about the Unthinkable* – a title to which Wack (1985a) alludes in one of the best known of his very few published writings (see also Ramírez, Selsky, and van der Heijden 2010). It's tempting as a consequence to read Wack as a disciple of Kahn. It would nevertheless be very misleading to do so. Kahn remained loyal throughout his career to a strategic vision that pressed towards determinate outcomes, often bordering on and sometimes crossing over into prediction. *On Thermonuclear War* inaugurates such ambitions. *The Year*

2000, which Kahn and Anthony Wiener (1967) co-authored, continues them. Scenarios are fundamental to both works, but their predictive dimensions ally them more with the general current of what is usually deemed futurology (see, for example, de Jouvenel [1963]; Gabor [1963, 1972]; Toffler [1970, 1980]) than with scenario planning in the mode of Wack. À la Wack, prediction is epistemically illegitimate. It is (thus) unwise: period.

Before visiting the principles that inform Wack's own deceptively simple "intuitive" methodology of scenario planning (see Mason 2019), it's worth taking a sidelong glance at less professional and more political (or politico-moral) expressions of the scenaristic enterprise that may not be as sophisticated as most of their professionalized counterparts, but do provide the broader epistemic context in which the latter must be situated. Such expressions have marked many of the new social movements from the 1960s forward to today. Key environmentalist texts in the genre include Poul Anderson and F.N. Waldrop's (1947) "Tomorrow's Children" and Anderson's (1961) later novel *Twilight World* – both of them somewhat fantastical, but precursors of more rigorous formulations of what would come to be known as "nuclear winter" (Turco et al. 1983). Rachel Carson's (1982) *Silent Spring*, which begins with the scenario of a small town suddenly deprived through insecticidal saturation of the songbirds and wildflowers that had formerly graced it, is more pivotal. It led to the banning of the use of DDT and remains among the primary points of reference for the rhetoric of sustainability. A key feminist text in the genre is Shulamith Firestone's (1970) *The Dialectic of Sex: The Case for Feminist Revolution*, though its passionate and rather mechanical Marxism perhaps aligns it more with the futurists (however antipathetic most of them were to Marxism) than with scenarists of less confident stripes. Such ecofeminists as Riane Eisler (1987) and Lori Gruen (see Gruen and Jamieson 1994) are the heirs of Carson and Firestone alike.

Ülrich Beck, Anthony Giddens, and Scott Lash's (1994) parsing of "reflexive modernization" offers a fairly convincing conceptualization of what is genuinely new about the new social movements – and, with them, what is new about the Wackean way of scenario planning. Reflexive modernizers, an otherwise motley crew, are effectively second-order observers (observers observing observers observing, in Niklas Luhmann's [1998] formulation), but with a particular focus. They are united in their suspicions, not merely that what the enthusiasts of modernization before them wrought have left us all in potentially grave peril, but also that the statisticophilic classe dirigiste of modernization past and present has been deceiving us, and on two fronts. On the one front, they've been pretending to be able to render calculable what isn't in fact calculable, a pretense grounded in the presumption that processes observable in the past and present are regular enough to allow at least limited generalization and stable enough to allow any reliable renderings of the future on the basis of the past and the present. On the other, they've always been giving themselves an out. "Silent spring? But I never represented it as being impossible. I only represented it as being exceedingly unlikely." For the reflexive modernizer – whether one longing for a more trustworthy modality of expertise or one who has had enough of "expertise" – these statisticophilic deceptions simply won't do. The analysts of reflexive modernization underscore that the statistician – a member of the classe dirigiste, like it or not – depends logically on the linearity of the relation between the past, present, and future.

Sophiology: Wack and His Successors

Whether or not he should properly be included among reflexive modernizers, Wack overtly eschews the ultimate – though it must be stressed, only the ultimate – authority of either statistical or system-theoretic representations of the future (and with it, the near-predictions that both often license). He is not anti-scientific (far from it), but he shares with the activists of the new social movements a suspicion of arithmetic linearism, whether statistical or system-theoretic. He posits instead the dynamic centrality of the irreducibly particular, the non-recursive, the always unpredictable surprise of the emergent.

The principle of non-linearity is his analytical entrée into scenaristic method, the first of the axiomatic presumptions that mark his sophiology as a whole. Wack (1985a, 1985b) puts forward his basic point of view in two brief papers appearing in sequence in the *Harvard Business Review*. He opens the initial installment with a skeptical glance at forecasting:

> Forecasts are not always wrong; more often than not, they can be reasonably accurate. And that is what makes them dangerous. They are usually constructed on the assumption that tomorrow's world will be much like today's. They often work because the world does not always change. But sooner or later forecasts will fail when they are needed most: in anticipating major shifts in the … environment that make whole strategies obsolete. (1985a: 73)

It's modest enough in tone, but its implications are very bold. All statistical projections hinge precisely, if more weakly than their neo-Cartesian counterparts, on the presumption that the future will manifest the same (or more or less the same) causal dynamics that have informed the past and inform the present (see Hacking 1976, 1990). Should the future instead prove to revert to or drift into what two of Wack's followers call "the feral" (Ramírez and Ravetz 2011), it will run afoul of the prerequisites of domestication that statistical representation demands (see Ramírez and Selin 2014: 59). Any coming to terms with such a feral future will require a different representational apparatus, an apparatus sensitive to its recalcitrance, its vagaries and savagery. As Rafael Ramírez and Jerome Ravetz put it, that may precisely be the "beginning of wisdom" (2011: 480). It will demand an apparatus whose designers put aside any passion for generalization in favour of a resolute dedication to the capturing of the future as an ensemble of cases. Whether or not they know a word of Ginzburg (or of *Zen in the Art of Archery*), its designers will have to accommodate themselves to the sophiological matrices of the evidential paradigm.

One might simply throw up one's hands at this point, but Wack adopts a more pragmatic – less wishful, more sophiological – response. A second axiom functions as its guidepost. Rather than looking to perfect the extant techniques of forecasting or hiring "more or better forecasters," he advises that we should "accept uncertainty, try to understand it, and make it part of our reasoning":

> Uncertainty today is not just an occasional, temporary deviation from reasonable predictability; it is a basic structural feature of the … environment. The method used to think about and plan for the future must be made appropriate to a changed … environment. (Wack 1985a: 73)

He credits a personified Royal Dutch Shell corporation with "believing" that "decision scenarios" constitute such a way forward, though of course he was instrumental in persuading the board and impressing on it that this was so.

The task of persuasion wasn't easy, for two chief reasons. The first is that the principle of the acceptance of uncertainty isn't merely a principle of the tolerance of the unknown but rather a principle of the intellectual and affective stimulus it might provide to the (corporate) imagination. Wack became well aware that business executives, like the rest of us, can tolerate only so much of such stimulation. Too much of it, too much information, and our inescapably finite psychic resources – at once cognitive and affective (see Wack 1985a: 81) – become overwhelmed. We devolve into a state of confusion and anxiety (Ramírez and Selin 2014: 65–6). Wack's approach to this problem is not to do everything he can to dispel confusion and anxiety; perhaps, as Ramírez and Selin (2014: 65–7) suggest, the approach does what it can to exacerbate it. Yet, the purpose is once again ultimately pragmatic. Wack doesn't expect business managers (or, it would seem, any other mere mortals) to be heroic in the face of complexity. He instead recommends that scenario planners themselves be sensitive to human finitude, and so limit themselves to constructing a constrained portrayal of scenaristic alternatives. After all, they're not merely describing "different outcomes in the same world," they're effectively describing "different worlds" (Wack 1985b, 146). They can't indulge in the baroque. Wack stipulates:

> Never more than four (or it becomes unmanageable for most decision makers), the ideal number is one plus two; that is, first the surprise-free view (showing explicitly why and where it is fragile) and then two other worlds or different ways of seeing the world that focus on ... critical uncertainties. (146)

To my knowledge, few if any practising scenario planners embrace Wack's ideal of two plus one. The construction of quadripartite scenarios is a professional working standard – a standard that nevertheless has many detractors.

The second reason why it wasn't easy to persuade Shell executives to embrace scenario planning was that the first step in the construction of scenarios proved not to be directive. It nevertheless had its impetus and justification in a third operative axiom. Wack (1985a) doesn't identify the axiom in any straightforward way, but one might think of it as the axiom of the out-of-the-question. "First-generation" scenarios (78) "presented ... raw uncertainties" (78). Their purpose was to "give insight into the system," to stimulate perception of "the connection among various forces" and "driving events" (78). Systems theory: so far, so good – and it was an indispensable tool in moving on to scenarios of a "second generation." Systems theory facilitated prediction – but, unlike for Kahn and his fellow futurists, it ultimately served Wack only as a tool of negation. It did not illuminate what might be. It instead illuminated only what could not be – or what could be only by way of a "miracle" (82–3). Fashioned in the light of impossibilities and miracles but without undermining the taken-for-granted, the second-generation scenarios that Wack and his team offered inspired little conviction.

Wack came late – and presumably only after his several encounters with Sufi and Buddhist masters – to the realization that, in every effort to engage his executives actively in scenario planning, he had to confront head-on those mental maps and interior microcosms (Wack 1985b: 140 and passim) that managers brought to the tables of their meetings. Again, however, he wouldn't be intimidated. He followed the way of his masters to the orchestration of an uncovering, a clearing, a lifting of the clouds of the taken-for-granted and all of the passions invested in the future repeating the past:

> I have found that getting to that management "Aha!" moment is the real challenge of scenario analysis. It does not simply leap at you when you've presented all of the possible alternatives, no matter how eloquent or how beautifully drawn your charts. It happens when your message reaches the microcosms of decision makers, obliges them to question their assumptions about how the business world works, and leads them to change and reorganize their inner models of reality. (140)

It might just take a real guru to pull that off (see Ramírez and Ravetz 2011).

Cynthia Selin (2007) appropriately notes the paradoxical quality of Wack's simultaneous commitment to a realist engagement with predetermination and a constructivist conceptualization of the mental maps and interior microcosms that mediate (and block and distort) perception. The quality dissipates only slightly when the temporal distance that must be traversed to get from cloudiness to more luminous skies is taken into account (a distance that Wack seems to have been confident that he had himself fully travelled). Of course, gurus don't typically balk at paradox, and some positively thrive on it. Wack for his part simply doesn't mention it (at least in his published writings). Nor, it must be noted, does he ever suggest that the goal of clearing is the goal that his own gurus held dear: mystical dissolution into plenitude, mystical communion with the All-In-One. As an orchestrator of scenario construction, Wack is not a mystic. He might instead be said to be a "reconstructionist" (or "reorganizationalist": see Wack 1985a: 77), whose labours are directed not towards the complete undoing of maps and microcosms but instead to their reformation. Here Hans-Georg Gadamer's (1975) theorization of the hermeneutical circle – which demands that one confront and bring consciously to the fore one's preconceptions in the process of bringing what first seems alien into one's perceptual horizons – is perhaps the most relevant analogue to Wack's own pedagogy. Perhaps it is, but with one significant qualification: Gadamer's hermeneutical undertaking is effectively personal and its outcome an ethical reformation, a broadening of the ethical imagination. Wack's undertaking is collective and its outcome a reformation facilitating decision and action.

That said, Gadamer's quest, like Wack's, is a quest for "insight" (Wack 1985a: 78, 84). For Wack, insight is achieved in arriving at the scenaristically "plausible" and at scenaristic alternatives that are "equally plausible" (1985b: 139). Wack's critics have generally regarded such a standard as hopelessly fuzzy-headed (and that many professional scenario planners refer to their methodology, in a Wackean spirit, as "intuitive" only adds fuel to the fires). Ramírez and Selin (2014) plausibly argue that the concept of plausibility suffers from a historically extended stigmatization in the face of the statisticophilic epistemology of the probable. This point is no doubt true – but Wack himself shows little concern to launch a counteroffensive. Or, to put it more carefully: plausibility functions in Wack's work first and foremost as a counteroffensive, but a counteroffensive in the manner of (Zen?) negation. Otherwise put: in Wack's work, whatever the plausible might or might not be, it is certainly not the same as the true, and cannot be, because sensu stricto scenarios are logically vacuous (see Durbin 2015); they are vacuous because they refer to states of affairs that do not exist. Nor – to underscore – is the plausible the same as the statistically probable. Wack doesn't explicitly say but seems to take for granted that the plausible acquires positive content only in the process of scenario construction itself. Thus, its semantics (à la Wack) cannot be construed in general. Its semantics are instead indexically relative, and an index of the particular case at hand.

Scenarism and Us

Ginzburg's conjectural paradigm thus remains very relevant. Two further issues demand immediate comment. The first is whether we can provide any additional elaboration of or supplement to Wackean sophiology. The second is whether, in seeking to provide such an elaboration, we can articulate any socioculturally broader conclusions about the distinctive features of the collective world in which we now live. Concerning the first: In what could be understood as an effort to supplement and refine Wack's sophiology, several analysts of scenario planning (Schwartz 1991; see also Vickers 1983; Ramírez and Ravetz 2011; Wade 2012) have had resort to narratology. Prima facie, it's a reasonable move. Kahn originally appropriated the term "scenario" from Hollywood. Hollywood had appropriated it from the theatre. Scenarios are indeed narratives, theatrical or novelistic in their way. Two modulations must nevertheless be registered. The first is that the stories told aren't grand narratives. They're little, specific to situation, specific to time and place. Beyond that, scenarists aspire to a realism that distinguishes their work from works of either theatrical or novelistic fiction. One can follow Ian Watt (1957) in identifying the chief characteristic of the latter (but the same can be said of the former) as "verisimilitude," a quality achieved in "bringing home to the reader" an object or scene "in all its concrete particularity, *whatever the cost in repetition or parenthesis or verbosity*" (29; my emphasis). Verisimilitude comes, in short, with excess, a hyperbole of detail that is independent of the essentials of plot.

Scenarist theatre and scenarist narratives may be lively and substantively rich (many professional scenarists advocate that it be so; liveliness sells), but they are not marked by evidential surplus or superfluity. They are evidentially restrained. Their master trope is not hyperbole. It is instead the trope that Kenneth Burke (1969) argues dominates all "scientific" rhetoric – metonymy, the distillation of a whole into one of its parts (recall Ginzburg's elucidation of the evidential paradigm). Information-theoretically, metonymy is indeed a device of the reduction of complexity and (in the "purer" sciences) a near or complete dissolution of it. In principle and in fact, however, scenarism doesn't go so far. It rests with a hazy version of metonymic reduction, and for two reasons. First, it is always working in the face of the unforeseen consequences of what has occurred or is occurring. Second, it is always working with a whole that is not itself graspable, because certain of its variables don't yet exist. Scenarists thus belong squarely within Niklas Luhmann's (1998) ecology of ignorance and, if Luhmann is correct, so do the rest of us. If not precisely in Luhmannean terms, scenarists know this very well. They know that they exercise their craft in the shorter rather than the longer term of the future. They engage in prognosis – but in prognosis the plausibility of which always erodes as the future grows more distant. Again, they are not futurologists, predictors, or confident forecasters. They are instead managers of complexity (see Samimian-Darash and Rabinow 2015). Every connection they make between past, present, and future is a partial connection; every reduction a partial reduction. The logic of their enterprise, moreover, is not assertoric – the logic of "is" and "will." It is modal – the logic of "could," "would," and sometimes "should." Their voice is subjunctive – the voice of "may" and "might."

The logic of scenarism cannot thus straightforwardly be compared to the logic of conventional historiography (which is assertoric, if in the past tense: the logic of "was" and "did"). Even so, David Staley (2002a, 2007) has argued compellingly that the historiographical enterprise and scenarism have many striking features in common: both are "imaginative," but of an imagination disciplined by "the evidence" (a dicey term, he rightly admits). Both are theatrical or narrativistic, but selectively, and of a selectivity that privileges the structures to be found within the cloud mass of the empirical manifold over the manifold in all its dewy density. Staley is prepared to assert an epistemological symmetry between the historiography of the past – especially the less conventional counterfactual historiography of the past, the logic of which he appears to recognize is not assertoric but modal – and the scenaristic exploration of the future. Both are devoted to the study and analysis of effectively unpredictable and almost surely uniterable sequences of events – of the sheerly serial (see the discussion of reflexive modernization supra).

Staley – not coincidentally – is the author of a projective "history" of greater gender equality in the near future of Japan, grounded in such present evidence as the decline of arranged marriage (Staley 2002b). His drawing of an analogy between the epistemics of (counterfactual) historiography and the epistemics (better, sophiology) of scenarism is, I think, much more productive and illuminating than the drawing of analogies between the logic of narrative and the logic of scenarism. Pressed to its limits, it carries us to endorsing the epistemological symmetry between variables that might be tracked down in accounting for what has happened in the past and those that – because they haven't yet been manifest – can only be posited. It carries us to a double recognition: a recognition of the asymmetry between our knowledge of what has already been realized and what is (at best) virtual (see Samimian-Darash 2013); and a recognition as well of our incapacity to transcend the epistemological difference between what we can claim to know of the past and its relationship to the present and what we can claim to know of the past and the present and the relation of both to the future – at least when the span is of "modest scope."

The question is what sort of scope a "modest" scope might be. Many, if not all, historiographers are ready – and ready as a matter of their profession – to extend the reach of their evidential hand into a distant past, as archives (written or otherwise materialized) might permit. Ginzburg could be read as endorsing the reach of their retrospection; his own historiographies reach back to the early Renaissance. The temporal restrictions of his conjectural paradigm – the hunter's extrapolation from the spoor of his prey, its scent, its spittle, to its hiding place – are a better model of the temporality of Wack's own sophiology. Wack's realism limits itself to "the near past" (1985b: 142), the present, and the "medium range" of projection, which is in fact a range of very modest scope. It extends only to roughly a decade or two in advance of the present – and establishes a temporal benchmark for all that I know of professional scenarists' projective or prognostic treatment of what might, in one or another alternative, lie ahead. It's completely in accord with the exemplar of case-based medical diagnostics that Ginzburg has put at the fore of his articulation of the evidential, the conjectural paradigm.

How I Spent One of My Summer Vacations, or, Sophiology to No End

I offer here a somewhat concentrated reprise of a tale that I have previously spun (Faubion 2018). So: I arrive in Athens in May 2004. The Olympic Games are three months away, but I haven't come to Athens to attend the Olympics Games. I've come instead to explore what the cadre of reformist intellectuals who had been the subject of the research I had conducted between 1986 and 1987 (Faubion 1995) might be making of them. Soon into my visit, I met with Demosthenes Agrafiotis, already a noted essayist, poet, and artist when I had conducted my initial research. He was also a professor of sociology at the National School of Public Health (NSPH). In 2004, Agrafiotis was serving as the chancellor of the NSPH. He was also in the later stages of serving as director of methodology for the team engaged in assembling the Greek platform of FORESIGHT. Endorsed at a convention of the European Council in Lisbon in 2000 (Lisbon European Council 2000; see also Rodrigues 2003), a landmark of anticipatory governance, FORESIGHT hinged and continues to hinge on the construction of scenarios of the ways and means by which a Europe of a not-too-distant future could nationally and federally assert itself as the leading player in a "knowledge economy" against the techno-economic top seed: then (and still now) the United States. This description sounds as if it's a market-driven initiative, and that rings true enough. Yet, the Greek architects of the FORESIGHT exercise were not alone in modulating the imperatives of the "Lisbon Strategy" to diverse ends: economic but also political, aesthetic, and ethical. The result was the transformation of an economistically driven political initiative into a more total social phenomenon. Wack's signature seems not to have been prominent in Lisbon. It is absent from the bibliography of the Greek exercise. It nevertheless marks that exercise in spirit throughout.

In May 2004, the Greek team appointed to undertake the exercise in FORESIGHT had just completed its mission. Agrafiotis put the results at my disposal: a more than 1,500-page document that included an articulation of the methodological principles, the parameters of analysis, and an ensemble of scenarios anticipating the future of Europe and the future of Greece within it. The scenarios were directed at two target dates: one eight years hence (2012) and the other nine years beyond that – 2021, the two-hundredth anniversary of the Greek declaration of independence from the Ottoman Empire (Agrafiotis 2016). Four general scenarios addressed Greece as a member among others of a globally embedded European Economic Community (EEC). Another four, more specific, addressed Greece as a bounded nation-state within the EEC. These latter scenarios construed Greece variously as a garden, an environmental preserve; as an active player in an unregulated (loosely, "neoliberal") market economy; as a bastion of civic entitlements; or as a dissolute subaltern, riven for one reason or another by turmoil and dependent on heavy-handed benefactors. In accord with the Lisbon Strategy, the project unfolded modularly, devoting specific attention to the intersections and dynamics among e-governance, "culture" and tourism, agriculture and fishing, the natural environment, health and the invigoration of scientific research (among other things), and the provision of a technological infrastructure adequate to the task of bringing the whole package to fruition.

None of the scenarios that Agrafiotis and his team produced were sheer inventions, creations ex nihilo. Agrafiotis has clarified for me in several exchanges that the first two of these scenarios – Greece as an environmental preserve and Greece as an active player in a neoliberal economy – were both inspired in thinking through the potential intersection of global and expansively European trends with what seemed at the time to be realistic national ambitions. The Olympics weren't their only inspiration, but featured saliently within them. Rumours – some coming from the highest governmental echelons – had it that the completion of more efficient highways, the Athens subway system, and the planting of more than a quarter million trees and over ten million shrubs in advance of the games would improve the habitability of the metropolis and its surroundings by some 35 per cent (but who knows who arrived at that number, and how?). In a past version of this paper, I cited several sources publishing such claims on internet sites. Those sites have subsequently disappeared. I now find only one author following the Greek government Center for Planning in claiming – again *avant l'heure* and wrongly – that the games would generate 65,000 permanent jobs (Janowski 2003). They did not.

The idyll of the Greek garden embedded a critique of the unleashing, under the license of market-pegged developmentalism, of private interests set free from the constraints of the public good. Indicative of the critical import of the idyll was the widespread accusation that the forest fires so often afflicting the country in its summer months were the result of arsonists intent on destroying the realm of the public trust in order to pave the way for private development projects. Occasionally at least, those accusations may well have been on the mark. Embedded in the accusation was nevertheless a certain collective confidence (if by no means unanimous) that Greece could realistically aspire to be an exemplar of green industry and white technology. The garden and the market weren't precisely two sides of the same coin, but they were complements, each of the other.

The latter two scenarios – a Greece of entitlements and a Greece reduced to politico-economic subjection – reflected, as Agrafiotis has put it to me, more "chronic" conditions. The third was welfarist. In 2004, as before, Greece had in place a variety of more or less functional perquisites for its citizens – a public health system and state-funded retirement pensions among them. They were costly – and rather more costly than a national budget office concerned to demonstrate compliance with the European Union benchmark of a deficit of no more than 3 per cent of the gross domestic product (GDP) officially disseminated. (Retrospective estimates of the Greek deficit, though always inflected by variable practices of accounting, range from between 4 per cent [Eurostat 2004] to more than 8 per cent of the GDP [Manessiotis 2011].) Still, that Greece would sustain its system of entitlements into an unfolding future would effectively amount to its continuing to conduct business as usual. The fourth scenario – that, whether due to military invasion or revolt, natural disasters, or economic turmoil, Greece would fall into disarray and debt-servitude – was itself hardly unimaginable. It was all the more imaginable if one cast one's historical eye all the way back to 1821. Indeed, it proved to be very close to the mark – a near bullseye. The scenarists could see it coming. More precisely, they saw that it could be coming. The fourth scenario did not, however, prove to win the clear conviction of any of the working groups assigned to develop the various modules of the FORESIGHT exercise. Trusting in the promise of the Olympic Games, the majority voices of all of those groups inclined instead towards more optimistic perspectives.

Even the wise can make mistakes. Even the most able hunter can go astray. Even that most iconic of sleuths, Sherlock Holmes, missed the mark on a few occasions. Yet, the Greek scenarists did not, again, really miss their mark. In a conversation I recently had with him, Agrafiotis could justly remark: "We got it right." The remark might seem arrogant, but it is not. It is tempered by the modesty inherent to the modal pluralism of the scenaristic enterprise itself. Sharon Ryan (2018), the author of the entry on wisdom in the *Stanford Encyclopedia of Philosophy*, assesses the ethos of the wise in terms with which "any acceptable theory of wisdom ought to be compatible": "Wise people ... possess epistemic self-confidence, yet lack epistemic arrogance. Wise people tend to acknowledge their fallibility, and wise people are reflective, introspective, and tolerant of uncertainty" (sec. 1). Ryan makes no reference to scenario planning, but Wack, his heirs, and – among them – Agrafiotis and his scenarist colleagues ex hypothesi were and probably remain wise people just so. The wise are one breed of people. Oracles are another.

Aristotle famously distinguishes three elements pivotal to the arts of persuasion: ethos (character), logos (reason), and pathos (passion, emotion). The Greek scenarists were certainly deploying such arts – if, in the middle and mix of their joint undertaking, deploying them no farther than each on the other. Ex hypothesi, ethos can be left aside. The diagram of scenario planning imposed confident modesty on the Greeks as and at work, even if it did not and could not despotically control de facto all of their characterological penchants while at work. Circumscribed by the imperative of confident modesty, logos was not so hampered in its activity that it shot itself in the foot (clumsy hunting, clumsy sleuthing). The Greek scenarists "got it right." The turbulence that afflicted their undertaking was the turbulence between logos and pathos. They got it right, but wanted it to be wrong. The upshot was not any error of scenaristic reasoning. It was instead the modulation of logos by pathos – the modulation of reason by a majoritarian hope, of what such Enlightenment philosophers as John Locke sometimes disparaged as "enthusiasm." It was not unwise per se, but perhaps unwisely biased. Pathos: we can't live with it (at least as wise people), but we can't live without it (even as scenario planners).

Bias is our human condition. Could the bias or biases of the aficionados of Greek FORESIGHT have been noticed, challenged, corrected? Perhaps they could have been – but the potentially corrective dialogue that the Greek scenarists sought to have with the official superiors to whom they might have submitted their disciplined speculations found their superiors unreceptive. Sociologically at least, Wack, the commissioned Buddhist guru, is not socio-politically instructive at this juncture. He was commissioned by superiors who were prepared, however reluctantly, to give him the floor. The Greek venture into FORESIGHT had as its primary board of sponsorship, reception, and review the decidedly technocratic Greek Secretariat of Research and Technology (GSRT). As with technocrats generally (see especially Touraine 1971), the governors of the secretariat would likely have wanted to have a program delivered at their doorstep: characterologically, logically, and passionately. The Greek venture could not fulfill any such expectation. Yet, even technocrats can be tolerant of less than programmatic perfection. Even they can engage in constructive assessments of and interventions into the ethos, logos, and pathos of persuasion. The GSRT seems not to have cared to have any such engagement. Nominally the superior party of Greek FORESIGHT, the agency left its executors to their own devices from the outset, and proved to be uninterested even in considering what they had formulated. Other governmental functionaries proved equally indifferent, even disdainful (Agrafiotis 2016; see also Amanatidou 2016). Agrafiotis is of the well-informed opinion that the top-down, Brussels-authorized mandate of FORESIGHT rankled the functionary GSRT powers-that-were as (yet another) imposition from on high and from without. They didn't themselves invite any coterie of sages to see for them what they thought they could already see. They also didn't invite any guru or any coterie of sages commissioned from the Bruxellean flatland to transform their mental – or better, their ethological or logical or passionate – microcosms. Whose fault was that? To invert and pervert Shakespeare, the fault lay less either with the scenarists or the functionaries of the GSRT than with the social and political stars, the circulations of which affect all of us more than we often care to acknowledge – the guru Wack among us. Greek FORESIGHT is an object lesson. What it teaches us is that, in its production as in its reception, wisdom depends not merely on the decryption of spoors, scents, spittle, and hiding places, but also on the decryption of a sociological astrology, of which none of us has and none of us is likely ever to have full command. Wisdom should be assessed accordingly.

REFERENCES

Agrafiotis, Demosthenes. 2016. "Cultural Blindness." Translated by James D. Faubion. In the series *Greece is Burning*, edited by J.D. Faubion, E. Georges, and G. van Steen. *Cultural Anthropology*. https://culanth.org/fieldsights/cultural-blindness.

Amanatidou, Elissabet. 2016. "Αποτίμηση της προοπτικής διερεύνησης" [Evaluation of Foresight]. In Επιστημονική και Τεχνολογική Προοπτική Διερεύνηση, Ελλάδα 2021 [Scientific and Technological Foresight, Greece 2021], edited by M. Chletsos and D. Agrafiotis, 374–404. Athens: Pedio.

Anderson, Poul. 1961. *Twilight World*. New York: Tor Books.

Anderson, Poul, and F.N. Waldrop. 1947. "Tomorrow's Children." *Astounding Science Fiction* 39 (1): 56–79.

Beck, Ülrich, Anthony Giddens, and Scott Lash. 1994. *Reflexive Modernization: Politics, Tradition and Aesthetics in the Modern Social Order*. Stanford, CA: Stanford University Press.

Boyer, Dominic. 2013. *The Life Informatic: Newsmaking in the Digital Era*. Ithaca, NY: Cornell University Press.

Brefi Group. 2018. "Scenario Planning – Some Definitions." https://www.brefigroup.co.uk/facilitation/scenario_planning_definition.html.

Burke, Kenneth. 1969. *A Grammar of Motives*. Revised edition. Berkeley: University of California Press.

Carson, Rachel. 1962. *Silent Spring*. Boston: Houghton Mifflin Harcourt.

Chletsos, Michalis, and Demosthenes Agrafiotis, eds. 2014. Επιστημονική και Τεχνολογική Προοπτική Διερεύνηση, Ελλάδα 2021 [Scientific and Technological Foresight, Greece 2021]. Athens: Pedio.

de Jouvenel, Bertrand, ed. 1963. *Futuribles: Studies in Conjecture*. 2 vols. Geneva: Droz.

Durbin, Trevor. 2015. "Big Ocean: Marine Conservation, Bureaucratic Practice, and the Politics of Vagueness in the Pacific Islands." PhD diss., Rice University Electronic Theses and Dissertations (10279).

Eisler, Riane. 1987. *The Chalice and the Blade: Our History, Our Future*. San Francisco: Harper & Row.

Eurostat. 2004. "Report by Eurostat on the Revision of the Greek Government Deficit and Debt Figures." http://ec.europa.eu/eurostat/documents/4187653/5765001/GREECE-EN.PDF/2da4e4f6-f9f2-4848-b1a9-cb229fcabae3?version=1.0.

Faubion, James D. 1995. *Modern Greek Lessons: A Primer in Historical Constructivism*. Princeton, NJ: Princeton University Press.

– 2018. "On Parabiopolitical Reason." *Anthropological Theory* (May 2018): 219–37. https://doi.org/10.1177/1463499618770558.

Firestone, Shulamith. 1970. *The Dialectic of Sex: The Case for Feminist Revolution*. New York: Farrar, Strauss and Giroux.

Foucault, Michel. 1973. *The Birth of the Clinic: An Archaeology of Medical Perception*. Translated by A. Sheridan. London: Tavistock.

Gabor, Dennis. 1963. *Inventing the Future*. London: Secker and Warburg.

– 1972. *The Mature Society*. London: Secker and Warburg.

Gadamer, Hans-Georg. 1975. *Truth and Method*. Translated by J. Weinsheimer and D.G. Marshall. New York: Crossroads.

Ghamari-Tabrizi, Sharon. 2005. *The Worlds of Herman Kahn: The Intuitive Science of Thermonuclear War*. Cambridge, MA: Harvard University Press.

Ginzburg, Carlo. 1989. "Clues: Roots of an Evidential Paradigm." In *Clues, Myths, and the Historical Method*, translated by J. Tedeschi and A. Tedeschi, 87–113. Baltimore, MD: Johns Hopkins University Press.

Global Foresight. n.d. "Foresight Graduate Programs – Global List." https://sites.google.com/site/globalforesightwiki/foresightprograms.

Gruen, Lori, and David Jamieson, eds. 1994. *Reflecting on Nature: Readings in Environmental Philosophy*. New York: Oxford University Press.

Guston, David. 2014. "Understanding 'Anticipatory Governance.'" *Social Studies of Science* 44 (2): 218–42. https://doi.org/10.1177/0306312713508669.

Hacking, Ian. 1976. *Logic of Statistical Inference*. Revised edition. Cambridge: Cambridge University Press.

– 1990. *The Taming of Chance*. Cambridge: Cambridge University Press.

Herrigel, Eugen. 1953. *Zen in the Art of Archery*. Translated by R.F.C. Hull. New York: Pantheon Books.

Ichikawa, Jonathan Jenkins, and Matthias Steup. 2018. "The Analysis of Knowledge." *The Stanford Encyclopedia of Philosophy*, 2018 (summer) ed., edited by Edward N. Zalta. https://plato.stanford.edu/entries/knowledge-analysis/#KnowJustTrueBeli

Janowski, Tomasz. 2003. "Olympic Dividends Not Yet Certain for Athens." *ekathimerini.com*. http://www.ekathimerini.com/16301/article/ekathimerini/business/olympic-dividends-not-certain-yet-for-athens.

Kahn, Herman. 1960. *On Thermonuclear War*. Princeton, NJ: University of Princeton Press.

– 1984. *Thinking about the Unthinkable in the 1980s*. New York: Simon & Schuster.

Kahn, Herman, and Anthony Weiner. 1967. *The Year 2000: A Framework for Speculation on the Next Thirty-Three Years*. New York: Macmillan.

Lisbon European Council. 2000. "Presidential Conclusions." http://www.europarl.europa.eu/summits/lis1_en.htm.

Luhmann, Niklas. 1998. *Observations on Modernity*. Translated by William Whobrey. Stanford, CA: Stanford University Press.

Manessiotis, Basil. 2011. "The Root-Causes of the Greek Sovereign Debt Crisis." Paper presented at the 2nd Bank of Greece workshop on the economies of Eastern European and Mediterranean countries, 6 May 2011. http://www.bankofgreece.gr/BoGDocuments/The%20root-causes%20of%20the%20greek%20sovereign%20debt%20crisis%2005%2005%202011(3).pdf.

Mason, Moya K. 2019. "Future Scenarios: The Art of Storytelling." http://www.moyak.com/papers/scenarios-future-planning.html.

Niles, David. 2009. "The Secret of Successful Scenario Planning." *Forbes*, 3 August. https://www.forbes.com/2009/08/03/scenario-planning-advice-leadership-managing-planning.html#4209d5498064.

Rabinow, Paul, and Anthony Stavrianakis. 2014. *Designs on the Contemporary: Anthropological Tests*. Chicago: University of Chicago Press.

Ramírez, Rafael, and Jerome Ravetz. 2011. "Feral Futures: Zen and Aesthetics." *Futures* 43 (4): 478–87. https://doi.org/10.1016/j.futures.2010.12.005.

Ramírez, Rafael, and Cynthia Selin. 2014. "Plausibility and Probability in Scenario Planning." *Foresight* 16 (1): 54–74. https://doi.org/10.1108/FS-08-2012-0061.

Ramírez, Rafael, John W. Selsky, and Kees van der Heijden, eds. 2010. *Business Planning for Turbulent Times: New Methods for Applying Scenarios*, 2nd ed. New York: Earthscan.

Rodrigues, Maria João. 2003. *European Policies for a Knowledge Economy.* Cheltenham: Edward Elgar.

Ryan, Sharon. 2018. "Wisdom." *The Stanford Encyclopedia of Philosophy*, 2018 (fall) ed., edited by Edward N. Zalta. https://plato.stanford.edu/archives/fall2018/entries/wisdom.

Saïd Business School. 2019. "Oxford Scenarios Programme." University of Oxford. https://www.sbs.ox.ac.uk/programmes/oxford-scenarios-programme.

Samimian-Darash, Limor. 2013. "Governing Future Potential Biothreats: Toward an Anthropology of Uncertainty." *Current Anthropology* 54 (1): 1–22. https://doi.org/10.1086/669114.

– 2016. "Practicing Uncertainty: Scenario-Based Preparedness Exercises in Israel." *Cultural Anthropology* 31 (3): 359–86. https://doi.org/10.14506/ca31.3.06.

Samimian-Darash, Limor, and Paul Rabinow, eds. 2015. *Modes of Uncertainty: Anthropological Cases.* Chicago: University of Chicago Press.

Schwartz, Peter. 1991. *The Art of the Long View.* New York: Doubleday.

Selin, Cynthia. 2007. "Professional Dreamers: The Past in the Future of Scenario Planning." In *Scenarios for Success: Turning Insight into Action*, edited by B. Sharpe and K. van der Heijden, 27–52. Hoboken, NJ: Wiley.

Shannon, Claude. 1948a. "A Mathematical Theory of Communication." *Bell Systems Technical Journal* 27 (3): 379–423.

– 1948b. "A Mathematical Theory of Communication." *Bell Systems Technical Journal* 27 (3): 623–66.

Staley, David. 2002a. "A History of the Future." *History and Theory* 41 (4): 72–89. https://doi.org/10.1111/1468-2303.00221.

– 2002b. "Japan's Uncertain Future: Key Trends and Scenarios." *The Futurist* 36 (2): 48–53.

– 2007. *History and Future: Using Historical Thinking to Imagine the Future.* Lanham, MD: Lexington Press.

Toffler, Alvin. 1970. *Future Shock.* New York: Bantam.

– 1980. *The Third Wave.* New York: Bantam.

Touraine, Alain. 1971. *The Post-Industrial Society. Tomorrow's Social History: Classes, Conflicts and Culture in the Programmed Society*. Translated by L.F.X. Mayhew. New York: Random House.

Turco, Richard P., Owen B. Toon, Thomas P. Ackerman, James B. Pollack, and Carl Sagan. 1983. "Nuclear Winter: Global Consequences of Multiple Nuclear Explosions." *Science* 222 (4630): 1283–92. https://doi.org/10.1126/science.222.4630.1283.

Vickers, G. 1983. *Human Systems Are Different*. London: Harper & Row.

von Neumann, John, and Oskar Morgenstern. 1944. *The Theory of Games and Economic Behavior*. Princeton, NJ: Princeton University Press.

Wack, Pierre. 1985a. "Scenarios: Uncharted Waters Ahead." *Harvard Business Review* 63 (September–October): 73–89. https://hbr.org/1985/09/scenarios-uncharted-waters-ahead.

– 1985b. "Scenarios: Shooting the Rapids." *Harvard Business Review* 63 (November–December): 131–42. https://hbr.org/1985/11/scenarios-shooting-the-rapids.

Wade, Woody. 2012. *Scenario Planning: A Field Guide to the Future*. Hoboken, NJ: Wiley.

Watt, Ian. 1957. *The Rise of the Novel: Studies in Defoe, Richardson and Fielding*. Berkeley: University of California Press.

8 Grappling with the Ineffable in Three African Situations: An Ethnographic Approach

WIM M.J. VAN BINSBERGEN

Introduction: The Topicality of Wisdom Today

In the context of the 2015 Pittsburgh conference and the present collection of papers based on it, I am conscious of a heavy responsibility to which I can scarcely hope to live up: I represent two continents here, not only Europe (with just one other representative, from Cambridge, UK – perhaps scarcely to be called Europe anymore, since the Britons opted for "Brexit" in 2016) but also Africa (not touched upon in any other contribution). Whereas most of the other contributions concentrate on what could be termed, somewhat too negatively, "literate traditions from various parts of the world but appropriated, canonized, and reified by North Atlantic specialist scholarship," my own focus here is on situations (typically outside the North Atlantic region: in Africa) that are not logocentric,[1] that are largely illiterate, and that are located where the researcher does not have a pre-existing text at her or his disposal but centrally aims at producing such a text (as ethnography) for the first time.

All our contributions deal with wisdom; but for all our contributions and certainly for my own, we may ask whether we deal with wisdom in a sufficiently wise way. For many decades, the notion of "wisdom" used to be confined in the general academic understanding and within the scope of philosophy, philology, and anthropology to either antiquated complexes of local esoteric knowledge devoid of objective truth or equally antiquated complexes that had relevance only within a limited context of space and time, and within a limited field of scholarship – such as the wisdom books of the תנך *Tanaḫ*, also incorporated in the Christian Old Testament, or 易經 *yì jīng* (*I Ching*) as a wisdom book widely used for divination in East and South East Asia.[2]

My own interest in wisdom was kindled, more than half a century ago, when my elder brother gave me an extensive introduction to the Presocratics (ancient Greek philosophers) for my fifteenth birthday (de Raedemaeker 1953); and much later, thirty years ago, by the writings of my close colleague and friend Richard Werbner (1973, 1989, 2015) on Kalanga wisdom divination in Botswana – a practice that was not text-based then, but whose textual basis in the medieval Arabic divination form called علم الرمل, *ᶜilm al-raml* (sand science) I was to explore extensively from 1990 onward (see, for example, van Binsbergen 1995, 1996, 2012a, 2012b, 2013).

In the last few decades, the intellectual landscape associated with wisdom has been transformed due to, among others, the following influences:

- *positive re-evaluation of wisdom in a spate of recent scholarly literature,* from psychology, psychiatry, anthropology, philosophy, and the like,[3] rethinking knowledge, truth, and agency (for an extensive overview, see van Binsbergen 2009a);
- *new technologies of information and communication*, especially the creation of the internet, which has brought about greatly increased worldwide access to, communication about, and attempted (often hegemonic, reductive, and superficial) appropriation of, as well as reification of, the wisdom traditions of remote regions and periods; and
- *aspects of globalization* (the dramatic reduction – mainly through recent technological means – of the effects of time and space on present-day actors) largely due to the just mentioned technology. Another aspect of globalization has been the erosion of hitherto habitual and moderately comfortable boundaries of knowledge, groups, and identities; in reaction, a new, increasingly insistent and violent politics of identity has emerged in which new identities and new distinctions proliferate in the face of their annihilation (real, apparent, feared, imminent, threatened) under conditions of globalization.

The amorphous and eclectic New Age movement[4] is an example of the now worldwide circulation of wisdoms that were earlier far more confined to their original cultural, linguistic, and geographical niche. In the same vein, fundamentalism, militant Islamism, and creationism are some examples of movements revolving on the retreat within hardening boundaries as a response to boundary- and identity-threatening globalization. On the one hand, such movements themselves rely on, and seek to militantly propagate, what they consider unique wisdoms; on the other hand, the combination of truth claims with physical and/or ideological violence requires from those not involved in such movements a new kind of wisdom: dealing with the dilemmas arising from the fact that now, again, the wisdom of others may take on life-threatening features.

Not for the first time, though. When a Christian mob, exhorted by monks, lynched, among others, the female "pagan" non-Christian philosopher Hypatia in Alexandria during the fourth century CE, it was a similar case; her conventional image adorns the cover of a book on African women philosophers we did a few years ago (Osha with van Binsbergen 2006). Other similar cases were the Crusades, the Inquisition, the genocidal auto-da-fés enacted by Christian religious orders among pre-Christian inhabitants of the New World, the witch craze of early modern Europe, and the witchcraft eradication movements of early twentieth-century sub-Saharan Africa. The violent aspects of the pursuit of (un)wisdom remind us of the close link between belief, language, and violence throughout history (see also Schroeder 1996).

This argument reflects my grappling with wisdom issues and intercultural epistemology during the past two decades and, especially, some of the ideas now being worked out in my book project in progress, "Sangoma Science: From Ethnography to Intercultural Ontology: Towards a Poetics of the Globalising Exploration into Local Spiritualities" (van Binsbergen In preparation [b]).

"On the Way to Language"

Wovon man nicht sprechen kann, darüber muss man schweigen.
Of what one cannot speak, thereof one must be silent.
– Wittgenstein, *Tractatus Logico-Philosophicus*, 1921 (Wittgenstein 1964)

With its emphasis on the ineffable, our collective project focuses on what cannot be said (what is considered too great to be said) in language. Implicitly, therefore, our project is about the critique and the limitations of language (Heidegger 1985). This topic is noteworthy in several ways.

In the first place, the production of scholarship and *a fortiori* that of anthropology is production in language – and, even in discursive written language, usually in one of the few international lingua francas of today, especially English. Whatever transformations anthropology as an academic subject may have undergone in the most recent decades (with its obsession with the politics of identity, with Foucault and Deleuze, with multisited fieldwork, and with its relative abhorrence of prolonged, expensive fieldwork in distant places),[5] anthropology originally came into being shortly before the twentieth century CE as the art of covering with texts the part of the world that was not already so covered out of its own internal literate dynamics. Hence, there is a marked and crucial contradiction between anthropology and the experience of the ineffable among most of the other participants in our project. For, contrary to the philosopher, the linguist, the (documentary) historian, the literature scholar, only the ethnographer has no text yet at her or his disposal – typically, such texts still need to be created as a result of the researcher's very own research efforts. The anthropologist thus casts into the wind Wittgenstein's admonition quoted earlier. Cases in point are the great anthropologist of religion, Victor Turner (1967, 1968), in his seminal analyses of South Central African symbols; or the Louvain School of Anthropology (for example, Devisch, De Boeck, and Stroeken),[6] reconstructing in words what never was expressed in so many words by the local participants themselves, with all the risks and uncertainties of such an ethnographic attempt.

From earliest childhood on, my own life as a literary and scholarly writer has been predicated on the assumption that nearly everything can be said (van Binsbergen 2015a). That assumption can hardly be considered personal and idiosyncratic: it is built into the very culture of my native city, Amsterdam, and reflects the unquestioned logocentricity of both the Protestant Christian and the Jewish strands that have helped to shape Amsterdam and Dutch culture over the last half millennium and before. Almost obsessively throughout my research career, I have been trying to extend the realm of what has been said – "creating history where previously there was none"[7] – but also producing ethnographic description on the same basis. Inevitably, I hit on contradictions:

- What was effectively expressed in the routinized, globalized discourse of professional anthropology (preferably in an international language, such as English – nearly all my anthropological publications have been in that language) on second thought turned out not to capture the existential thrust of the fieldwork encounters with fellow human beings on which it was based; and, what was even more regrettable, my professional texts did not make much sense to my original fieldwork hosts, and, if they became yet a source of pride and identity to them (van Binsbergen 1987, 1992b, 2003a), it was not because of the details of their contents or because of the specific nature of my commitment

but simply because other rival ethnic groups had possessed and boasted such texts for decades already.
- What came closer to the existential thrust of the fieldwork encounter (for example, my 1988 novel in Dutch, *Een Buik Openen*, on my first fieldwork in North Africa, 1968, and many of my poems) was, with some exceptions, considered irrelevant to the furtherance of anthropology.

Although my first identity as an intellectual producer has been (and largely remained) that of a poet, in my anthropological and intercultural-philosophical work, language has increasingly appeared to me as a trap and a danger – as "violence" inflicted on my research hosts and upon myself in my role as fieldworker; in the process, language revealed itself as utterly unable to express many of the most important aspects of the human experience. Having acceded to the Rotterdam chair of intercultural philosophy in 1998, the results of my sustained probing into the possibilities and the epistemological conditions for valid knowledge production across cultural boundaries has highlighted language (because of its high levels of specificity and social markedness, which makes it the perfect tool for othering and exclusion) as a principal factor, not for genuine intercultural exchange (as is often pretended) but, on the contrary, as a principal factor for the hegemonic, subordinative thwarting of intercultural encounter (van Binsbergen 2003a).

Thus, the ineffable, in other words, what could not be said in language, has constituted the inevitable and conscious boundary condition of all my fieldwork and ethnography since the late 1960s. How did it manifest itself? Let me highlight some of the main instances by serially discussing the following three African situations: the Ḫumiri highlands of North West Tunisia (North Africa); the Nkoya of South Central Africa (rural West Zambia and urban Zambia); and the *sangoma* ecstatic healing cult in urban and peri-urban North East Botswana. After each ethnographic summary, we shall assess how wisdom manifests itself in each context and how people considered wise are identified there. These three case studies will be our stepping stones to more fundamental theoretical issues:

- Is wisdom truly an indigenous *emic* concept,[8] or is it merely an alien *etic* imposition on the part of us North Atlantic analysts?
- Ethnography appears to be, among other things, the art of explicit language-based articulation and transmission of the ineffable that manifests itself, in the local participants' actions including speech acts, as self-evidence.

- Although science may be the systematic pursuit of communicable empirically grounded truth, truth can be argued to be culturally bounded and to proliferate and fragment (under today's conditions of globalization, localization, and "glocalization")[9] into numerous local "truth enclaves," whose truth cannot be transmitted intactly "as truth" across cultural and linguistic boundaries towards other such truth enclaves.
- Under the circumstances, and in addition to the descriptive and analytical tasks the social sciences have defined for the ethnographer on the impetus of their own intra-disciplinary paradigmatic development, a unique and globally pivotal task seems to have fallen upon today's ethnographer: that of becoming a spokesperson for apparently peripheral wisdoms.

Let us now first turn to the three case studies.

Three African Situations

Ḫumiriyya, the Highlands of North West Tunisia, North Africa

WISDOM IN ḪUMIRIYYA

In Ḫumiriyya, the highlands of North West Tunisia,[10] I did participatory and oral historical research into popular Islam and local social organization (van Binsbergen 1980b).[11]

This trip was my first encounter, as a child of the Amsterdam urban slums, with peasants' popular religion (rather similar to the folk Roman Catholicism that, along with diffuse folk Judaism, had been a major influence during my childhood). The fieldwork took place well before the revival of formal Islamism in the late 1970s. Except in terms of prestige, I had little benefit from the Arabic I had studied, for this folk complex "was largely illiterate, and [had] millennia-old regional traits" (which decades later I was to subsume under the heading of "Pelasgian")[12] blended almost imperceptibly with the stipulations of a much more recent (late first millenium CE), and still somewhat alien, formal Islam. I was immensely impressed by the way in which the local women, especially, and the male attendants of the formalized, white-washed local domed shrines[13] understood the local landscape, their privileges and obligations as peasants, the shrines and their invisible saints, and the likewise invisible army of جنون *jnūn* (jinns) all as one coherent and meaningful system for the production and distribution of البركة *al-baraka* (blessing) – thus sanctifying the jinn-haunted steep hills and rivulets where I was learning to be an anthropologist.

A major aspect of the administration of blessing was the ecstatic cult of the local فوقره *fūqra* (faqirs), who were nominally members of the قدرية Qadiriyya brotherhood found all over the world of Islam. Under the trance-producing music from the الطبلة *tabala* (frame drum) and the القصبة *quṣba* (reed) flute, nocturnal séances were staged in which the faqir entered into trance, summoning the (spirit of the) local saint from his tomb and, without injury, manipulating thorny cactus leaves, pointed women's claps, and fiery coals and scythes as a sign of the saint's *baraka*-emanating presence. Just turned twenty-one years of age, I was impressionable, and I was immensely impressed indeed, successfully joining the *fūqra* at their repeated invitation, experiencing my first trance, opening up my urban eyes to the sacred and meaningful beauty of the countryside, studying pilgrimage practices in much detail, and entering into a ritual obligation towards the valley saint Sidi Mḥammad, which I and my family have kept up ever since. However, I soon steered away from the original sacred and existential inspiration by concentrating on a highly formalized, statistical approach to observable social and religious interaction in this community, allowing myself to be alienated from its wisdom until much of that found its way into my 1988 novel. Moreover, in order to understand the myriad local shrines within the landscape and its history, I had to reconstruct, from scratch, a detailed local history of over twenty agnatic descent groups with their socio-political struggles in the course of two centuries. Though this work made me an oral historian and a proto-historian, it meant that the promise of wisdom deriving from this fieldwork remained dormant for a long time.

When engaged in this first fieldwork, I was a very young anthropological apprentice, shy, inexperienced in interviewing, and at a loss as to how to manage my participation and observation in an alien environment of people twice or thrice my age. I had not yet even begun to think through the violence that my incessant emphasis on verbal utterances was imposing on the largely implicit, scarcely ever verbalized worldview of my informants. Although many of my insights came from observation, participation, and unobtrusive conversation ("small talk," where my assistant Ḥasnāwi bin Ṭahar حسناوي بن طاهر compensated in a masterly way for the severe limitations of my knowledge of local spoken Arabic), I insisted on conducting formal interviews, recording all the utterances verbatim and exploring (especially with the aid of spun-out hypothetical cases laid before my informants) what the uses and semantic fields were of such basic concepts as *baraka*, ولي *ulī/wali* (saint), حَرَام *ḥarām* (polluted, forbidden), and other such ideas. In fact, most of my interpretation of the

Figure 8.1 The leading elder ᶜAmer bin Mabrūk and his grandson photographed in the village of Hamraya, *ᶜomdat* ᶜAṭaṭfa, ᶜAin Drāham, Tunisia, in 1968; in the background, a neighbour's house. (© 1968/2017 Wim van Binsbergen)

interview data thus gathered took place not immediately and on the spot, but much later, back in my North Atlantic academic environment. It was a most unwise approach, largely based on the implicit false assumption that a one-to-one relationship should exist between local *emic* terms and their ethnographic *etic* rendering. Even though I was closely supervised in the field by teachers from my home institution, I remained – for such were the times, and such was anthropology in the 1960s – unaware of the hegemonic and artefact-producing effects of such a strategy in the field. Going through the myriad ways in which the word "*baraka*" could be used in everyday local parlance and persecuting the peasants with ever more refined alternatives put before them to choose between, I found their complaint was not only boredom and fatigue, but also the reproach that it appeared as if I thought they were lying to me about their own culture. What little wisdom I ultimately (years later) managed to thresh out of the experience came not from verbal utterances but from accepting the lead of one of my key informants in her enthusiastic exclamations about the local saint in his tomb: جدودنه "They are our grandfathers/our ancestors" (figures 8.1–8.5).

Figure 8.2 A sacralized landscape: Ḫumiri women harvesting rye in the outskirts of the village of سيدي محامد Sidi Mḥammad, *ᶜomdat* ᶜAṭaṭfa, ᶜAin Drāham, Tunisia, in 1968; in the background, along the path on the crest of the hill under the larger tree, the main shrine of سيدي بوقصبية Sidi Bu-Qasbaya can be made out; it is of the مزارة *mzara* type, with Bronze Age megalythic connotations. (© 1968/2017 Wim van Binsbergen)

Figure 8.3 The shrine of Sidi Mḥammad Sr., North West Tunisia, 2002. (© 2002/2017 Wim van Binsbergen)

Figure 8.4 The valley of Sidi Mḥammad as seen from my house, ᶜAṭaṭfa, ᶜAin Drāham District, Tunisia, 1979. Note the domed saint's grave (middle ground, centre left); another, more senior shrine finds itself on the nearest hilltop in the background. (© Wim van Binsbergen)

Figure 8.5 The *mzara* ᶜAin Raml (2002), an originally megalithic type of shrine in the valley of Sidi Mḥammad, ᶜAin Drāham, Tunisia. (© 2002/2017 Wim van Binsbergen)

WISE PERSONS IN ḤUMIRIYYA

In the context of our 2015 Pittsburgh conference, it became increasingly interesting to consider what the "wise person" looks like in a specific local culture and society. In Ḥumiriyya, the answer to this question would (in a way perhaps characteristic of wisdom and its ambivalences) be divided between two possibilities.

In the first place, there is the category of "the elder" (الكبير *al-kabīr* masc. / الكبيرة *al-kabīra* fem.) – leading personalities marked by advanced age, high status (with secular power and wealth as an unmistakable prerequisite), and exemplary public behaviour, exercising wide-ranging authority (from prayer, healing, and pilgrimage to conflict regulation, the management of oral traditions and traditional knowledge, marital arrangements, and the coordination of everyday productive activities) at the ward and village level and within the various hierarchical levels of (nominally) agnatic descent groups. Ḥumiriyya is a profoundly segmentary society, and secular elders of greater and lesser scope would be found at every segmentary level. Agnatic segments in the course of their dynamics over time might straddle and outgrow the geographic boundaries in the landscape, but usually, in the 1960s (half a century after the imposition of colonial rule, the end of open warfare and feuding, land scarcity, and population increase had led to sedentarization), agnatic and territorial segments would tend to coincide. At the highest segmentary level, the العمدة *ᶜomdat* (šayḫdom, in fact: mayoralty), there would be only one or two generally recognized elders. I was fortunate, as a very young man, to become close with one of the very principal elders of the عطاطفة ᶜAtatfa shayḫdom: العمر بن مبروك ᶜAmer ben Mabrūk, a lean and very tall man in his mid-seventies, rich in land, cattle, descendants, and stories, an indispensable key figure in any major social and political event in the valley and endowed with a great and contagious sense of humour. Although generally admired and revered, his style of behaviour would often be indecorous. Thus, one day he treated us to the story of the first human conflict over land:

> Būni Ādam [Our Father Adam, the first man] and Sīdī Ibrahīm [St. Abraham] had decided to try and terminate their continuous fighting over land by erecting a boundary stone. But scarcely had the stone been placed when the two started fighting again, and while wrestling and rolling over the ground, Būni Ādam surreptitiously kicked the stone to a more advantageous position.

And without interrupting the flow of his story, the near-octogenarian epitome of wisdom suddenly lay down on the dusty ground and laughingly imitated the kicking action of our common ancestor.

Offset against this secular ideal of the elder-as-wise is the wise person whose claim to wisdom resides in that person's exceptionally intimate links with the sacred and supernatural: in the first place, the warden (الوكيل *al-ukīl*) of the major domed local shrine(s); and, secondly, the invisible deceased saint himself or herself, alleged to be buried in that shrine and the object of an intensive cult of invocations, sacrifices, pilgrimages, and ecstatic dances, all justified by the stereotypified account of that saint's life as a path to sanctity and to public recognition of that sanctity. In this time-honoured world of popular Islam in the late 1960s (not yet affected by the general, dramatic shift towards formal Islam following the 1979 Iranian revolution, the oil crises of the 1970s, and the subsequent international rise of modern Islamism), the saint was considered to display some (certainly not all) of the characteristics of a pious adherent of formal Islam (notably the prayer five times a day – even to the local peasants, such a simple observance of a general Islamic prescription was already an uncommon, unprecedented sign of piety; pilgrimage to Mecca [الحج *al-hajj*] was not even contemplated as a saintly characteristic), but especially the display of miracle signs (الكرمات *al-karamāt*) such as stone balls, birds (as celestial messengers) alighting on his shoulders, the power to protect the cattle entrusted to him as a herdsman even if he took a nap, or the power to bestow fertility on barren women. These all constituted signs of special blessing deriving from an exceptionally close relationship with الله/ Allah.

The two categories of wisdom, elder and saint, would not be strictly separated. Secular elders would be considered to bestow blessing hence healing, whereas shrine wardens would also engage (not always successfully) in conflict regulation and marital arrangements. In a society that still vividly remembered having been torn, as recently as the beginning of the twentieth century, by frequent and life-threatening violent conflict, the religious wise, however, would be strictly pacifist (they could afford to be so because they were considered to be sacrosanct, untouchably protected by the invisible saints they were serving) and, moreover, characterized by a quality called النيه *al-nīya*: a simpleton piety bordering on naïve madness.

Finally, beyond these roles occupied by insiders belonging to the local community and local kin groups, there were outsider roles dispensing sacred wisdom: (1) the principal (الشاوش *al-shawush*) of the Qadiri lodge situated, since the late nineteenth century, on the other side of the mountain range of ᶜAin Fellus in the adjacent valley; (2) the soothsayers (التكازة *tekeza*) who, with adulterated cleromantic techniques that had circulated for centuries in the world of Islam, offered villagers a momentary private refuge for the expression of their problems at the distant, segmentarily neutral market of the district's capital عين دراهم ᶜAin Drāham; and (3) the Qur'ānic teacher (لمدب *meddeb*), whose privileged position of being literate had allowed him, a stranger, to take up residence in the valley and teach the local children the rudiments of reading in his ramshackle private school – but who besides dabbled in divination and other forms of magic with the help of gross, mass-produced magical books that were available in every bookshop, but which inspired the villagers with a sense of religious awe. Although as ancestors the saints' characteristics as locals had to be stressed (only locals could make legitimate claims to local land), the general understanding was that, as representatives and bringers of formal Islam (soon to relapse into popular forms), the saints had to have come from far away: for example, from Kairwan or Sequiat al-Hamra in Mauretania.

The Nkoya of South Central Africa (Rural West and Urban Zambia)

ETHNOGRAPHIC SUMMARY

Among the Nkoya of Zambia (South Central Africa), my research has concentrated on ecstatic healing cults (rather in continuation of the research line on trance and mediumship I had started in North Africa), kingship, and (as an indispensable key to these two topics) the details of a complex kinship system and a regional settlement history over an area larger than my (admittedly small) home country, the Netherlands.[14] This time, leaders in the major ecstatic cults were no longer "informants" but my close fictive kinsmen, and my association with them was to last from early 1972 to today; in the process, I became an effective member[15] of several villages and kin groups, adoptive member of a royal family, sponsor of ecstatic ritual, and (after my apprenticeship in Botswana) even an active local diviner and healer. I edited and published in both Nkoya and English *Likota lya Bankoya* (the standard Nkoya ethnohistory, compiled in the 1950s by Rev. Jehosophat Shimunika, the first Nkoya Christian pastor) and played a certain role in the Nkoya's remarkable ethnic resilience over the decades. I have internalized Nkoya language, culture, and society to a much greater extent, and over a much longer time, than I have the Ḫumiri equivalents. Although the Nkoya are small-scale agriculturalists, the main identity, especially of the Eastern group (Mashasha) on whom I have concentrated, is that of hunters, and their ties with the land are limited and shifting. The Nkoya setting entirely lacked the idea of a sacralized landscape as the main vehicle of wisdom, as it was among the Ḫumiris (and among the Manjacos of Guinea Bissau, where I did fieldwork between 1981 and 1983). Nkoya society even had a trait that struck me as utter unwisdom in the first place: the framing of *all* primary relationships in the kin group and the local community in terms of an idiom of potential sorcery – with the attending actual magical practices of sorcery and the incessant suspicion of sorcery practices in others. The atmosphere of immense paranoia that this outlook generates (and from which I found it often impossible to distance myself as a fieldworker over the years) lends an edge of bitter doubt and disappointment to even the most intimate and trusted relationships.

However, in the several extensive discussions I have devoted to the Nkoya kinship system, I have identified sorcery, not as the "core" of the social process within Nkoya villages and kin groups (also extending into urban contexts) but as a vital "boundary condition," inside of which the unmistakable riches of care, reciprocity, transgenerational continuity, altruism, self-sacrifice, non-violence, unconditionality, and reticence would nonetheless thrive. Considering myself (in ways that are immaterial here) a lifelong victim of the North Atlantic kinship system in modern transition, I had from the beginning the greatest admiration for the Nkoya kin system, considering it a locus of great wisdom and also of personal comfort and signification. After a few decades of Nkoya research, I began to ask more fundamental questions: for example, I wondered if my initial impression was true that "transcendence" – the backbone, I would say, of the North Atlantic experience under Christianity and even further developed since early modern times – has no proper place in Nkoya life. Explicit thoughts on this point are scarcely verbalized by the Nkoya, so ethnographically reconstructing and rendering their wisdom is truly an application of the art of "capturing the ineffable."[16] Initially, I thought their worldview to be entirely immanent, incapable or unwilling to reach beyond the common limitations of the human existence, but, as I probed deeper into the question (van Binsbergen 2012c), I had to admit that their rituals, music, and dance indicated a profound desire to rise above the human condition; these elements of expressive culture turned out to amount to an affective spiritual technology to fulfil such desire and even (notably, in the *ushwana* name-inheritance ritual [van Binsbergen 1990b; In press (b)]) to defeat death, albeit only conceptually and ritually. In their ecstatic cults of the last hundred years, such as *Bituma*, *Moba*, *Mwendapanchi*, and other similar ones, impersonal spirits of alienness and contagion have come to largely replace the ancestral and royal spirits that – according to my painstaking ethnohistorical reconstructions – were locally considered to be in control of the lifeworld until late precolonial times. The Nkoya know a creator god, Nyambi,[17] but Nyambi's gender is undetermined (the Nkoya language knows no gender). Nyambi is not, or scarcely any more,[18] the object of a cult and (except in the Christian context) is rarely prayed to or otherwise invoked. The deep forests (where, kilometres away from the village, big game used to be hunted – or poached, depending on who is speaking – until the 1980s) are considered to testify vocally to the creative presence, glory, and beauty of Nyambi and, moreover, are the haunts of a unilateral being Mwendanyangula (The One Whose Identity Is On High), often conceived as snake-like and difficult to distinguish from Nyambi. But, although they are thus both epiphanies of the sacred, in nearly half a century now, very few participants volunteered specific comments on their nature. A famous song in the royal orchestra's repertoire chides Nyambi as a clumsy creator, proving unable to prevent the speaker from falling in love with his sister (the standard mode of address between lovers being that of siblings). Mwendanjangula may happen upon you in the deepest forest, and, if you are the first to greet him, he will bestow great riches and healing powers upon you – but, in the opposite case, he will destroy you. For an iconographic study of a statuette representing, among other supernatural beings, Mwendanjangula, see van Binsbergen 2011e.

These Nkoya examples unproblematically remind us of millennia of North Atlantic/West Asian cultural traditions during which those regions have also associated the ineffable with epiphanies of the sacred (figures 18.6–18.9). One other peculiar way, however, in which the ineffable has manifested itself in the Nkoya context is in isolated enclaves of apparently concentrated and conventionalized meaning that no contemporary competent bearer of Nkoya culture manages to explain or translate any more. When editing the *Likota lya Bankoya*, I hit on many such instances, provisionally but lamely translated as, for example, "the snuffbox of Nyambi's child"; the personal names of royals, praise-names of kings, and names and epithets of clans (suggestive of a transformative element cosmology with catalysts – with parallels only in East Asia in the last few millennia) would offer many more instances. Having grappled with such elusive nuggets of meaning for decades, I finally resigned myself to the idea – admittedly anathema and politically incorrect to most modern Africanists – that (like much of the Nkoya musical and mythical repertoire) these cases represented substrate transcontinental borrowings, especially from South Asian Hindu and Buddhist contexts, once firmly established in South Central Africa

Figure 8.6 Do the rural cosmology and ritual practices constitute the principal referents of urban puberty rites? Coming-out dance of a girl (standing, left, with head scarf), escorted by her under-age second (standing, right, with bead scapular), under the encouraging eyes of her mentrix (centre, with beads in her hair), Mukunkike village, Kaoma, Zambia, 1978. (© Wim van Binsbergen)

Figure 8.7 Although the global economy is omnipresent (notice the enamel basin, petrol drums, plastic bucket, manufactured textiles, next to locally grown calabash containers), viable agricultural production, a selection of which is shown in the picture, continues to provide relevance to the ancient rural cosmology; Nkeyema, Kaoma District, Zambia, 1978. (© Wim van Binsbergen)

Figure 8.8 Seconded by her infant granddaughter, the white-robed *Bituma*-cult leader, my adoptive mother Mrs. Mayatilo Shiyowe, at the end of her sacred path and in front of her sacred pole hung with strings of white beads; Shumbanyama village, Kaoma District, 1973. Note the fly switch and the enamel container with sacrificial beer. Bringing a new, amoral (for guiltless) interpretation of misfortune, modern proto-globalization-inspired cults of affliction offer a practical wisdom enshrined in bodily movements, drumming rhythm, and songs. (© Wim van Binsbergen)

but long since expelled from conscious collective memory there (van Binsbergen 2012b, 2017: ch. 10; In press [b]) – and likewise expelled from conscious collective memory among the Southern African *sangoma* diviner-healers, on which my fieldwork was to concentrate subsequently.[19]

Graduating over the decades from an erring young fieldworker to a Nkoya elder and royal, guardian of a locally recognized treasure of historical and cultural knowledge, I may have succeeded somewhat in some of my writings to afford Nkoya wisdom the informal and largely tacit, yet central, place it has in its original context. One important way for the Nkoya to bring out and transmit implicit wisdom is by the teachings and admonitions of elders (*ku longesha*, for example, as part

Figure 8.9 Virtuality reigns at the Kazanga festival. A clerk of the district branch of the Department of Cultural Services, dressed up in the historic attire of the court jester (*kayoni ka Mwene*, the king's bird – a cosmogonic evocation), reminds uniformly dressed village girls to position themselves in a regular grid and to keep in line – spatial patterns without roots in any Nkoya rural situation. In the back, a poorly dressed chief's court official wields a tape recorder of ghetto blaster size, so as to record the dance troupe's song. Kazanga festival, Kaoma District, 1994. (© Wim van Binsbergen)

of the wedding ceremony and in girls' puberty training). My gradual incorporation into Nkoya life was marked by an increasing number of instances in which I myself have become the object of such admonitions, having failed to live up to common local standards of conduct in sexual, marital, and communicative matters and in anger management. Here, like in court cases, the emphasis is on verbal expressions, often with the aid of proverbs, so apparently the opposite of the ineffable – but the underlying principles and their cosmological anchorage remain hidden and can only be guessed at through introspection à la Turner and the Louvain School.

WISE PERSONS AMONG THE NKOYA

In Ḥumiriyya, notions of implied wisdom were to a considerable extent predicated on the presence of a Great Tradition that (under the heading of Islam) had commanded respect and religious authority for over a millennium, even though periodically sinking to a low ebb and even though much of the implied contents of that Great Tradition, as

Pelasgian, is likely to have predated Islam by two millennia. Among the Nkoya, however, such a Great Tradition was[20] apparently[21] absent – although, since the advent of Christian missionaries in the 1910s and local labour migrants' exposure to many varieties of Christianity in distant places of work from about 1860, Christianity has come to assume the quality of a recent and optional Great Tradition in the face of historic practices and representations of ancestral, royal, and ecstatic cults, which had continued virtually unabated.

Among the Nkoya, too, elders combined roles of productive management, healing, management of oral traditions and custom, and economic power – but invariably with a twist: no person would be called wise unless he or she was also surrounded by the connotations of witchcraft and sorcery that inevitably accrue to any exalted position (van Binsbergen 1981a, 2001). Rising above the crowd, in whatever respect, implicitly requires the magical powers to ward off the crowd's equalizing magical violence towards redistribution of scarce resources. The wise person is necessarily also a sorcerer, and mobilizing that person's specialist knowledge carries considerable risk from which only the white missionary, medical worker, administrator, or anthropologist are supposed to be exempt and immune.[22] The greatest achievement of my fieldwork (extending, intermittently, from 1972 to 2011) was not to learn the previously almost totally undocumented Nkoya language, culture, and social organization, nor to retrieve fragments of proto-historical knowledge otherwise lost forever, nor even to very gradually discover the hidden strands of transcontinental continuity in Nkoya culture and society, but, very simply, to be allowed to graduate from a white outsider immune to sorcery to an insider, adoptive kinsman and aristocrat, in other words, a *muntu*, locally considered to be subjected to the same cosmological categorization and supernatural forces as his hosts.

Given the local insistence on the ambivalence, the terror even, of wisdom, the idealized figure of the eminently wise exemplary person is virtually absent among the Nkoya, except in an alien, imported context of Christian biblical models (where Joseph, Solomon, and Jesus, among others, qualify as such). What, among the Nkoya, comes closest to global notions of wisdom is the art of managing productive and social relations, where there are hardly any binding, transcendent norms and values, so that all authority is based on capabilities of negotiation, persuasion, self-presentation, and impression management. Perhaps the firm direction yet loving care with which a mature woman teaches domestic, social, and sexual and reproductive matters to the non-kin girl who has been entrusted to her during the latter's puberty also comes close to global notions of wisdom. Among the Nkoya's regional neighbours, the Lunda, Luvale, Mbunda, and Chokwe, formal teaching of adolescent men on ontological, cosmological, historical, and reproductive matters has been locally contained within the formal initiation process of *Mukanda*,[23] but, among the Nkoya, *Mukanda* and the attending male genital mutilation were abolished in the early twentieth century.

In the second half of the twentieth century, some elderly headmen and leading women in puberty rites and cults of affliction could perhaps meet, among the Nkoya, the criteria of the "village sage" presented as a model of African wisdom by the Kenyan anthropologist/ philosopher Odera Oruka (1990; see also Mosima 2016). Beyond the paucity of explicit cosmological, ontological, mythical, and historical discourse at the village level, such sages would personally, originally, and idiosyncratically reflect on life, existence, God, evil, and death and sometimes informally share their ideas with their fellow villagers – but these sages would scarcely reap recognition for their insights and would rather acerbate the reputation as sorcerers, which would tend to adhere to their status and age anyway.

The Sangoma *Cult in Urban and Peri-Urban North East Botswana*

THE ETHNOGRAPHIC SETTING

I skip here my experiences, however instructive, as a fieldworker investigating local psychiatric healing methods among the Manjacos of Guinea Bissau (for relatively short periods in the years 1981, 1982, and 1983; see van Binsbergen 2017: 243–90) and immediately proceed to my third major fieldwork experience in the context of urban healing cults in modern Francistown, Botswana.[24] Although my research there was initially conceived in far more secular and sociological terms, my own specialist orientation as an anthropologist of religion, in combination with my professional network involving such colleagues as Richard Werbner, Terence Ranger, Inus Daneel, Matthew Schoffeleers, and Renaat Devisch;[25] with the vicissitudes of our urban experiences as a family (especially medical tribulations and the considerable ostracism to which we as whites were subjected in a local all-black residential area); and with the peculiar way in which traditional spiritual orientations had been forced to go underground in this globalized, commodified, South Africa–dominated boom town in North East Botswana, led me soon to concentrate on historic religious practices, especially the *sangoma* ecstatic ancestral cult.[26] Within a few years (1988–91), I graduated from being a distressed client seeking redress (in itself already scarcely a stance of hegemonic ethnographic detachment) to being an initiated, publicly qualified, certified, and even state-recognized ritual leader and diviner (figures 8.10–8.13).

Figure 8.10 *Sangomas* in action: The younger sister, Kwani, expresses her genuine surprise at the particular fall of the divination tablets from the hands of her elder sister, Molly; Monarch Township, Francistown, Botswana, 1988. Being our first encounter, this event must have been (although it was not disclosed to me until a year later) the moment when – with tremendous impact on my life and career – the oracle predicted my becoming a *sangoma* and identified me as the incarnation of these young women's great uncle, Johannes. (© Wim van Binsbergen)

Figure 8.11 Fellow *sangomas* supervise one of the principal acts marking Wim van Binsbergen's (left, squatting) final initiation as a *sangoma*: the sacrifice of a goat at the male ancestors' shrine in Matshelagabedi village, North East District, Botswana, 1991. (© Wim van Binsbergen)

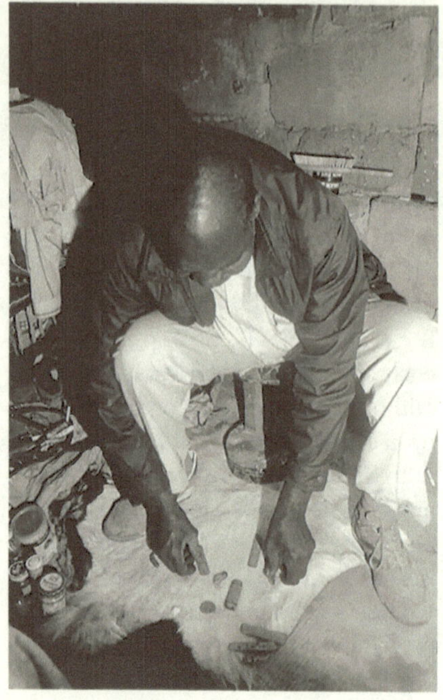

Figure 8.12 Operating under the smoke of Francistown's magnificent Nyangabgwe hospital, an urban diviner, in what is locally known as "his surgery," casts his divination tablets (ultimately derived from Arabian and Chinese geomancy, but entrenched in African localization since circa 1500 CE) in order to diagnose a case of suspected witchcraft. Somerset East squatment, Francistown, Botswana, 1989. (© Wim van Binsbergen)

Figure 8.13 Dr. Smarts Gumede's surgery, Francistown, Botswana, 1989. (© Wim van Binsbergen)

The wisdom proffered in the context of this cult – although much later found to border, as always perhaps, on unwisdom – included the possibilities and strategies of precognition, veridical divination, telekinesis, far-reaching healing capabilities, and the sense of being one of the very rare (roughly, one in a thousand) living people who had been elected by the ancestors to wield these powers among the living as sign of the ancestors' presence and of being elected by them. Learning to divine means spending weeks, even months, on end at the *sangomas'* lodge, practising every afternoon with one's fellow novices, until coherent readings and interpretations can be made of the successive falls of the oracular tablets[27] – readings out of which the learner can finally produce a convincing liberating and redressive verbal account of what is wrong with the client and what is to be done (in terms of ritual action, medicines, and other forms of redress, for example, taking a different name) to remedy the client's predicament.

This practice, in particular, is the local wisdom that I have propagated (van Binsbergen 2003a: ch. 7) in my writings and as a practising *sangoma* through face-to-face sessions with Africans and Europeans and through the internet, far outside its original cultural and linguistic niche in Southern Africa – while discovering, in the process, that that wisdom is far from originally Southern African but belongs to a very widespread family of geomantic divination systems, whose history and transmission I have since traced in several scholarly studies. However, divining and healing are part of a more comprehensive practice of caring for clients' existential problems, and there was a "bedside manner" to be learned, as well as performative self-presentation in dancing, ritual, sacrifice, and dress; the gathering, preparation, and administration of herbal medicine; and the intricacies of detecting the influence of the dead (and of sorcerers) in the vicissitudes of the lives of the living.

Even so, *sangoma*hood proved to be a wisdom with limitations. It allowed me to help others in their existential, social, or medical crises, but not myself. And the post-graduation token bonus that was extended to me by my spiritual leader, in the form of a big gold nugget,[28] did not survive a goldsmith's professional scrutiny – it turned out to be a pebble covered with gold paint. But the huge black bull my lodge leader had freely thrown in to add splendour to my graduation had been real, and priceless. I was taken by her to the Mwali cult's distant regional headquarters and there confirmed as an accomplished *sangoma*, even cloaked in a leopard skin, where most others had been refused and rejected. When I brought to bear my (fortunately unimpaired – or so it seemed) scientific methods of objectivity and statistics onto the results I was getting as a diviner, I could only admit that *sangoma*hood did enable me – very much to my surprise – to produce what my clients, and I myself, were persuaded to consider veridical divination, not just once but almost invariably in many dozens of cases![29]

WISE PERSONS IN THE CONTEXT OF THE *SANGOMA* CULT OF SOUTHERN AFRICA

Speaking related languages of the Bantu branch of the Niger-Congo linguistic macrophylum and sharing largely in the same proto-historic Bantu substrate cultural heritage, the urban, peri-urban, and rural communities in North East Botswana, which I have studied since 1988, displayed, as far as wisdom is concerned, a pattern rather reminiscent of the Nkoya. Moreover, both regions have undergone substantial Asian influence in the most recent millennia – as has all of South Central and Southern Africa. Also, among the *sangomas*, the culturally constructed ambivalence of power and knowledge meant that every diviner-healer-priest, while offering insights into clients' life and the manifestations of ancestors and evil forces therein, was at the same time inevitably a specialist in evil, destruction, and sorcery. *Sangomas* would periodically stage collective manifestations outside their lodges (typically situated in the midst of densely populated urban neighbourhoods) and, when doing so, would make a point of inspiring supernatural fear with their black cloaks, fly-switches, drumming, intimidating gaze, dancing, and singing. For their non-initiated neighbours, the *sangomas'* wisdom in divination and healing, although often considered indispensable, was only applied to as a last resort, and the worst that could happen to a family was to see one of their children elected to the status of apprentice *sangoma* as a necessary stage in the course of ancestral healing of very serious cases of affliction. At the remote Nata lodge in Central Botswana – the national branch of the Mwali cult, whose headquarters are in the Matopos Hills in neighbouring Zimbabwe – the high priest had to confirm, in a personal ritual at the High God shrine he administered, the final initiation of all new *sangomas* (and of all African independent church leaders too, for that matter). Some leading *sangomas* were (without in the least being defrocked) debarred from entering the shrine, because these leaders were generally known to engage in ritual murder towards the preparation of success medicine for the benefit of their affluent and politically active clients. Unmistakably, the leering, cunning voice of the High God, which those admitted could hear making elaborate and articulate pronouncements at the shrine in an obsolete Shona dialect, was that of the high priest himself, who was an immigrant from Ilaland, Zambia – the eastern neighbours of the Nkoya and, in many respects, hardly distinguishable from the latter.

Let us proceed from these obvious performative aspects of the *sangomas'* public presentation (an element continually stressed in *sangoma* training at the lodges) to their common public perception as being wise. There are only feeble indications that wisdom was attributed to them locally as a genuine *emic* category. Southern African dictionaries, written by specialists on the basis of many years of global formal education and therefore somewhat to be mistrusted as renderings of local non-specialist thought, tend to present lexical items to be translated as "wisdom," for example, *botlhale, tlhalefô* (Tswana; Matumo 1993: 643); *uchenjeri, ungwaru* (Shona; Hannan 1974: 933). For the clients, the *sangomas'* wisdom consists in the ability "to see one's life," to weave – out of scraps of private (and usually not consciously disclosed) biographical data whose accuracy only the client can assess and affirm – a detailed meaningful story naming specific circumstances, victims, and perpetrators, thus casting light on what hitherto were diffuse troubling factors in life and linking the perceived misfortune of the past and the present to a brighter, redeemed near future, with specific ritual action stipulated by the *sangoma* as the nexus between troubled past and bright, redeemed future. For the clients, this ability springs from the *sangomas'* link (privileged, immediate, and periodically renewed through offerings, trance ritual, and dreams) with ancestors, both their own and the clients'. The *sangomas'* knowledge of sources of pollution, and of natural and sacrificial remedies for redress and healing, further reinforces their fame of wisdom. One of my teachers in the Francistown context, Mr. Smarts Gumede, though not a *sangoma* himself, was a herbalist who did not rely on trance but merely on cleromantic, geomantic divination; an aspect of his wisdom was that he engaged in herbalist research and experimentation, identifying and testing hitherto unrecognized medicinal herbs on the basis of thinking through their symbolic characteristics such as long and entangled stems or violent physical effects when ingested. A display of cunning and the presentation of arrogant authority in specialist-client interaction is part of the *sangomas'* public act; and, if the *sangomas* put these qualities to profitable use in secular activities, for example, the retail trade or a transport company, that usage is not held against them. Yet, perhaps their greatest claim to wisdom is the piety with which they go about representing the ancestors and empathically, compassionately, yet reticently revealing and redressing the hidden chains of connection in their clients' life. It took me years to realize and be able to prove the originally Buddhist strands in Southern African *sangoma*hood, but once perceived, their entire presence appeared in a milder, less entrepreneurial, and more spiritual light (van Binsbergen 1990a, 2003a: ch. 8; 2005b).

Having prepared the ground ethnographically with these three vignettes of wisdom, let us now discuss their possible implications for our collective project.

Discussion

Wisdom: Indigenous Emic Concept or Alien Etic Analytical Imposition?

By and large, our little survey of wisdom in three cultures where I did intensive and prolonged fieldwork over the decades suggests that, rather than being an indigenous *emic* concept (see title of this section) whose definitions and situational use in the local context might be traced from the local participants' explicit verbal statements and observed actions, wisdom in these three cultures turns out to be largely an externally imposed *etic* category, no doubt inspiring to the extent that it may highlight tendencies within the ethnographic data and may be conducive to cross-cultural comparison, but always remaining at the analytical *etic* level.

I suspect that this apparent state of affairs owes much to the fact that the three cultures in question are effectively, on the ritual and divinatory level, non-literate – the written word is not absent there, and there is some awareness of a distant Great Tradition of literate religion, yet established and transmitted sacred texts hardly play a manifest role.[30]

The Ḫumiri worldview appears to be largely continuous with a Neolithic, Pelasgian society based on early food production through rudimentary agriculture and animal husbandry; what I have perceived in my first fieldwork as "the wisdom of the landscape" is conceived within the scope of perennial productive and reproductive forces, to which later symbolic complexes (Phoenician/Carthaginian, Hellenistic, and Imperial Roman shrine cults; early Christianity; and Islam) have added an explicit, text-based superstructure. The latter now dominates the conceptualization but not the management and administration of wisdom.

The ambivalence of power, knowledge, and healing that is to be at the heart of any wisdom-orientated analysis of the Nkoya and *sangoma* situations is, on the one hand, the manifestation of a perennial and ubiquitous characteristic of the sacred as inherently ambivalent (recognized and emphasized by such early theoreticians of the sacred as Durkheim and Otto[31]), but, on the other hand, reveals a widespread worldview (an attempt to trace its global manifestations was made in my *Before the Presocratics* [van Binsbergen 2012a]) that is largely immanentalist, amoral, and cyclical and has managed to stay aloof from the tendency (so marked in literate world religions) towards firm categorization and transcendence. Once again, I revert to my view already stressed in my earlier writings on wisdom, transcendence, and evil: that these concepts are largely predicated upon the literate traditions of the interrelated world religions of the last few millennia (with transcendence in part[32] a by-product of textuality – the text as a means to think beyond the chaotic, boundary-effacing here and now), and therefore, while inspiring and reminding us of the literate, transcendent thrust of our own North Atlantic and Asian cultural backgrounds, these concepts should not be allowed to pose as cultural universals.

Let us stop a moment to ask why so much that is assumed to be self-evidently expressible in speech and writing in North Atlantic society today, and *a fortiori* in anthropological discourse, is not so expressed in many of the societies we study. Several reasons combine here:

- *Cosmological reasons.* The lifeworld that is reality within a specific culture in space and time is largely constructed, maintained, and transmitted to new generations and to adult newcomers by non-verbal means: gestures, artefacts, rites, and symbols inscribed onto the body both consciously – for example, genital mutilation – and subconsciously; the underlying concepts are not so much absent but mostly remain implied; it requires local "sages" (see Odera Oruka 1990) to try and articulate them and to develop a (personal and idiosyncratic) discourse about them – such sages are by definition few and far between and their pronouncements idiosyncratic.
- *Non-verbality consciously associated with a social category or consciously prompted by the specifics of time and place.* In much of Bantu-speaking Africa, children before formal initiation/maturity have no right to talk about sexuality in any form; before a king, one cannot speak of death nor greet or address him at night; one cannot call one's spouse by the latter's given name, even though the latter is commonly, publicly known; some words cannot be said at night; some not by women; some not by members of a specific clan; and so forth. The ineffable is not only part of the local cosmological construction but is also a product of the explicit local production and regulation of social categories, their interaction, and the rules and prohibitions governing such interaction. Early travellers, missionaries, and administrators writing about local cultures outside the North Atlantic must have remained unaware of the verbal taboos involved, condescendingly and even racistically

attributing the non-response they met with to the local people's ignorance and impaired mental faculties.

- *The comparatively exceptional verbality of the North Atlantic tradition.* This tradition of verbality, and *a fortiori* its academic subculture, would make it most likely that the central position which writing, the state, proto-science, and organized relation have accorded to Western verbal expression for five millennia has no counterparts in most of the societies anthropologists study.
- *The ineffable as a result of cultural amnesia.* The ineffable from this source, notably vis-à-vis substrate cultural layers no longer consciously perceived by the participants (or actively censored out of overt expression in the light of socio-political pressures), has already been briefly discussed earlier.
- *Religious reasons.* The ineffable is commonly (perhaps globally and universally?) associated with epiphanies of the sacred, which tend to be heavily restricted, tabooed.[33]
- *Cultural contents programmed deeply and near universally in humans.* Finally, it cannot be a priori ruled out – although the idea runs counter to anthropology's standard conception of culture (Tylor 1871) as everything that is learned, retained, and transmitted through conscious, overt, sensorily based communicative learning mechanisms – that some cultural contents (primary bodily responses, emotions and what triggers them – see Devisch 1987 – perhaps also basic models of relationships and basic myths)[34] are programmed so deeply and so near universally in humans that it is in the most literal sense beyond the reach of the words of the participants' themselves and thus also cannot be directly and reliably captured in ethnography.

If it is therefore rather difficult to encounter and recognize the wisdom of our hosts in societies outside the North Atlantic region, could we say that this other region, in engendering ethnography and its methods, has developed a methodologically underpinned strategy to solve at least some of the problems just listed concerning the limited articulation of wisdom? This question is the one to which we now turn.

Ethnography as the Art of Articulating and Transmitting the Ineffable

In all three situations evoked earlier, Ḫumiriyya, the Nkoya, and the Botswana *sangomas*, the ineffable in fieldwork manifested itself in the first place by the near-total absence of "subtitles": the local actors were scarcely structuring their society and reality in terms of explicit verbalizations, and I had the greatest difficulty (especially during my first fieldwork) generating texts that seemed to fit their practice and experience and were manifestly grounded in their own recorded verbal utterances.

I began to understand why, as already alluded to, in his analysis of ritual symbolism Victor Turner (doing research among the Ndembu Lunda, who are closely related in culture and language to the Nkoya) had to rely so much on his own introspection, on reading between the lines of a non-existent text, and could hardly rely (as would have been sound ethnographic practice) on recorded utterances from his informants. Also, the Louvain School, Belgium, mainly researching the northern extensions of the Lunda complex of Central Africa, worked largely on the same principles and the ethnographic method of "speaking like a Yaka" (Devisch 1984) – where a fieldworker would produce ethnographic pronouncements in the vernacular based on the local linguistic and cultural knowledge gathered and internalized – much like a non-native speaker may teach the language he has acquired as an adult; by the Louvain School, such pronouncements have been considered neither artefacts nor anathema (as many other anthropologists would consider them to be), but privileged self-evident knowledge.

Among the *sangomas*, similar handicaps attended the fieldwork – even though by that time I had already graduated from being an ethnographer, looking for data and desperately, publicly wielding my little notebook in formal interviews, to being an apprentice unobtrusively seeking spiritual enlightenment and spiritual techniques including four-tablet divination. There was never any explicit elaboration of the underlying principles of the ancestral cult, nor of the fixed and named interpretations associated with each of the sixteen (2^4) basic divination configurations in which the four tablets (each differently marked on one site) could fall – the spiritual leader's non-subtitled mere example was supposed to suffice. This model for knowledge transmission bewildered me until, in the course of my subsequent explorations into Asian proto-historic influences on Africa and my short spells of actual fieldwork in South Asia and South-East Africa, I recognized that it was very much the model of the आश्रम *aśram* – one of the many jigsaw pieces of Asian-African continuities gradually falling into place, ill-prepared though I was for them as an Africanist. More recently, I have even been able to identify the very considerable South Asian strands in Nkoya society, culture, and occasionally even language, but I have only partially addressed (van Binsbergen 2017: ch. 10, 361–412; and In press [b]) the question as to what such South Asian influence means for Nkoya wisdom.

The shadow – or should I say, the invitation? – of the ineffable hangs over the entire practice of ethnography, especially in the classic extended fieldwork–based form,[35] which this form of intellectual production acquired from the 1930s on (at least in Europe; in the United States, the Boasian School reached this point somewhat earlier). As stated in my introduction to the present argument, anthropology is a verbal, textual practice, projected onto human phenomena that are often not, or scarcely, verbal or textual. A central tension derives from the contradiction between

1 the prolonged, day-to-day practice of *fieldwork as near-total social, cultural, and linguistic immersion in a local community* (when the acquisition of discursive, cognitive, and distancing insights in that local situation is constantly accompanied and guided by a process of social control: the fieldworker publicly displays emulations of local practices, including speech acts, which are noticeably approved or disproved by the fieldwork hosts to the extent to which these emulations give signs of the fieldworker having absorbed and taking into account, or having ignored and rejected, the collective representations and tacit conventions that, in that community, produce the self-evident lifeworld – in other words, constitute reality as the ineffable); and
2 the violent distancing from this day-to-day intercultural interaction; its patterns of obligation, reciprocity, and identification; its displays of submission to locally publicly shared representations, values, and beliefs *in the process of the construction of ethnographic text*, which is meant for academic circulation outside the host community and is structured by conventions (including choice of language, conceptual apparatus, and stylistic register) totally alien to the host community and, in the first place, conducive to career objectives and ulterior existential concerns likewise alien to the host community.

My childhood experiences had served to free me from excessive chauvinistic identification with the North West European society and languages in which I was reared; I was a published poet before I became a successful anthropologist; and it was thanks to the exhortations by my gifted and generous teachers of anthropology in the 1960s,[36] and the patience and loving understanding of my spouses and children as fieldwork companions, that I have generally tried to conduct my fieldwork in such a way as to let the locally ineffable seep in with maximum effect while in the field and to salvage as much as possible from that ineffable content in my subsequent discursive, anthropological writing. When the conventions of academic ethnography initially seemed to thwart that intention, I used poetry, short stories (notably *Zusters dochters*), a novel (for example, *Een Buik Openen*, on my North African fieldwork),[37] photography, and, more recently, video[38] as media. And, failing all that, I have eagerly and wholeheartedly adopted locally available statuses and roles to internalize experience and to pay homage to the ineffable I was encountering in fieldwork. Thus, I have been privileged to become (albeit only occasionally)[39] a North African ecstatic faqir dancing to the honour of the deceased local saint Sidi Mḥammad; a Zambian adopted royal; and a Botswana *sangoma* diviner-healer. These identities – among other ones – I have kept up over the decades as sources of anchorage, identification, and inspiration in the midst of my North Atlantic urban existence and as sites of introspection-based ethnographic experiment and increasing understanding.

The Cultural Boundedness of Truth and Its Proliferation Today

The collective representations being generated within a specific local context of language and culture are, in the most literal sense, "world-creating": they install the local self-evidences based on which sense phenomena and human utterances become endowed with local meaning. They are therefore the criteria for the generation and evaluation of truth. There is a cherished (though, since the work of Gettier, somewhat dated and to be amended)[40] definition of knowledge as "justified true belief." In our present context, we may take the implied step to the extent that wisdom is eminent, sublime truth. Justification of knowledge, and its assessment as being true, may take place on the basis of strictly formal criteria from logic and mathematics; or, again, on the basis of the unquestioned authority attributed to the person mediating the knowledge in question; yet, in all cases, *real justification and truth must be locally acknowledged and felt to be justified* – in other words, *must be culturally supported in terms of the local self-evidences*. Hence, truth is inherently tied to local cultural domains and, in principle, cannot simply be affirmed or verified outside the affirmer's or verifier's own truth domain, that is, outside the latter's culture and language.

From a viewpoint of interculturality, this conclusion is a most depressing thought. The idea of one global truth for all of humankind is evidently naïve and has been, for millennia now, a source of much conflict and violence. Eminently typical especially of our contemporary, globalized world is the fragmentation of myriad truth domains ("truth enclaves," we might call them) and the increasingly complex, intolerant, and violent struggle between their respective representatives, who tend to be driven by a nostalgic, essentialist assumption of one all-embracing, all-overriding truth. While we may easily identify incomplete globalization (the shattering of local cultural horizons and the microcosms contained within them, but failure, as yet, to arrive at an integrated world culture) as the cause of such fragmentation, the relativism that, since the middle of the twentieth century, has been anthropology's main contribution to this debate is not a convincing way out. For whatever the promises of relativism as a theoretical tool, at the level of the thinker's and actor's existence, the inevitable self-evidences she or he lives by in a more or less coherent and meaningful world are inevitably surrounded by a halo of utter and non-negotiable truth – *of relativism-defeating self-evidence*. By the same token, even the formal criteria such as logic and mathematics are peculiar to specific truth enclaves only (notably those of North Atlantic/global specialist academic life) and need not be considered universal.[41]

The challenge of wisdom-seeking approaches in our time and age is therefore to both (1) affirm the local truth of the self-evidences constituting local cultural domains; and (2) find a way to negotiate these local truths into a wider context, where they simply cannot be the whole truth and nothing but the truth, yet may be allowed to contribute their modicum of fragmentary truth to the knowledge heritage of humankind as a whole.

I was educated half a century ago as a specialist in the anthropology of religion, which then was dominated by Durkheim's work. Here, the solution was very simple – so simple as to be both hegemonic and impotent. All religion was supposed to be a figment of the imagination; its truth claims were (half a century after Feuerbach's [1945] deconstruction of Christian religion in 1841 and a few decades after Nietzsche's [1973] proclamation of the death of God in 1882) only to be dismissed, and instead we were facing an interesting charade of the "social" imposing its authority "through man-made but divinized symbols." Much of my work in the anthropology of religion (see van Binsbergen 2017) followed Durkheim's inspiration, but was increasingly intended to expose the dismissive hegemonic claims accrued to it and to formulate an alternative. In fieldwork, I had come into contact – repeatedly, intensely, and in a handful of cultural and linguistic settings rather different from one another – with local religiously generated truths, which I allowed to spill over, eclectically and situationally, into the many non-scientific, non-academic aspects of my life, even if these truths turned out to work havoc, initially had a bewildering effect on my marriage, risked destroying my colleagues' respect for me, and militated against each other. I felt[42] that supporting these truths was, in the last analysis, nothing but remaining faithful to the field hosts' expectations of sociability and reciprocity engendered and utilized in my fieldwork. Religion, then, is not so much about cosmological and metaphysical truths, but about local groups constituting themselves through basically arbitrary symbols and offering their members the protection and self-esteem of belonging (this view is still very much Durkheim). Denouncing these truths would be only too easy, but it would require excessive reliance on one truth enclave (that of North Atlantic/Aristotelian binary logic, global natural science) and thus would separate us from the majority of humankind; at the same time, such denouncing would amount to social distancing ourselves from those holding these truths – and, if these were truths acquired in classic anthropological fieldwork, would amount to betrayal of the expectations and practices of sociability via which these truths were transmitted and acquired by the fieldworker in the first place. On the other hand, affirming these truths would put one at the charmed level of the simple believer – and would, at the same time, risk academic and intellectual suicide.

I have arrived at the view that a wisdom approach can offer a way out of these tantalizing dilemmas, which, beyond the academic ivory tower, dominate our time and age in that they inform the very real and increasingly violent struggles on the ground between the North Atlantic cultural, intellectual, economic, and military status quo and their defiance by militant Islamism and other forms of fundamentalism (including the belief in intelligent design, creationism, the market, racism, and so forth). The way out seems to be as follows: instead of the common-sense conception of binary logic, which – built around the principle of the "excluded third," in other words, "you cannot have your cake and eat it too" – has dominated Western thinking about truth ever since Aristotle, we need a different (more kaleidoscopic, situational, and oscillating) conception of truth and a different ontology – a different conception of how reality is constituted and how we may situate ourselves in reality.

It is considered absurd to leave open the possibility that existence – in other words, "being" – does not exclude the possibility of "not-being."[43] Still, both ontological modes appear as complementary in many cosmogonies – while the oscillation between invisible beings ("non-being" or "not-yet-being") to which tangible effects are yet attributed ("being") is at the heart of all religious imagination and practice, and of all cosmogony.

Part of the promise of wisdom as a focus is that "truth enclaves" may, after all, turn out not to be totally local and disparate; rather, a form of relevance may be found across several such enclaves. This idea certainly smacks of New Age and would not sit well in an academic environment. Yet, if we could spell out the conditions under which the truth of one truth enclave could be received and admitted to be somewhat relevant in another truth enclave, it would mean that we would have found truth that does not just apply to one language and one culture but that (after selection and transformation) may be shared by larger sections of humankind, perhaps by humankind as a whole. A solution on this point would also take us beyond the facile relativism that is anthropology's principal stock-in-trade: for some local truth will turn out to be capable of generalization, even universalization. But, here again, there would be a constant oscillation, in my experience at least, between two extreme conditions: (1) truth that can be subjectively recognized and affirmed; and (2) the same truth subjectively evaporating into untruth.

The dilemma of wisdom is that we typically find such truths "outside" what is culturally and linguistically familiar to us from childhood, so these truths are almost inherently condemned to be non-truth, too, at the same time.

Does not this thinking explode the kind of truth that is being generated by supposedly universal, rational, and objective "science"? Such scientific truth is very much based on complex applications of chains of binary logic, and this epistemic foundation seems to guarantee that what is true in one part of the world and one period is still true in others. Here, the impossibility of substantiating Einstein in the Nkoya language remains pertinent. Yet, the airplane based on sound principles of aerodynamics and engineering does not just fly properly over the part of the world where modern natural science is accepted and dominant, but continues to do so over other parts of the world where the global/North Atlantic natural sciences are less known and less accepted. There is a big problem here to be considered. Is science just another truth enclave from a cultural-relativist perspective at a par with the others – with African systems of magic and divination, with Indian tantra, with a Native American spirit quest? Is it, to use Sandra Harding's (1997; see also van Binsbergen 2007b, 2015b) provocative (and ultimately, though reluctantly, rejected by herself) expression, just an "ethnoscience"? Or can it, contrary to these local truths enclaves, lay truth claims that are more comprehensive – that are, in fact, universal? And that are "free" from the otherwise so common oscillation to and fro between truth and non-truth? Is the discovery of such generalizable, metacultural wise truths not the real goal of science, beyond its present North Atlantic ethnocentric complacency?

Most scientists have no time (nor the epistemological background) to grapple with these kinds of questions. They would simply assume unrivalled universality for what they produce as science – unhindered by the high probability that their science of today will be the superstition or pseudoscience of tomorrow. Let us not forget that once, four thousand years ago, in ancient Mesopotamia, extispicy (divination by reading a sheep's liver) and astrology (making predictions based on the apparent positions of celestial bodies as seen in heaven) constituted the first proto-sciences. Yet, today (although astrology was taught in the West at the university level well into the Enlightenment, that is, the eighteenth century CE) these two sciences are no longer recognized as being scientific and are widely held to be pseudosciences (Popper 1959). Modern science, and most epistemologists, are satisfied that natural laws apply invariably, universally, and timelessly (in the sense that they are considered not to evolve or change, not even over gigantic stretches of time such as the fourteen billion years estimated to be the age of our present universe), and, as a result, miracles cannot exist. However, most defendants of science (especially its many popular, journalistic, and lay defendants) fail to take into account that the edges of the thinkable and the scientifically permissible have been stretched immensely with the revolution in physics through relativity theory and quantum mechanics a century ago to such an extent that precognition and prediction now seem to have acquired (notably in the field of "non-locality")[44] a scientific basis still inconceivable in the totally deterministic universe of the late nineteenth century CE. And, beyond such a theoretical basis "within" science, it is possible (at least "thinkable") that natural laws can be temporarily suspended – that scientific truths can also occasionally be seen to apply selectively and kaleidoscopically, and to sometimes oscillate towards being non-truths; or that natural laws do differ depending on the specific of space and time, and do evolve.

Let us consider the following statements as truth claims:

- Dead ancestors may actively and significantly intervene in the world of their still living descendants – a truth shared in many parts of the world including sub-Saharan Africa and China, but rejected in the North Atlantic, especially among the educated classes.
- Telepathy, telekinesis, and precognition exist to such an extent that it can be firmly demonstrated in the world of the senses (a widespread claim wherever divination is being practised by ritual specialists).

Is it possible that both these two statements are actually and literally true, although only within the truth enclaves where such claims are taken for granted and with a kind of truth that *cannot* intactly – that is, as truth – cross cultural and linguistic boundaries to a truth enclave of non-believers on these points? My extensive experiences and practice as a *sangoma* from 1990 onward have suggested to me (see van Binsbergen 2007a, In preparation [b]) the following tentative answer (which admittedly raises more questions than it can answer!):

> Ancestors do not in the least exist in the sense of autonomous entities capable of intervening in tangible reality; but, once a kin group has conceived that they do and once the group engages in the cult of such ancestors (notably under ritual leadership by a priest, diviner, *sangoma*, shaman, and the like), the ancestors' initial and essential virtuality[45] may oscillate, transform, into a real and tangible presence and power, which can then temporarily and situationally manifest itself in the empirical world.

I propose that a possible way out of the plurality and mutual incompatibility of truth enclaves is the assumption of the kaleidoscopic flip-flop nature of reality: "Now you see them, now you don't" (a common expression in Bantu languages for the "little people," whose existence many – but certainly not all, not, for example, on the British Isles – inhabitants of the North Atlantic region would deny). According to my difficult and drastic proposal, even statements that are held to be true, proven to be true ("Socrates is mortal") may yet be untrue under certain circumstances ("Yet, Socrates's name is still on everybody's lips 2,400 years after his alleged death"). Again, under what conditions can the truth claims of one specific truth enclave be true outside that enclave? Both always, and never. From here, it is only a small step to considering the nature of symbols: sometimes they unmistakable refer to and are determined by the referent they signify, but sometimes they are effectively independent from the referent and take on a life of their own. By the same token, beliefs may often appear to be merely erroneous and fantastic, but yet, sometimes they may reshape reality in such a way as to make these beliefs have a tangible effect on reality – for instance, when ancestors appear to be offering the paranormal information that makes veridical divination possible.

The last paragraph could pass as an example of whatever has remained ineffable in modern global scientific discourse – as forbidden scholarship[46] to end all scholarship. It sounds, admittedly, like the ravings of a lunatic, but, at the same time, it may begin to account for the subjective experience of billions of people in many parts of the world and during many periods. The creative, generative principle implicitly invoked here[47] would be the human mind, and the whole proposition again sourly smacks of New Age. Still, we may be tempted to think that, since we as self-reflective humans constitute one of the instances (so far, the only instance documented) in which the universe has become conscious of itself, it would not be unthinkable that the human mind, on our apparently insignificant and far from unique planet, may yet serve to funnel through, to mediate, the inconceivably immense creative and productive power of the universe (of God?) and thus may be a catalyst in sometimes achieving what we would not give credit for to humans out of their own limited capabilities.

> Though this be madness, yet there is method in't. (Shakespeare, *Hamlet*, 2.2)

Becoming a Spokesperson for (Apparently) Peripheral Wisdoms

Already, many years before thinking all these ideas through to the (admittedly, still shaky, far from conclusive) point summarized just now, and before articulating it in terms of a comparative wisdom discourse, I have made it a priority in my scholarly and literary work to seek to mediate, to a worldwide audience, the local wisdoms I have been privileged to encounter in fieldwork; mediating them, while admitting some of the attending theoretical, methodological, and political difficulties. This mediation I have sought to do, in the first place through ethnographic and intercultural-philosophical texts, but also through pictures, moving images, literary prose and poetry, and especially by repeatedly presenting myself as someone who, although a fairly successful North Atlantic scholar, yet embraces these wisdoms and considers them worthy of global circulation and appropriation. I have considered this stance an important one in the global politics of knowledge, accomplishing the following:

- affirming forms of knowledge that, given the hegemonic and sometimes even racialist (Harding 1993) tendencies of North Atlantic knowledge formation over the past few centuries, have tended to be pushed to the periphery, discarded even, by mainstream global scholarship as figments of the imagination, as mere ideology, as the "poor man's" thought of peripheral populations and peripheral continents;
- experimenting with, and affirming, the extent to which such peripheral knowledges are capable of being formulated in a

globally understandable form and thus are capable of contributing to the sum total of valuable human knowledge;

- affirming the extent to which knowledges that have been considered local and peripheral may, on closer scrutiny, turn out to be part of a widespread, even worldwide complex – so, even if we are most familiar with the European or North Atlantic manifestations of that complex, it does not mean these knowledges originated there in the first place;

  A standard example would be geomantic divination, which (with the probable exception of Oceania) has a practically global distribution today and, despite having been an important format of divination in Western and Southern Europe since medieval times, clearly was not of European but of West and East Asian, perhaps also African, origin (van Binsbergen 2012b, 2017: ch. 9, 329–60). But divination would not be the only example. Judaism, Christianity, and Islam are cases in point – emerging outside Europe, even though they have grown into major European/North Atlantic expressions in recent centuries. And I have suggested (van Binsbergen 2003a, 2015b: ch. 15; In preparation [b]) that my African colleagues, fellow *sangomas*, have discovered already centuries ago strands of the kind of non-locality effects that have only very recently been formulated in North Atlantic natural science.

- freeing the peripheral knowledges of Africans, Asians, inhabitants of the New World, and of Oceania from the unjustified burden of historic irrelevance and affirming their place among the uniquely valuable knowledge traditions of humankind.

This stance has granted me considerable recognition and esteem among my African colleagues and African intellectuals at large – while the expected punishment and ostracism on the part of my North Atlantic colleagues has been relatively moderate, although certainly not negligible.[48]

Yet, fundamental questions remain here. Can one transmit wisdom and at the same time retain it as a personal resource? Can wisdom be transmitted across cultural boundaries at all? Does not the format of language-based representation kill wisdom? The purpose of gatherings like the 2015 Pittsburgh one, and of the present collection, would be defeated if the answer were to be "no." Perhaps wisdom is not so much about contents, but about oscillating strategies of transmission and selective representation/acceptance/challenge; and not about the art of writing, but of listening attentively.[49]

NOTES

1 Compare Rorty 1989; Derrida 1967a, 1967b.
2 An important implication of my argument is that the representation of a local truth domain in a North Atlantic lingua franca and in terms of scholarly analytical categories entails a crucial imposition of a distortive and hegemonic nature. Merely in order to constantly remind the reader of this state of affairs, I have insisted on rendering, in my recent scholarly writing, local concepts and names in local scripts whenever in existence and whenever available to me. I am not much of a linguist, and such training as I have received in this field has been in general linguistics, hardly (with the exception of Greek and Arabic) in the specifics of the world's language families and their orthographies. My use of scripts from outside the present-day North Atlantic is likely to be wrought with orthographic errors. It is mainly an embellishment reminding the reader (who may also be assumed to be a non-specialist in the languages in question) of the immense distance between the North Atlantic/global scholarly rendering and what takes place in and among the original participants.
3 Much of this re-evaluation was explored in my extensive earlier work on wisdom: van Binsbergen 2008, 2009a, 2009b.
4 Of the extensive literature on the New Age movement, I mention Aldred 2000; Callewaert 2007; Hanegraaf 1996, 1999; Hunt and McMahon 1988; van Wersch 1990; Wood 2007; York 2003; Zinser 1987.
5 One of the striking developments in recent anthropology has been that theoretical inspiration is no longer exclusively generated from inside the discipline on the basis of the incessant critical revisiting of a corpus of classic texts (Durkheim, Frazer, Tylor, Boas, Malinowski, Evans-Pritchard, Radcliffe-Brown, Gluckman, and so on); instead, the half-digested texts of French philosophers, usually only cursorily read in ramshackle American translations, have been adopted as a new canon – a new scholastics exempted from critical and theoretical evaluation. This depiction is no doubt a caricature on my part and one that I have set out more elaborately (along with detailed discussions of selected post-structuralist philosophers) in van Binsbergen 2011b, 2015b.
6 Compare the writings by Devisch as cited in this argument's bibliography and de Boeck and Devisch 1994; de Boeck 1991a, 1991b, 1993; Stroeken 2000; Okere, Njoku, and Devisch 2005. I have repeatedly represented and assessed the Louvain School as a commendable and daring, yet risky, form of ethnography through introspection; see van Binsbergen 2017: n83; 2015b: 138, 363; 2003a: 516; and 1992a (more specifically on de Boeck).
7 Here we shall consider the relevant ethnographic settings in more detail. (1) My first fieldwork, Tunisia 1968, envisaged a detailed reconstruction

of the residential history of an Eastern Atlas valley and its many shrines over two centuries – in a peasant sociocultural context that was effectively illiterate and in which myriad fragments of ideologically manipulated and distorted oral-historical testimonies constituted my main data (van Binsbergen 1971, 1980a, 1980b, In preparation [a]). My subsequent projects aimed at (2) the reconstruction of late precolonial political and religious history in South Central Africa from circa 1500 CE onward (van Binsbergen 1981a, 1992b); (3) tracing the submerged and largely obliterated transcontinental influences that South Central African (and, more recently, West African) cultures have undergone from South East, South, and East Asia (van Binsbergen In press [b], In press [d]); (4) tracing the history of ancient Mesopotamian magic (van Binsbergen and Wiggermann 1999); (5) contributing to the *Black Athena* debate (van Binsbergen 1997a, 2011a) and, more specifically, exploring ethnicity in the Bronze Age Mediterranean, especially with a bid to identify the homeland(s) of the so-called Sea Peoples (van Binsbergen and Woudhuizen 2011); (6) tracing the genealogy and history of geomantic divination across the three continents of the Old World and linking it with the postulated substrate cosmology of the transformative cycle of elements which is even attested in the New World and appears to have Upper Palaeolithic antecedents (van Binsbergen 2012a). Finally, my boldest attempts at creating history where previously there was none have been (7) in reconstructing – inspired by the seminal work of Michael Witzel (2001, 2012) and often in direct conjunction with him – humankind's earliest intellectual history from the Middle Palaeolithic onward by bringing to bear the recently revived comparative mythology upon iconographies and other ancient symbolic patterns revealed to us by archaeology (van Binsbergen 2006a, 2006b, 2011d; van Binsbergen with Lacroix 2000).

8 On the relevance of the distinction between *emic* (in the local actors' conceptualizations) and *etic* (in imposed external alien conceptualizations, for example, those of North Atlantic/global science) for intercultural/transcultural analysis, see Headland, Pike, and Harris 1990; van Binsbergen 2003a: 22 f.

9 I shall forgo giving an overview here of the familiar recent literature on globalization; essential readings are cited in Robertson 1994, who also seems to have coined the term "glocalization"; see also van Binsbergen 2003a, 2015b, 2017 – the indexes will guide the reader to a relevant selection of the literature.

10 See van Binsbergen 1971, 1980a, 1980b, 1988, 2017: 49–115, and In preparation (a).

11 I am indebted to the Musée des Arts et des Traditions Populaires, Tunis, Tunisia; Muḥammad Suudi, who taught me elementary Arabic; my

untiring assistant Ḥasnāwi bin Ṭahar حسناوي طاهر بن; the people of the ᶜAtatfa šayẖdom, especially those of the villages of Sidi Mḥammad and Mayziyya; and Amsterdam University and specifically its Anthropological Sociological Centre, whose staff (led by Douwe Jongmans and Klaas van der Veen) organized the research training facility in whose context my Ḫumiri research was initially conducted, with follow-ups in 1970, 1979, and 2002. Apart from a small subsidy from Amsterdam University, this research was self-sponsored.

12 See van Binsbergen and Woudhuizen 2011; van Binsbergen 2011a, 2012a, 2017. In van Binsbergen In preparation (a), which is essentially a thorough revision of my 1971 text, I have inserted a new chapter discussing Ḫumiri religion as Pelasgian. This perspective is admittedly a possible source of confusion, for both in antiquity and in modern scholarship there has been a wide range of opinion as to what constitutes Pelasgian culture or language. Yet, the Pelasgian hypothesis allows us to appreciate Ḫumiri culture's continuity, not only with ancient Europe in the Neolithic and Bronze Ages (the Northern shore of the Mediterranean, the British Isles, the Baltic region) but also with West Asia including the Iranian Plateau – a distribution pattern sporadically extending all the way east to the South Asian peninsula, Bangladesh, China, Indonesia, the Pacific, and even the New World.

13 Besides these standard shrines acceptable to formal Islam, there were many more lesser shrines (مزارة *mzara*), mainly frequented by women. These were mostly megalithic structures dating from the Bronze Age, and I suspect the attending practices were largely so as well.

14 Extending from early 1972 to the present day, this research was initially (1972–4) self-sponsored, but subsequentlty (from 1977 on) adopted by the African Studies Centre, Leiden, the Netherlands; and (through the intercession of A.J.F. Köbben) by WOTRO, the tropical branch of the Netherlands Research Foundation. It was greatly facilitated by the unfailing support, over all these years, of my sometime research assistant and subsequently elder brother Mr. Dennis Shiyowe (now Mwene Shumbanyama) and his family; King Mwene Kahare Kabambi (my adoptive father), his successors, and his court; King Mwene Mutondo and his court, where I was nominated a sub-chief in 2011; in general, the Nkoya people of Kaoma District and of Lusaka, Zambia; Rev. Mary Nalishuwa and her family; Rev. Jehosophat Shimunika and his family; Dr. Stanford Mayowe; and a network of educated middle-class Nkoya people organized (since the early 1980s) within the Kazanga Cultural Society. Henny van Rijn and Patricia Saegerman shared the Nkoya fieldwork as my successive spouses, making essential contributions, as did our children. From among my numerous publications on the Nkoya, I may mention van Binsbergen

1979, 1981b, 1990b, 1992b, 1993, 2014, In press (b). A fairly complete list is available in the end bibliography of van Binsbergen In press (b).

15 To explain why, among the Nkoya, one is a "member" of a village rather than an inhabitant requires an extensive argument, which I have presented in my study of Mabombola village (van Binsbergen 2014); In press (b) incorporates the English version.

16 "Capturing the ineffable" was the subtitle of the 2015 Pittsburgh workshop convened by Alter and Kao.

17 This theonym, with minor phonological variations, is ubiquitous throughout West and Central Africa (van Binsbergen 2015b: 18–22, and passim). I have repeatedly suggested that this name (associated with solar/spider symbolism, but etymologically relegating to a Common Bantu root – *amb-*, to speak) is continuous with a series of female theonyms attested, since the Bronze Age, for a range of North African, West Asian, and South West European cultures, including, among others, Antinea, Neith, Athena, Anat, and Anahita, and associated with women's domestic tasks, especially spinning and weaving, but also with military prowess and weaponry.

18 Mutumba Mainga (1972) describes a rudimentary solar cult (centring on Nyambi) for the neighbouring Luyi/Lozi/Barotse, with reference to a precolonial period (eighteenth to nineteenth century CE) when these Western neighbours were still very close to the Nkoya, notably, speaking a closely related language, sharing a royal cult, a divination system, and so on. Traces of such a solar cult are found in *Likota lya Bankoya* (notably King Mwene Kayambila's dedication of his newborn child to the rising sun; *Likota lya Bankoya*, 25:1) and, in fact, survived in Nkoya rural practice in the 1970s. The latter's royal cult and court etiquette are still closely related to an (otherwise submerged) solar cult: the king is equated with the sun and cannot be venerated at night. There are many indications that the parallels with ancient Egypt are not merely typological but reveal genuine historical continuity (see van Binsbergen 2011c).

19 A few examples will suffice (van Binsbergen 2003a, 2017, and In press [b]): among Nkoya royals, personal names circulate that are unmistakably those of South Asian gods, such as Mangala (the planet Mars) and Skanda (war god and brother of Ganeša). Nkoya court culture, including gestures/stances and verbal expressions of respect, the format of court chronicles, and the dynastic numbering of royal incumbents, follows South Asian literate patterns. *Keye-keye*, one of the principal songs in the repertoire of the Nkoya royal orchestras, has an almost literal counterpart in a Buddhist text from Sri Lanka. Nkoya music in itself suggests many South Asian (and South East Asian) reminiscences (van Binsbergen 2015b: 159 ff.). A central *sangoma* hymn closely follows the *Lotus Sutra* of Buddhism, while (with a

surprising play on Bantu nominal prefixes) the High God Mwali has many features of Kali. The differential initiation rites of *sangomas* from various strata of Southern African society follow a caste pattern described in a classic South Asian text, *The Questions of King Milinda* (Rhys Davis 1988); and so forth. The South Asian connection may also go some way to explain the Mongolian (via the Moghul Empire) and Celtic strands I detected (van Binsbergen 2010) in Nkoya mythology, for example, the cauldron of kingship, stealing the moon, deadly royal sibling rivalry involving an artificial woman, but, by and large, I would consider these Pelasgian effects.

20 Although fieldwork continued until 2011, the ethnographic present of my Nkoya summary is primarily that of the 1970s, hence my occasional shift here to the past tense.

21 Apparently, because – as set out in a previous note – my research of the last two decades has brought to light many strands of hitherto secret, forgotten, or overlooked transcontinental cultural continuities (especially with Hinduism, Buddhism, and Taoism), which might well be interpreted in terms of an implicit, substrate Great Tradition. See van Binsbergen 2003a: ch. 8; 2012a; 2017: ch. 10, 361–412; and In press (b). In addition to these proto-historic influences dating from the first millenium BCE to the second millenium CE, Pelasgian diffusion might be considered, going back to West Asia and the Mediterranean region during the late Bronze Age and possibly accounting for the wide distribution of certain mythological and ritual themes, for example, male and female puberty rites, sun worship, and the abhorrence of pork (which, of course, could also be a trace of Islamic, Jewish, and Hindu Vishnuist influence). The difference between the Great Tradition in the contexts of Hinduism, Buddhism, and Islam and such a submerged, substrate postulated Great Tradition, apparently underlying considerable parts of Africa including Nkoyaland, is that the former is locally enshrined in written documents whereas the latter, being submerged and largely eclipsed from local consciousness, cannot explicitly be invoked by the participants to justify particular beliefs and actions.

22 The reasons for this exemption are not immediately clear. The standard explanation is that, cosmologically, whites (Nkoya: *bakuwa*), along with Arabs, Chinese, Indians, and other somatic/ethnic types sporadically spilling over the horizon into the Nkoya awareness, are not real "human beings" (designated *bantu* in Nkoya and in Common Bantu generally), but constitute an indeterminate and liminal freak category of animate beings somewhere between animals, evil spirits, and the supernatural. This language use (eponymous – Bleek 1851 – for the large Bantu-speaking linguistic cluster, which is at least a few millennia old) is certainly much older than the colonial period, which in Zambia only started in 1900 CE.

However, the ancient classification may subsequently have been redefined in light of the incomparably greater power of whites in the colonial period under the hegemony of the colonial state and the Christian church.

23 *Mukanda* is the regional name of the male puberty rite (including genital mutilation) among selected peoples in South Central Africa; until the advent of the twentieth century CE, the Nkoya overlapped with this cluster, from which they subsequently dissociated in the course of the twentieth century. For a detailed discussion of this process and its background, see van Binsbergen 1992b, 1993, where a selection of the extensive literature on the topic is also cited.

24 Largely at the instigation of Richard Werbner, my research in Francistown, North East District, Botswana, was initiated in early 1988, with one year of fieldwork 1988–9 and many subsequent follow-up visits. I am indebted to the African Studies Centre, Leiden, for research funding; to the Applied Research Units, Ministry of Local Government, Lands and Housing for providing a stimulating research context; to the people of Francistown and surrounding peri-urban and rural areas for welcoming me and my family; to MmaShakayile, MmaNdhlovu, and Mr. Smarts Gumede for extending their profound esoteric knowledge to me; and to Patricia Saegerman and our children for living through the first spell of fieldwork. The *sangoma* complex of Southern Africa has been the subject of an extensive scholarly literature, much of which is cited in my own relevant publications, including van Binsbergen 1990a, 1991, 1995, 1996, 2003a, 2015b: 179–88, 505, 518; 2017: 145–86.

25 See Werner 1973, 1989, 2015; Ranger 1968, 1972, 1975, 1979, 1985, 1999; Daneel 1970, 1971, 1974, 1988; Schoffeleers 1972a, 1972b, 1978, 1979, 1985, 1991, 1992; Devisch 1978, 1984, 1985, 1987, 1991, 1993, 2004, 2008; de Boeck and Devisch 1994.

26 In Botswana, the *sangoma* cult is considered a recent (twentieth century CE) introduction from South Africa and from Ndebele-speaking regions in Zimbabwe, but, in Southern Africa as a whole, the cult has a venerable history of at least several centuries, partly as a cult sustained by court priests. Ultimately shamanic and thus sharing in the global history of shamanism ever since the Upper Palaeolithic, its more specific origin may lie in Hindu and especially Buddhist practices in South Asia.

27 Already in 1561, the Roman Catholic missionary Father Gonçalo da Silveira SJ was condemned to death at the court of Monomotapa (the Shona ruler of a large part of today's Zimbabwe), only a few hundred kilometres from present-day Francistown, on the basis of the outcome of the very same four-tablet oracle. By an interesting parallel, the apostle of the Frisians, my Roman Catholic patron St. Willibrord, was also condemned (circa 700 CE) by a cleromantic oracle when accused

of sacrilege by his heathen royal host in an island north of Frisia, but subsequently acquitted.

28 Southern Africa, especially the Zimbabwe Plateau, has been a gold-producing and (transcontinentally) gold-exporting region for millennia, and the earliest South Asian cultic influences ultimately producing the *sangoma* cult are likely to have been in the context of Indian gold prospecting and trading. See van Binsbergen In press (d), especially the contributions by Thornton and by Hromnik.

29 However, this fact (or illusory appearance?) of producing veridical divination was only brought about under conditions of genuine bona fide practice, going through the prescribed motions in the prescribed ritual attire after proper ritual preparations, spontaneously and with a relaxed, open state of mind (although my panic-stricken awareness that the client could at any moment be disappointed by my furtive or non-existent divinatory powers was difficult to dispel). I could never *at will* produce specific results – but that is a common finding in research on the occult and the paranormal and the reason why objectifying experimental devices to test paranormal phenomena have invariably failed. I submit that the mechanism behind this phenomena is more or less the following: Wisdom, including the capability of performing veridical divination, consists in the acquired ability (not exactly learned overnight!) to let one's own human person effortlessly yet transformatively coincide with the structure of the universe. Compassion is an implied, though secondary, aspect of such connectedness. Rational thought, by contrast, consists in the demarcation and idiosyncratic articulation of one's own sense of self – the Cartesian *cogito ergo sum* (which, however, does not cover altered states of consciousness, when, for instance, the medium in trance exists whilst being temporarily unconscious of herself or himself; in *sangoma* circles the test of true ancestral trance – sometimes yet performatively faked – is precisely that the medium must have no conscious memory of acts and utterances made while in trance). My mind's rational self-affirmation juxtaposes, opposes, confronts, and commits to othering, everything that is not me, and thus rents the texture of, and my own being embedded in, universal connectedness on which paranormal phenomena including veridical divination depend. See Descartes 1984 (1637); Hintikka 1968; Williams 1968. In ways that I cannot go into now (but that I have discussed *in extenso* elsewhere: see van Binsbergen 2003b, 2004a, 2004b, 2012a, In press [d]; van Binsbergen and Woudhuizen 2011: 412–15), we here hit on, demonstrably, very old themes in the history of human thought: the slow but traceable emergence of the capability of affirming fundamental difference – in other words, the emerging capability of thinking binary opposition; the incredibly wide distribution in space and time, and the

equally incredible linguistic convergence, of granulation symbolism (for which the spotted leopard skin – my very own – the star-spangled night sky, rainfall, and plant seeds are near-global natural pointers), with smooth, unarticulated, unstructured continuous extension (as the lion's skin; as if untouched by human thought), set off against articulated, pinpointed, discontinuous speckledness (as if the latter brings out reality under the disruptive, separating impact of human thought). Related phenomena, perhaps prematurely canonized in specialist circles, have been the interpretation of patterns in rock art in psychedelic, trance-inducing terms (see Huffman 1983; Lewis-Williams 1985; Clottes and Lewis-Williams 1998); as well as the very widespread theme of therianthropy (see Jolly 2002; Parkington 2003; Hollmann 2005), where humans (often dressed in animal skins, including leopard skins – the first known case being circa 60 kilo annum before present; de Lumley 1972) impersonate animals in an implied mental play on identity/continuity/merging/binary opposition between humans and animals.

30 Only one exception comes to mind. When, after graduation, I was taken to Nata for final confirmation, I was at first sent back for I had not presented myself there in "the traditional attire of [my] people," a leopard skin. Francistown being a centre of skin tannery and wildlife trophies, this puzzling omission (which set me on the long trail of my subsequent leopard-skin research and the discovery of the South Asian strands in *sangoma*; van Binsbergen 2003a, 2003b, 2004a, 2004b, In press [a]) was remedied within a week, and during that liminal week I was told by the Nata high priest (a graduate of a Rhodesian/Zimbabwean minor seminary for the Roman Catholic priesthood) to recite, a few times a day, Psalm 121:

1 I will lift up mine eyes unto the hills, from whence cometh my help.
2 My help cometh from the LORD, which made heaven and earth.
3 He will not suffer thy foot to be moved: he that keepeth thee will not slumber.
4 Behold, he that keepeth Israel shall neither slumber nor sleep.
5 The LORD is thy keeper: the LORD is thy shade upon thy right hand.
6 The sun shall not smite thee by day, nor the moon by night.
7 The LORD shall preserve thee from all evil: he shall preserve thy soul.
8 The LORD shall preserve thy going out and thy coming in from this time forth, and even for evermore (Psalms 121:1–8).

31 See Durkheim 1912 (also Smith and Alexander 1996; van Binsbergen In press [c]).

32 But not totally so: the use of a more or less fixed and stable lexicon depends on the ability to refer, with a word, to what is not necessarily here and not necessarily now; this essentially transcendent quality is a

fundamental characteristic of all language, not just of text. Therefore, some diffuse form of transcendence is already implied in all human language.

33 Hence, the important tradition of negative theology in Western thought, concentrating on what *cannot* be said about the godhead, with an early expression in pseudo-Dionysius (1910 [fifth and sixth century CE]) and recently revived in post-structuralist philosophy (Derrida 1996, 2002; Bulhof and Ten Kate 1992; see also van Binsbergen 2005a).

34 See van Binsbergen 2015b: n557. Cultural drift – changes in culture due to chance fluctuations – is a commonly observed fact and one that makes us suspicious if we encounter claims of cultural constancy over long stretches of space or time: thousands of miles, tens of thousands of years. Yet, there is considerable evidence of very long-term cultural inertia in certain aspects of human culture, notably in the fields of comparative mythology, initiation rites, material culture (lithic industries remaining virtually unchanged for dozens of millennia, and so forth) and modes of production (notably hunting and gathering). Seldom can we identify the precise social institutions and communicative procedures bringing about such massive continuity – but time-honoured, highly sanctioned, and densely controlled central institutions such as puberty rites are likely to have served as repositories for cultural contents of very long standing (van Binsbergen 2011d). Such rites tend to have a secluded and secret character, therefore not only *transmitting* the ineffable but also *producing it in the first place.* Invoking, in addition, genetic factors to explain long-term cultural inertia (as Jung did – in a time and a discipline where the modern anthropological concept of culture had hardly yet penetrated) gives a biological twist to the ineffable, but probably without solid grounds.

35 The last three decades, under the influence of globalization, the rise of the internet, reduced budgets for prolonged fieldwork, and lessening awareness of the severe limitations of approaching a local lifeworld in one of the world's lingua francas (which, admittedly, have considerably gained in scope in that period – today one can somehow get by in English even in Indonesia, and France!), we have seen in many ways adulteration of the classic fieldwork model through a number of recent developments, including, *inter alia,* "multisited" approaches, internet searches, reliance on Big Data, commissioned applied research by unqualified researchers, and lessening recognition of the local cultural and linguistic specifics of communities and the need to approach them, unobtrusively and humbly, on their own terms. Many European candidates today seeking a doctorate on the basis of their ethnographic fieldwork in distant places have remained largely incompetent in the local language and the general culture of their host society. I suspect that the situation in the United States is not dramatically different. Needless to say, I greatly regret these

developments – as someone who, in the course of nearly half a century and at the cost of very considerable effort, medical risks, and existential commitment, has gained local cultural and linguistic competence in three or four local African settings and has ventured into a handful of Asian research sites in a more limited manner. This chapter, however, is not the place to engage in a critical discussion of this new mode of fieldwork. Suffice it to say that it is not only methodologically shallow, but also reinforces North Atlantic hegemony – as does so much in globalization.

36 Among whom I should mention, in the first place, Douwe Jongmans, André Köbben, and Klaas van der Veen. See Jongmans and Gutkind 1967; Köbben 1965; Jongmans and van der Veen 1968.

37 See van Binsbergen 1984, 1988.

38 See my personal channel at the video portal YouTube. My personal website http://www.quest-journal.net/shikanda, especially its weblog section http://www.quest-journal.net/shikanda/topicalities/topicali.htm, contains hundreds of photographs from my various research locations.

39 But, in a non-specialist sense, I and my family have continued to routinely observe, like local villages, the semi-annual cult of this saint for half a century.

40 See Gettier 1963 and subsequent discussions, including Conee 1988; Lehrer 1979; Moser 1992.

41 In my oral presentation at Pittsburgh, 2015, I gave at this point the example of vainly trying to substantiate Einstein's (1960) special and general theory of relativity, originally published in 1917, among the Nkoya, arguing that this theory could not possibly be made into "justified true belief" in Nkoya language and culture on the simple grounds that the conditions for justification (the specialized physics concepts of mass, velocity, and time and the particular mathematical procedures employed to compellingly relate these and other concepts) were absent there or (even if present in the minds of some Nkoya secondary school or university graduates) at least had not the slightest compelling validity in Nkoya society at large. The Pittsburgh audience of philologists and anthropologists (with no philosopher, mathematician, or physicist present, let alone any other African) readily misunderstood my point as denouncing the Nkoya's logical capabilities, as a hegemonic and ethnocentric statement. But such a reproach was unjustified, for I meant the very opposite: Einstein is made true on the basis of truth criteria that are justified in the North Atlantic/global academic natural science subculture, but they are not justified, not even justifiable, not even meaningful in Nkoya culture. Einstein is implicitly assumed to be universally applicable, but that in itself is a largely unwarranted hegemonic claim, largely (but not entirely; see

Harding 1997; van Binsbergen 2007b, 2015b) reflecting the North Atlantic region's dominance in the modern world.

42 This feeling arose from an intuitive application of what I later, as a philosopher, encountered as the "principle of charity" (Lepore 1992): "if this is what other people think and do, who am I to reject these thought and actions?"

43 By definition, it is the principle of the excluded third state: "where P, there not not-P." Where A is alive, there A is not dead. One of the most frequently cited thought experiments in quantum mechanics (though recently called into question), however, is that of Schrödinger's cat, where the state of a cat locked in a box, whose unlocking releases gas instantly lethal to the cat, remains undetermined between living or dead until the box is actually opened (Przibram 1967; Gribbin 1984). Another major source of inspiration away from binary logic would be post-structuralist philosophy, where Derrida's claim (also with reminiscences of Marxian dialectics) that everything carries inside itself its own opposite or negation appears to revive some of humankind's oldest forms of reasoning. A semantic exploration of the Borean lexicon (a language reconstruct supposed to have been spoken in Central to East Asia in the Upper Palaeolithic) brings out its frequent reliance on what I have called (van Binsbergen 2012a; van Binsbergen and Woudhuizen 2011) "range semantics" – where the meaning of a lexical item consists of the entire range from A to A's opposite, for example, the same word being used for both "white" and "black," "wet" and "dry," "light" and "dark," "vulva" and "penis," and so on.

44 In present-day thought, the concept of "non-locality" is used in two largely unrelated ways: (1) as the dissolution – under conditions of globalization – of locality as a central principle of social organization (see Appadurai 1995); and (2) as the theoretical implication of quantum mechanics (notably, the implication that renders veridical divination scientifically possible; see van Binsbergen 2013, 2015b: ch. 15, 505–18) to the effect that any object in the universe has an impact on any other object, instantaneous and unmitigated by physical distance (see Einstein, Tolman, and Podolsky 1931; Einstein, Podolsky, and Rosen 1935; Bell 1964; Walker 1977; Bohm and Hiley 1993; Aerts 1985; Nortmann 2008: 160 ff.). For the bold-hearted, non-locality is simply another word for God. This statement is not merely flippant, but also yet another example of how the wisdom discourse in some truth enclaves may well correspond, even coincide, with, for instance, scientific discourse in other truth enclaves – a pet New Age idea (see, for example, Capra 1978; Zukav 1979).

45 On the pivotal concept of virtuality, see van Binsbergen 1997b, 2015b, 1998.

46 By "forbidden scholarship," I am making an oblique reference to Cremo and Thompson's (1993) *Forbidden Archaeology*, arguing (on the basis of the Hindu cosmology of repetitive aeons) the presence of apparently man-made artefacts in terrestrial geological contexts predating the accepted appearance of humans by many millions, even several billions, of years. My book in progress, "Sangoma Science," is inter alia an attempt to deal with such impossible claims as Cremo and Thompson's or Edith Turner's (1993) as to "the reality of spirits." A trained nurse, and more recently the charismatic major force behind the journal *Anthropology of Consciousness*, Mrs. Turner is the life companion, co-fieldworker, co-author, and widow of the leading twentieth century anthropologist of religion Victor Turner.

47 This principle is invoked as a paroxysm of idealism: the claim that the mind creates the world in the most literal sense.

48 Thus, the first account of my own "becoming a *sangoma*" (van Binsbergen 1991; see also 1990a, 2017 for a less egocentric account of the same urban religious setting) was publicly ridiculed and dismissed in front of my long-standing colleagues in Africanist religious anthropology by the then convener of the annual Satterthwaite Colloquium on African Religion and Ritual, 1991; however, in the very same session, it was co-opted for publication in the authoritative *Journal of Religion in Africa*. A similarly negative experience, after I had much input at two preparatory conferences at Brussels (see Decouter et al. 2000), was my fate when I was excluded from a book on comprehensive approaches in science and scholarship, subsequently published by Aerts, D'Hooghe, and Note (2005). Also, within my home institution (the African Studies Centre, Leiden, the Netherlands, with which I have been associated since 1977, holding positions of leadership from 1980 to 2002), three of the last five years before my retirement were marred by similar exclusion, although this situation was subsequently redressed and I was made a life Honorary Fellow instead. On the other hand, my explorations into *sangoma*hood and my continuing active practice as an African diviner have also gained much praise (see, for example, Devisch 2008; Osha 2005, 2011–13; Mosima 2016).

49 In the last pages, and perhaps throughout my argument, there is a play on several meanings of wisdom that ultimately should be told apart:

- wisdom as a quality of persons and explicitly formulated by the local participants as a local cultural ideal;
- wisdom as a quality of persons but only imputed, not explicitly formulated, by the local participants as a local cultural ideal;
- wisdom as a universal category to which North Atlantic scholars contemplating cultural manifestations of wisdom do themselves consciously aspire;

- wisdom as a quality attributed, by external analysts such as the participants in this workshop, to social and cultural arrangements; and
- otherwise.

However, at this point, I shall refrain from taking my explorations any further.

REFERENCES

Aerts, D. 1985. "The Physical Origin of the Einstein-Podolsky-Rosen Paradox." In *Open Questions in Quantum Physics: Invited Papers on the Foundations of Microphysics*, edited by G. Tarozzi and A. van der Merwe, 33–50. Dordrecht: Kluwer Academic.

Aerts, D., B. D'Hooghe, and N. Note, eds. 2005. *Worldviews, Science and Us: Redemarcating Knowledge and Its Social and Ethical Implications.* Singapore: World Scientific.

Aldred, L. 2000. "Plastic Shamans and Astroturf Sun Dances: New Age Commercialization of Native American Spirituality." *The American Indian Quarterly* 24 (3): 329–52.

Appadurai, A. 1995. "The Production of Locality." In *Counterworks: Managing the Diversity of Knowledge*, edited by R. Fardon, 204–25. London: Routledge.

Bell, J.S. 1964. "On the Einstein-Podolsky-Rosen Paradox." *Physics* 1 (3): 195–200.

Bleek W. 1851. "De Nominum Generibus Linguarum Africae Australis, Copticae, Semiticarum Aliarumque Sexualium." PhD diss., Bonn University.

Bohm, D., and B.J. Hiley. 1993. *The Undivided Universe: An Ontological Interpretation of Quantum Theory.* London: Routledge.

Bulhof, I.N., and L. Ten Kate, eds. 1992. *Ons Ontbreken Heilige Namen: Negatieve Theologie In De Hedendaagse Cultuurfilosofie.* Kampen, NL: Kok Agora.

Callewaert, Winand. 2007. "The Upanishads and the New Age Literature." Paper presented at the international symposium "Expressions of Tradition Wisdom," Royal Academy for Overseas Sciences, Royal Museum for Central Africa, and Royal Museums of Art and History, Palais des Académies, Brussels, Belgium, 28 September 2007.

Capra, F. 1978. *The Tao of Physics: An Exploration for the Parallels between Modern Physics and Eastern Mysticism.* 3rd ed. London: Fontana/Collins.

Clottes, J., and D. Lewis-Williams. 1998. *The Shamans of Prehistory: Trance and Magic in the Painted Caves.* Translated by Sophie Hawkes. New York: Harry N. Abrams.

Conee, E. 1988. "Why Solve the Gettier Problem?" In *Philosophical Analysis*, edited by D. Austin, 55–8. Dordrecht, NL: Kluwer.

Cremo, M.A., and R.L. Thompson. 1993. *Forbidden Archeology: The Hidden History of the Human Race.* San Diego: Bhaktivedanta Institute.

Daneel, M.L. 1970. *The God of the Matopo Hills: An Essay on the Mwari Cult in Rhodesia.* The Hague/Paris: Mouton for African Studies Centre.

– 1971. *Old and New in Southern Shona Independent Churches.* Vol. 1, *Background and Rise of the Major Movements.* The Hague/Paris: Mouton.

– 1974. *Old and New in Southern Shona Independent Churches.* Vol. 2, *Church Growth – Causative Factors and Recruitment Techniques.* The Hague/Paris: Mouton for African Studies Centre.

– 1988. *Old and New in Southern Shona Independent Churches.* Vol. 3, *Leadership and Fission Dynamics.* Gweru, ZI: Mambo Press.

de Boeck, F. 1991a. "From Knots to Web: Fertility, Life-Transmission, Health and Well-Being among the Aluund of Southwest Zaire." PhD diss., Catholic University Louvain.

– 1991b. "Therapeutic Efficacy and Consensus among the Aluund of Southwestern Zaire." *Africa: Journal of the African Institute* 61 (2): 159–85.

– 1993. "Symbolic and Diachronic Study of Intercultural Therapeutic and Divinatory Roles among Aluund and Cokwe in the Upper Kwango (Southwestern Zaire)." *Afrika Focus* 9 (1–2): 73–104.

de Boeck, F., and R. Devisch. 1994. "Ndembu, Luunda and Yaka Divination Compared: From Representation and Social Engineering to Embodiment and Worldmaking." *Journal of Religion in Africa* 24: 98–133.

Decouter, S., R. Devisch, I. Maso, R. Oldemans, and W. van Binsbergen. 2000. *Hoe anders is "anders": Over wereldbeelden en Afrikaanse kennissystemen. Monografieën over interculturaliteit.* Berchem/ Mechelen: EPO/ CIMIC (Centrum voor Interculturaeel Management en Interculturele Communicatie).

de Lumley, H. 1972. *La grotte moustérienne de l'Hortus.* Études quaternaires, mémoire 1. Marseille: Laboratoire de Paléontologie Humaine et de Préhistoire, Université de Provence.

de Raedemaeker, F. 1953. *De philosophie der Voorsocratici.* Antwerpen/ Amsterdam: Standaard.

Derrida, J. 1967a. *L'écriture et la différence.* Paris: Seuil. English translation: *Writing and Difference.* Translated by A. Bass. Chicago: University of Chicago Press, 1978.

– 1967b. *De la grammatologie.* Paris: Minuit. English translation: *Of grammatology.* Translated by Gayatri Chakravorty Spivak. Baltimore: Johns Hopkins University Press, 1974.

– 1996. "Foi et savoir: Les deux sources de la 'religion' aux limites de la simple raison." In *La religion,* edited by J. Derrida and G. Vattimo, 9–86. Paris/Rome: Seuil/Laterza.

– 2002. *Jacques Derrida: Acts of Religion*. Edited by Gil Anidjar. London: Routledge.

Descartes, R. 1984. Discours de la methode et les essais (Leiden, 1637); Meditationes de prima philosophia (Paris, 1641); Principia philosophiae (Amsterdam, 1644). Translated by J. Cottingham, R. Stoothoff, and D. Murdoch. In *The Philosophical Writings of Descartes*, vols. I–II. Cambridge: Cambridge University Press.

Devisch, R. 1978. "Towards a Semantic Study of Divination: (1) Trance and Initiation of the Yaka Diviner as a Basis for his Authority; (2) Authority in the Yaka Diviner's Oracle." *Bijdragen: Tijdschrift voor Filosofie en Theologie* 39: 173–89, 278–88.

– 1984. *Se recréer femme: Manipulation sémantique d'une situation d'infécondité chez les Yaka*. Berlin: Reimer.

– 1985. "Perspectives on Divination in Contemporary Sub-Saharan Africa." In *Theoretical Explorations in African Religion*, edited by W.M.J. van Binsbergen and J.M. Schoffeleers, 50–83. London/Boston: Kegan Paul International.

– 1987. "Le symbolisme du corps entre l'indicible et le sacré dans la culture yaka." *Cahiers des Religions Africaines* 20–21 (39–42): 145–65.

– 1991. "Mediumistic Divination among the Northern Yaka of Zaire: Etiology and Ways of Knowing." In *African Divination Systems: Ways of Knowing*, edited by P.M. Peek, 112–32. Bloomington: Indiana University Press.

– 1993. *Weaving the Threads of Life: The Khita Gyn-Eco-Logical Healing Cult among the Yaka*. Chicago: University of Chicago Press.

– 2004. "Reading Wim van Binsbergen's Intercultural Encounters." *Quest : An African Journal of Philosophy/Revue Africaine de Philosophie* 17: 141–52.

– 2008. "Divination and Oracles." In *New Encyclopedia of Africa*, vol. 2, edited by J.M. Middleton and J. Miller, 128–32. New York: Scribner/Gale.

Durkheim, E. 1912. *Les formes élémentaires de la vie religieuse*. Paris: Presses Universitaires de France.

Einstein, A. 1960. *Relativity: The Special and the General Theory*. London: Methuen.

Einstein, A., B. Podolsky, and N. Rosen. 1935. "Can Quantum-Mechanical Description of Physical Reality Be Considered Complete?" *Physical Review* 47: 777–80.

Einstein, A., R.C. Tolman, and B. Podolsky. 1931. "Knowledge of Past and Future in Quantum Mechanics." *Physical Review* 37: 780–1.

Feuerbach, L. 1945. *Das Wesen des Christentums*. Edited by D. Bergner. Leipzig: Reklam.

Gettier, E.L. 1963. "Is Justified True Belief Knowledge?" *Analysis* 23: 121–3.

Gribbin, J. 1984. *In Search of Schrödinger's Cat: Quantum Physic and Reality*. New York: Bantam Books.

Hanegraaf, W.J. 1996. *New Age Religion and Western Culture: Esotericism in the Mirror of Secular Thought*. Leiden: Brill.

– 1999. "New Age Spiritualities as Secular Religion: A Historian's Perspective." *Social Compass* 46 (2): 145–60.

Hannan, M. 1974. *Standard Shona Dictionary*. 2nd ed. Salisbury/Bulawayo: Rhodesia Literature Bureau.

Harding, S., ed. 1993. *The "Racial" Economy of Science: Toward a Democratic Future*. Bloomington: Indiana University Press.

– 1997. "Is Modern Science an Ethnoscience? Rethinking Epistemological Assumptions." In *Postcolonial African Philosophy: A Critical Reader*, edited by E.C. Eze, 45–70. Oxford: Blackwell.

Headland, T.N., K.L. Pike, and M. Harris, eds. 1990. *Emics and Etics: The Insider/Outsider Debate*. Frontiers of Anthropology no. 7. Newbury Park /London/New Delhi: Sage.

Heidegger, M. 1985. *Unterwegs zur Sprache* (1950–1959). *Gesamtausgabe*, 262. Frankfurt am Main: Klostermann.

Hintikka, J. 1968. "Cogito Ergo Sum: Inference or Performance?" *Philosophical Review* 72 (1964): 3–32.

Hollmann, J.C. 2005. "'Swift-People': Therianthropes and Bird Symbolism in Hunter-Gatherer Rock-Paintings, Western and Eastern Cape Provinces, South Africa." *South African Archaeological Society, Goodwin Series* 9: 21–33.

Huffman, T.N. 1983. "The Trance Hypothesis and the Rock Art of Zimbabwe." *South African Archaeological Society, Goodwin Series* 4: 49–53.

Hunt, D., and T.A. McMahon. 1988. *America, the Sorcerer's New Apprentice: The Rise of New Age Shamanism*. Eugene, OR: Harvest House.

Jolly, P. 2002. "Therianthropes in San Rock Art." *South African Archaeological Bulletin* 57 (176): 85–103.

Jongmans, D.G., and P.C.W. Gutkind, eds. 1967. *Anthropologists in the Field*. Assen: van Gorcum.

Jongmans, D.G., and K.W. van der Veen. 1968. "Het leeronderzoek in Tunesië." *Sociologische Gids* 15: 75–183.

Köbben, A.J.F. 1965. *Van primitieven tot medeburgers*. Assen: van Gorcum.

Lehrer, K. 1979. "The Gettier Problem and the Analysis of Knowledge." In *Justification and Knowledge: New Studies in Epistemology*, edited by G. Pappas, 65–78. Dordrecht/Boston/London: D. Reidel.

Lepore, E. 1992. "Principle of Charity." In *A Companion to Epistemology*, edited by J. Dancy and E. Sosa, 365–6. Oxford/Cambridge MA: Blackwell.

Lewis-Williams, J.D. 1985. "Testing the Trance Explanation of Southern African Rock Art: Depictions of Felines." *Bolletino del Centro Communo di Studi Preistorici* 22: 47–62.

Matumo, Z.I. 1993. *Setswana/English/Setswana Dictionary*. rev. ed. Gaborone: Macmillan/Boleswa/Botswana Book Centre.

Moser, P.K. 1992. "Gettier Problem." In *A Companion to Epistemology*, edited by J. Dancy and E. Sosa, 157–9. Oxford/ Cambridge, MA: Blackwell's.
Mosima, P.M. 2016. "Philosophic Sagacity and Intercultural Philosophy: Beyond Henry Odera Oruka." PhD diss., Tilburg University.
Mutumba Mainga. 1972. "A History of Lozi Religion to the End of the Nineteenth Century." In *The Historical Study of African Religion*, edited by T.O. Ranger and I. Kimambo, 95–107. London: Heinemann.
Nietzsche, F. 1973."Die frohliche Wissenschaft (1882)." In *Werke*, vol. 2, edited by K. Schlechta, 7–274. München/Wien: Hanser.
Nortmann, U. 2008. *Unscharfe Welte: Was Philosophen ueber Quantenmechanik wissen moechten*. Darmstadt: Wissenschaftliche Buchgesellschaft.
Okere, T., C.A. Njoku, and R. Devisch. 2005. "All Knowledge Is First of All Local Knowledge: An Introduction." *Africa Development* 30 (3): 1–19.
Oruka, Odera. 1990. *Sage Philosophy: Indigenous Thinkers and Modern Debate on African Philosophy*. Leiden: Brill.
Osha, Sanya. 2005. "The Frontier of Interculturality: A Review of Wim van Binsbergen's Intercultural Encounters." *Africa Development* 30 (1–2): 239–50.
– 2011–13. *Parricide and a Hardened Forrester: Wim van Binsbergen, Valentin Mudimbe, and African Knowledge Systems*. Haarlem: Papers in Intercultural Philosophy and Transcontinental Comparative Studies, No. 3. http://www.quest-journal.net/PIP/Osha%20%203rd%20round.pdf.
Osha, Sanya, ed., with the assistance of Wim M.J. van Binsbergen. 2006. *African Feminisms*, special issue of *Quest: An African Journal of Philosophy / Revue Africaine de Philosophie* 20 (1–2): 200. http://www.quest-journal.net/2006.htm.
Parkington, John. 2003. "Eland and Therianthropes in Southern African Rock Art: When Is a Person an Animal?"*African Archaeological Review* 20 (3): 135–47.
Popper, Karl. 1959. *The Logic of Scientific Discovery*. London: Hutchinson.
Przibram, K., ed. 1967. *Letters on Wave Mechanics: Schrödinger, Planck, Einstein, Lorentz*. Translated by Martin J. Klein. New York: Philosophical Library.
Pseudo-Dionysius, the Areopagite. 1910 (fifth and sixth century CE). *Mysticism, Its True Nature and Value*. With a translation of the "Mystical theology" of Dionysius, and of the letters to Caius and Dorotheus (1, 2, and 5). Translated and edited by A.B. Sharpe. London: Sands; St. Louis: B. Herder.
Ranger, T.O. 1968. "Connexions between 'Primary Resistance Movements' and Modern Mass Nationalism in East and Central Africa." *Journal of African History* 9: 437–53, 631–41.
– 1972. "Mcape and the Study of Witchcraft Eradication." Paper presented at the Conference on the History of Central African Religious Systems, organized by the University of Zambia and the University of California Los Angeles, Lusaka, Zambia.

– 1975. "The Mwana Lesa Movement of 1925." In *Themes in the Christian History of Central Africa*, edited by T.O. Ranger and J. Weller, 45–75. London: Heinemann.
– 1979. "Developments in the Historical Study of African Religion: Relations of Production and Religious Change in Central Africa." In *Religion and Change in African Societies: Proceedings of a Seminar Held in the Centre of African Studies, University of Edinburgh, 27th and 28th April, 1979*, 1–18. Edinburgh: Centre of African Studies, University of Edinburgh.
– 1985. "Religious Studies and Political Economy: The Mwari Cult and the Peasant Experience in Southern Rhodesia." In *Theoretical Explorations in African Religion*, edited by W.M.J. van Binsbergen and J.M. Schoffeleers, 287–321. London/Boston: Kegan Paul International for African Studies Centre.
– 1999. *Voices from the Rocks: Nature, Culture History in the Matopos Hills of Zimbabwe*. Oxford: James Curry.
Rhys Davis, T.W., trans. 1988. "The Questions of King Milinda." 2 parts. In *Sacred Books of the East*, edited by F.M. Müller. Translated by various oriental scholars. vols. 35–6. Delhi: Motilal Banarsidass; first published in 1879–1910, Oxford: Clarendon Press.
Robertson, Roland. 1994. "Glocalisation: Time–Space and Homogenity–Heterogenity." In *Global Modernities*, edited by Mike Featherstone, Scott Lash, and Roland Robertson, 25–44. London: Sage.
Rorty, Richard. 1989. "Two Meanings of 'Logocentrism': A Reply to Norris." In *Redrawing the Lines: Analytic Philosophy, Deconstruction, and Literary Theory*, edited by Reed Way Dasenbrock, 204–16. Minneapolis: University of Minnesota Press.
Schoffeleers, J.M. 1972a. "The Chisumphi and M'bona Cults in Malawi: A Comparative History." Paper presented at the Conference on the History of Central African Religious Systems, organized by the University of Zambia and the University of California Los Angeles, Lusaka, Zambia. Published in Schoffeleers 1979, 147–86.
– 1972b. "The History and Political Role of the M'bona Cult among the Mang'anja." In *The Historical Study of African Religion*, edited by R.O. Ranger and I. Kimambo, 73–94. London: Heinemann.
– 1978. "A Martyr Cult as a Reflection on Changes in Production: The Case of the Lower Shire Valley, 1590–1622 AD." In *Social Stratification and Class Formation*, edited by R. Buijtenhuijs and P.L. Geschiere, 19–33. Leiden: Afrika-Studiecentrum.
–, ed. 1979. *Guardians of the Land: Essays on African Territorial Cults*. Gwelo: Mambo Press.
– 1985. "Oral History and the Retrieval of the Distant Past: On the Use of Legendary Chronicles as Sources of Historical Information." In *Theoretical*

Explorations in African Religion, edited by W.M.J. Binsbergen and J.M. Schoffeleers, 164–88. London/Boston: Kegan Paul International for African Studies Centre.

– 1991. "Ritual Healing and Political Acquiescence: The Case of Zionist Churches in Southern Africa." *Africa* 61 (1): 1–25.

– 1992. *River of Blood: The Genesis of a Martyr Cult in Southern Malawi*. Madison: Wisconsin University Press.

Schroeder, B. 1996. *Altared Ground: Levinas, History, and Violence*. New York London: Routledge.

Smith, Philip, and Jeffrey C. Alexander. 1996. "Durkheim's Religious Revival." *The American Journal of Sociology* 102 (2): 585–92.

Stroeken, K. 2000. "Bringing Home the Heat: An Anthropological Study of Bewitchment and Mediumship in Sukumaland." PhD diss., Catholic University Louvain.

Turner, Edith. 1993. "The Reality of Spirits: A Tabooed or Permitted Field of Study?" *Anthropology of Consciousness* 3 (1): 9–13.

Turner, V.W. 1967. *The Forest of Symbols: Aspects of Ndembu Ritual*. Ithaca, NY: Cornell University Press.

– 1968. *The Drums of Affliction: A Study of Religious Processes among the Ndembu of Zambia*. Oxford: Clarendon Press.

Tylor, E.B. 1871. *Primitive Culture: Researches into the Development of Mythology, Philosophy, Religion, Art, and Culture*, 2 vols. London: Murray.

van Binsbergen, Wim M.J. 1971. "Religie en samenleving: Een studie over het bergland van N.W. Tunesië." PhD diss., University of Amsterdam, Anthropological Sociological Centre. http://www.quest-journal.net/shikanda/Berber/access.htm.

– 1979. "The Infancy of Edward Shelonga: An Extended Case from the Zambian Nkoya." In *In Search of Health: Six Essays on Medical Anthropology*, edited by J.D.M. van der Geest and K.W. van der Veen, 19–90. Amsterdam: Anthropological Sociological Centre. http://quest-journal.net/shikanda/publications/ASC-1239806-041.pdf.

– 1980a. "Interpreting the Myth of Sidi Mhammad." In *Using Oral Sources: Vansina and Beyond*, edited by K. Brown and M. Roberts, 51–73. Special issue of *Social Analysis* 4. Adelaide: University of Adelaide.

– 1980b. "Popular and Formal Islam, and Supralocal Relations: The Highlands of Northwestern Tunisia, 1800–1970." *Middle Eastern Studies* 16 (1): 71–91. https://openaccess.leidenuniv.nl/handle/1887/8940.

– 1981a. *Religious Change in Zambia: Exploratory Studies*. London/Boston: Kegan Paul International.

– 1981b. "Theoretical and Experiential Dimensions in the Study of the Ancestral Cult among the Zambian Nkoya." Paper presented at the symposium on Plurality in Religion, International Union of

Anthropological and Ethnological Sciences Intercongress, Amsterdam, 22–5 April 1981. http://www.quest-journal.net/shikanda/african_religion/ancest.htm.
– 1984. *Zusters, dochters: Afrikaanse verhalen*. Haarlem: In de Knipscheer.
– 1987. "*Likota Lya Bankoya*: Memory, Myth and History." *Cahiers d'Etudes Africaines* 27 (107): 359–92. https://doi.org/10.3406/cea.1987.3410.
– 1988. *Een buik openen: Roman*. Haarlem: In de Knipscheer.
– 1990a. "Church, Cult, and Lodge: In Quest of Therapeutic Meaning in Francistown, Botswana." Paper presented at the 6th Satterthwaite Colloquium on African Religion and Ritual, Cumbria, UK, 21–4 April 1990. http://www.quest-journal.net/shikanda/publications/church_cult_lodge_1990.pdf. Final version now incorporated in van Binsbergen 2017: 147–86.
– 1990b. "Oesjwana [Ushwana]: het naamvererfingsritueel bij de Nkoja van westelijk Zambia." Foto presentatie bij de gelegenheid van de opening van het Pieter de la Courtgebouw, Faculteit Sociale Wetenschappen, Rijksuniversiteit Leiden, mei 1990. Text and photographs available at http://www.quest-journal.net/shikanda/african_religion/ushwana/ushwana.htm.
– 1991. "Becoming a *Sangoma*: Religious Anthropological Field-Work in Francistown, Botswana." *Journal of Religion in Africa* 21 (4): 309–44. Revised version in van Binsbergen 2003: 155–93. http://quest-journal.net/shikanda/intercultural_encounters/index.htm.
– 1992a. "De onderzoeker als spin, of als vlieg, in het web van de andere cultuur: Naar aanleiding van Filip de Boecks medische etnografie van het Lunda gebied." *Medische Antropologie* 4 (2): 255–67. www.quest-journal.net/shikanda/publications/spin_web_1992.pdf.
– 1992b. *Tears of Rain: Ethnicity and History in Western Central Zambia*. London/Boston: Kegan Paul International. http://www.quest-journal.net/shikanda/ethnicity/Tearsweb/pdftears.htm.
– 1993. "Mukanda: Towards a History of Circumcision rites in Western Zambia, 18th–20th century." In *L'invention religieuse en Afrique: Histoire et religion en Afrique noire*, edited by J.-P. Chrétien, avec collaboration de C.-H. Perrot, G. Prunier, and D. Raison-Jourde, 49–103. Paris: Agence de Culture et de Coopération Technique/Karthala. http://www.quest-journal.net/shikanda/ethnicity/mukanda.htm.
– 1995. "Four-Tablet Divination as Trans-Regional Medical Technology in Southern Africa." *Journal of Religion in Africa* 25 (2): 114–40. http://quest-journal.net/shikanda/publications/ASC-1239806-059.pdf.
– 1996. "Regional and Historical Connections of Four-Tablet Divination in Southern Africa." *Journal of Religion in Africa* 26 (1): 2–29. http://quest-journal.net/shikanda/publications/ASC-1239806-062.pdf.

– 1997a. "Black Athena Ten Years After: Towards a Constructive Re-Assessment." In *Black Athena: Ten Years After*, edited by Wim M.M. van Binsbergen, 11–64. Hoofddorp: Dutch Archaeological and Historical Society. http://www.quest-journal.net/shikanda/publications/ASC-1239806-017.pdf.
– 1997b. *Virtuality as a Key Concept in the Study of Globalisation: Aspects of the Symbolic Transformation of Contemporary Africa*. The Hague: WOTRO [Netherlands Foundation for Tropical Research, a division of the Netherlands Research Foundation NWO]. Final version in van Binsbergen 2015b: ch. 1, 85–168.
– 1998. "Globalization and Virtuality: Analytical Problems Posed by the Contemporary Transformation of African Societies." In *Globalization and Identity: Dialectics of Flow and Closure*, edited by B. Meyer and P. Geschiere, 273–303. Oxford: Blackwell. http://www.quest-journal.net/shikanda/publications/ASC-1239806-064.pdf.
– 2001. "Witchcraft in Modern Africa as Virtualised Boundary Conditions of the Kinship Order." In *Witchcraft Dialogues: Anthropological and Philosophical Exchanges*, edited by G.C. Bond and D.M. Ciekawy, 212–63. Athens, OH: Ohio University Press. http://www.quest-journal.net/shikanda/african_religion/witch.htm.
– 2003a. *Intercultural Encounters: African and Anthropological Lessons towards a Philosophy of Interculturality*. Berlin/Boston/Muenster: LIT. http://quest-journal.net/shikanda/intercultural_encounters/index.htm.
– 2003b. "The Leopard and the Lion: An Exploration of Nostratic and Bantu Lexical Continuity in the Light of Kammerzell's Hypothesis." http://www.quest-journal.net/shikanda/ancient_models/leopard_lion_nostratic_bantu_kammerzell.pdf.
– 2004a. "The Leopard in the Garden of Eating: From Food for Thought to Thought for Food – Towards a World History of Difference." Paper presented at "The Garden of Eating: Experiencing the Thought of Gilles Deleuze in Cultural Practices," Faculties of Philosophy/History and Art, Rotterdam, 29 May 2004. http://www.quest-journal.net/shikanda/general/webpage_deleuze/deleuze_leopard_www.htm.
– 2004b. "Long-Range Mythical Continuities across Africa and Asia: Linguistic and Iconographic Evidence Concerning Leopard Symbolism." Paper presented at the Round Table on Myth, Department of Sanskrit and Indian Studies, Harvard University, Cambridge, MA, 8–10 May 2004. http://www.quest-journal.net/shikanda/ancient_models/leopard_harvard_return.pdf.
– 2005a. "Derrida on Religion: Glimpses of Interculturality." *Quest: An African Journal of Philosophy/Revue Africaine de Philosophie* 19 (1–2): 129–52. http://www.quest-journal.net/QUEST_XIX/QUEST_XIX_binsbergen.pdf.

– 2005b. "'We Are in This for the Money': Commodification and the Sangoma Cult of Southern Africa." In *Commodification: Things, Agency and Identities: The Social Life of Things Revisited*, edited by Wim M.J. van Binsbergen and Peter Geschiere, 351–78. Berlin/Muenster: LIT. http://www.quest-journal.net/shikanda/topicalities/Wim_van_Binsbergen_Commodification_and_sangoma_cult.pdf.
– 2006a. "Further Steps towards an Aggregative Diachronic Approach to World Mythology, Starting from the African Continent." Paper presented at the International Conference on Comparative Mythology, organized by Peking University (Research Institute of Sanskrit Manuscripts and Buddhist Literature) and the Mythology Project, Asia Center, Harvard University (Department of Sanskrit and Indian Studies), Peking University, Beijing, China 10–14 May 2006. http://www.quest-journal.net/shikanda/ancient_models/Further%20steps%20def.pdf.
– 2006b. "Mythological Archaeology: Situating Sub-Saharan African Cosmogonic Myths within a Long-Range Intercontinential Comparative Perspective." In *Proceedings of the Pre-symposium of RIHN [Research Institute for Humanity and Nature] and 7th ESCA [Ethnogenesis in South and Central Asia] Harvard-Kyoto Roundtable*, edited by Toshiki Osada with the assistance of Noriko Hase, 319–49. Kyoto: RIHN. http://www.quest-journal.net/shikanda/ancient_models/kyoto_as_published_2006_EDIT2.pdf.
– 2007a. "Experiential Anthropology, and the Reality and World History of Spirit: Questions for Edith Turner." Expanded version of a contribution to the symposium "Healing and Spirituality," Research Institute for Religious Studies and Theology (RST)/Research Institute for Social and Cultural Research (NISCO), Radboud University Nijmegen, the Netherlands, 30 January 2007; revised version: paper presented at the European Council for African Studies conference, Leiden, July 2007. http://www.quest-journal.net/shikanda/african_religion/questions_for_Edith_Turner.pdf.
– 2007b. "The Underpinning of Scientific Knowledge Systems: Epistemology or Hegemonic Power? The Implications of Sandra Harding's Critique of North Atlantic Science for the Appreciation of African Knowledge Systems." In *La rationalité, une ou plurielle*, edited by Paulin J. Hountondji, 294–327. Dakar: CODESRIA [Conseil pour le développement de la recherche en sciences sociales en Afrique]/UNESCO [Organisation des Nations Unies pour l'éducation, la science et la culture]. http://www.quest-journal.net/shikanda/general/porto_novo_for_hountondji_2-2003_bis.pdf. Final version in van Binsbergen 2015b: ch. 13, 445–82.
– 2008. "Traditional Wisdom – Its Expressions and Representations in Africa and Beyond: Exploring Intercultural Epistemology." *Quest: An African Journal of Philosophy/Revue Africaine de Philosophie* 22 (1–2): 49–120. http://www.quest-journal.net/volXXII/Quest_XXII_Binsbergen_wisdom.pdf.

– 2009a. *Expressions of Traditional Wisdom from Africa and Beyond: An Exploration in Intercultural Epistemology.* Brussels: Royal Academy of Overseas Sciences/Academie Royale des Sciences d'Outre-mer. http://quest-journal.net/shikanda/topicalities/wisdom%20as%20published%20ARSOM_BETTER.pdfb.
– 2009b. "Expressions of Traditional Wisdom: What Africa Can Teach the World Today." *Bulletin des Séances de l'Académie Royales des Sciences d'Outre-Mer/Mededelingen Zittingen Koninklijke Academie voor Overzeese Wetenschappen* 55 (2009–3): 281–305. http://quest-journal.net/shikanda/topicalities/wisdom_ARSOM_55.3_2009.pdf.
– 2010. "The Continuity of African and Eurasian Mythologies: General Theoretical Models, and Detailed Comparative Discussion of the Case of Nkoya Mythology from Zambia, South Central Africa." In *New Perspectives on Myth: Proceedings of the Second Annual Conference of the International Association for Comparative Mythology, Ravenstein (the Netherlands), 19–21 August, 2008,* edited by Wim M.J. van Binsbergen and Eric Venbrux, 143–225. Papers in Intercultural Philosophy and Transcontinental Comparative Studies, no. 5. Haarlem: Shikanda Press. http://www.quest-journal.net/PIP/New_Perspectives_On_Myth_2010/toc_proceedings_IACM_2008_2010.htm.
–, ed. 2011a. *Black Athena Comes of Age: Towards a Constructive Re-Assessment.* Berlin/Boston/Munster: LIT.
– 2011b. "Existential Dilemmas of a North Atlantic Anthropologist in the Production of Relevant Africanist Knowledge." In *The Postcolonial Turn: Re-Imagining Anthropology and Africa,* edited by René Devisch and Francis B.Nyamnjoh, 117–42. Bamenda/Leiden: Langaa/African Studies Centre. http://www.quest-journal.net/shikanda/topicalities/postcolonial_turn/binsbergen_existential_dilemmas_postcolonial_turn.pdf.
– 2011c. "Is There a Future for Afrocentrism despite Stephen Howe's Dismissive 1998 Study?" In *Black Athena Comes of Age: Towards a Constructive Reassessment,* edited by Wim M.J. van Binsbergen, 253–82. Berlin/Boston/Munster: LIT. http://www.quest-journal.net/shikanda/topicalities/chapter_10_Black%20Athena_COMES_OF_AGE_.pdf.
– 2011d. "Shimmerings of the Rainbow Serpent: Towards the Interpretation of Crosshatching Motifs in Palaeolithic Art: Comparative Mythological and Archaeoastronomical Explorations Inspired by the Incised Blombos Red Ochre Block, South Africa, 70 ka BP, and Nkoya Female Puberty Rites, 20th c. CE." http://quest-journal.net/shikanda/ancient_models/crosshatching_FINAL.pdf.
– 2011e. "A Unique Nkoya Statuette Associated with Cults of Affliction (Western Zambia)." http://www.quest-journal.net/shikanda/topicalities/Mwendanjangula_final.pdf.

– 2012a. *Before the Presocratics: Cyclicity, Transformation, and Element Cosmology: The Case of Transcontinental Pre- or Protohistoric Cosmological Substrates Linking Africa, Eurasia and North America.* Special issue, *Quest: An African Journal of Philosophy/Revue Africaine de Philosophie* 23–4 no 1–2 (2009–2010): 1–398. Book version: Haarlem: Shikanda, 2012. http://www.quest-journal.net/2009-2010.htm.
– 2012b. "The Relevance of Buddhism and Hinduism for the Study of Asian-African Transcontinental Continuities." Paper presented at the International Conference "Rethinking Africa's Transcontinental Continuities in Pre- and Protohistory," African Studies Centre, Leiden, 12–13 April 2012. Final version: van Binsbergen, Wim M.J. 2017. "The Relevance of Taoism, Buddhism and Hinduism for the Study of Asian-African Transcontinental Continuities." In *Religion as a Social Construct*, ch. 10, 361–412. Haarlem: Shikanda. http://www.quest-journal.net/shikanda/topicalities/rel%20bk%20for%20web/g.pdf.
– 2012c. *Spiritualiteit, heelmaking en transcendentie: Een intercultureel-filosofisch onderzoek bij Plato, in Afrika, en in het Noordatlantisch gebied, vertrekkend vanuit Otto Duintjers Onuitputtelijk is de Waarheid.* Papers in Intercultural Studies and Transcontinental Comparative Studies, no. 10. Haarlem: Shikanda Press. www.quest-journal.net/PIP/spiritualiteit.pdf.
– 2013. "African Divination across Time and Space: Typology and Intercultural Epistemology." In *Realities Re-Viewed: Dynamics of African Divination*, edited by Walter E.A. van Beek and Philip M. Peek, 339–75. Zuerich/Berlin/Muenster: LIT. http://quest-journal.net/shikanda/ancient_models/divination_space_time_2008.pdf.
– 2014. *Het dorp Mabombola: Vestiging, verwantschap en huwelijk in de sociale organisatie van de Zambiaanse Nkoya.* Papers in Intercultural Philosophy and Transcontinental Comparative Studies, no. 15. Haarlem: Shikanda Press. www.quest-journal.net/PIP/Mabombola%20TEXT%20lulu3%20%20ALLERBEST.pdf.
– 2015a. *Een lekker sodemietertje: Een kind op weg naar de poezie (autobiografie 1947–1963).* Haarlem: Uitgeverij Shikanda.
– 2015b. *Vicarious Reflections: African Explorations in Empirically-Grounded Intercultural Philosophy.* Papers in Intercultural Philosophy and Transcontinental Comparative Studies, no. 17. Haarlem: Shikanda Press. http://www.quest-journal.net/shikanda/topicalities/vicarious/vicariou.htm.
– 2017. *Religion as a Social Construct: Asian, African, Comparative and Theoretical Excursions – A Testament in the Social Science of Religion.* Papers in Intercultural Philosophy and Transcontinental Comparative Studies, no. 22. Haarlem: Shikanda Press. http://www.quest-journal.net/shikanda/topicalities/rel%20bk%20for%20web/webpage%20relbk.htm.

– In press (a). *The Leopard's Unchanging Spots: A Pictorial Account of Comparative Research on the Transcontinental History of Leopard-Skin Symbolism, Shamanism, and African Agency*. Papers in Intercultural Philosophy and Transcontinental Comparative Studies. Haarlem: Shikanda Press.

– In press (b). *"Our Drums Are Always on My Mind": Nkoya History, Culture, and Society, Zambia*. Papers in Intercultural Philosophy/Transcontinental Comparative Studies, no. 11. Haarlem: Shikanda Press.

– In press (c). *The Reality of Religion: Durkheim Revisited*. Papers in Intercultural Philosophy and Transcontinental Comparative Studies, no. 25. Haarlem: Shikanda Press.

–, ed. In press (d). *Rethinking Africa's Transcontinental Continuities in Pre- and Protohistory*. Leiden: Brill.

– In preparation (a). *Religion and Social Organisation in North-Western Tunisia*. Vol. 1: *Kinship, Spatiality, and Segmentation*. Volume 2: *Cults of the Land, and Islam*.

– In preparation (b). *Sangoma Science: From Ethnography to Intercultural Ontology: Towards a Poetics of the Globalising Exploration into Local Spiritualities*.

van Binsbergen, Wim M.J., with the collaboration of Jean-Pierre Lacroix. 2000. *Cupmarks, Stellar Maps, and Mankala Board-Games: An Archaeoastronomical and Africanist Excursion into Palaeolithic World-Views*. http://www.quest-journal.net/shikanda/ancient_models/gen3/starmaps_3_2000/cupmarks_0.html.

van Binsbergen, Wim M.J., and F.A.M. Wiggermann. 1999. "Magic in History: A Theoretical Perspective, and Its Application to Ancient Mesopotamia." In *Mesopotamian Magic*, edited by T. Abusch and K. van der Toorn, 3–34. Groningen: Styx. http://www.quest-journal.net/shikanda/topicalities/rel%20bk%20for%20web/f.pdf.

van Binsbergen, Wim M.J., and Fred C. Woudhuizen. 2011. *Ethnicity in Mediterranean Protohistory*. British Archaeological Reports (BAR) International Series No. 2256. Oxford: Archaeopress. http://www.quest-journal.net/shikanda/ethnicity_mediterranean_protohistory/ethnicit.htm.

van Wersch, S. 1990. *De gnostisch-occulte vloedgolf: Van Simon de Tovernaar tot New Age: Een kritische beoordeling*. Kampen: Kok.

Walker, E.H. 1977. "The Compleat Quantum Mechanical Anthropologist." In *Extrasensory Ecology: Parapsychology and Anthropology*, edited by J.K. Long, 53–95. Metuchen, NJ/London: Scarecrow Press.

Werbner, Richard P. 1973. "The Superabundance of Understanding: Kalanga Rhetoric and Domestic Divination." *American Anthropologist* 75: 414–40.

– 1989. "Making the Hidden Seen: Tswapong Wisdom Divination." In *Ritual Passage Sacred Journey: The Process and Organization of Religious Movement*,

19–60. Washington/Manchester: Smithsonian Institution Press/ Manchester University Press.
– 2015. *Divination's Grasp: African Encounters with the Almost Said.* Bloomington: Indiana University Press.
Williams, B. 1968. "The Certainty of the Cogito." In *Descartes: A Collection of Critical Essays*, edited by W. Doney, 88–107. London: Macmillan.
Wittgenstein, L. 1964. *Tractatus Logico-Philosophicus: Logisch-Philosophische Abhandlung.* Frankfurt am Main: Suhrkamp. First published 1921. English translation: *Tractatus Logico-Philosophicus.* Translated by F.P. Ramsey and C.K. Ogden. London: Routledge and Kegan Paul, 1922.
Witzel, Michael. 2001. "Comparison and Reconstruction: Language and Mythology." *Mother Tongue* 6: 45–62.
– 2012. *The Origins of the World's Mythologies.* New York: Oxford University Press.
Wood, Matthew. 2007. *Possession, Power and the New Age.* Belfast: Theology and Religion in Interdisciplinary Perspective.
York, Michael. 2003. *Historical Dictionary of New Age Movements.* Lanham, MD: Scarecrow Press.
Zinser, Hartmut. 1987. "'Schamanismus im New Age': Zur Wiederkehr Schamanistischer Praktiken und Seancen in Europa." *Zeitschrift fur Religions und Geistes-Gesch*ichte 39 (1): 319–27.
Zukav, G. 1979. *The Dancing Wu-Li Masters: An Overview of the New Physics.* New York: Morrow.

Contributors

Joseph S. Alter teaches anthropology and is the director of the Asian Studies Center at the University of Pittsburgh. He has published a number of books, including *The Wrestler's Body, Knowing Dil Das, Gandhi's Body, Yoga in Modern India*, and *Moral Materialism*. Beyond the study of yoga in contemporary practice, his interests include the cultural history of nature cure as a system of medicine, the political ecology of health, and biosemiotics. A new project focuses on yoga understood from the vantage point of a critical sociology of knowledge, asking what constitutes the elementary forms to enlightenment and how should we understand embodiment in relation to philosophy.

Clark Chilson is an associate professor in the Department of Religious Studies at the University of Pittsburgh, where he teaches about religion in Asia and the relationship between Buddhism and psychology. He is the author of *Secrecy's Power: Covert Shin Buddhists in Japan and Contradictions of Concealment* (2014) and the co-editor of two books: *The Nanzan Guide to Japanese Religions* (with Paul Swanson) and *Shamans in Asia* (with Peter Knecht). He has published articles on Shin Buddhism, Kuya, Ikeda Daisaku, and non-religious spiritual care in Japan. His publications on Naikan include "Naikan: A Meditation Method and Psychotherapy" in the *Oxford Research Encyclopedia of Religion* (Oxford University Press, 2018) and "Naikan's Path" in *Pure Lands in Asian Texts and Contexts: An Anthology*, edited by Georgios Halkias and Richard Payne (University of Hawaii Press, 2019). He has given presentations on Naikan in Japan, Canada, Denmark, and the United States, and has also done intensive Naikan five times at two different Naikan centres in Japan.

Richard Doyle (aka Mobius), author of scores of scholarly articles and seven books, has been awarded grants from the National Science

Foundation and the Mellon Foundation while winning acclaim and accolades as a classroom teacher in the United States, the United Kingdom, Germany, and China. In 2002, he was healed of lifelong severe asthma in an ayahuasca ceremony, and has since devoted his life to synthesizing the world's spiritual practices into a practical, open source and empirically verifiable pathway available to all. He is currently Edwin Erle Sparks Professor at Penn State, and his recent books include *The Genesis of Now*, *Darwin's Pharmacy*, and *Looking Upside Down at Nothing*.

James D. Faubion is Radoslav Tsanoff Chair and Professor of Anthropology at Rice University. He is the editor of *Rethinking the Subject: An Anthology of Contemporary European Social Thought*; the second and third volumes of *Essential Works of Michel Foucault*; *The Ethics of Kinship: Ethnographic Inquiries*; the second edition of Michel Foucault's *Death and the Labyrinth*; with George E. Marcus, *Fieldwork Is Not What It Used To Be: Learning Anthropology's Method in a Time of Transition*; *Foucault Now: Current Perspectives in Foucault Studies*; and with Dominic Boyer and George Marcus, *Theory Is More than It Used to Be*. He is the author of *Modern Greek Lessons: A Primer in Historical Constructivism*; *The Shadows and Lights of Waco: Millennialism Today*; and *An Anthropology of Ethics* (Cambridge University Press, 2011).

Richard D.G. Irvine is a lecturer in social anthropology at the University of St Andrews. His research explores religious life, rationalization and disenchantment, environmental change, and the relationship between human life and geological temporality in the United Kingdom and Mongolia. He is the author of *An Anthropology of Deep Time* with Cambridge University Press.

Philip Y. Kao is a research associate in the Department of Anthropology at the University of Pittsburgh. He obtained his PhD from the University of St Andrews and is a lifetime member of the Association for Anthropology, Gerontology, and the Life Course (AAGE). In addition to his research on wisdom and aging, Philip Kao served several years as an editor for the journal *Anthropology & Aging*. He is a former University of Pittsburgh Provost Postdoctoral Fellow and has taught a variety of courses on contemporary topics in sociocultural anthropology at the University of Pittsburgh and at Harvard University.

Charlotte Linde has been a senior research scientist at NASA, studying issues of cockpit and air traffic control communication, learning among the science team members of the Mars Rover, and knowledge management for long-term space missions. Before that, she was a senior researcher at the Institute for Research on Learning and founded and ran a research and consulting company, Structural Semantics. Her research projects include narrative in the development of individual and group identity and the negotiation of authority conflicts in emergency aviation situations. Publications include *Life Stories: The Creation of Coherence* and *Working the Past: Narrative and Institutional Memory* (Oxford University Press). Her current research focuses on the anthropology of wisdom, including the social negotiation of wisdom through the creation and use of stories of exemplary members of a community, the movement of stories of religious founders across time and cultures, and the importation and creation of spiritual activities on the internet. She has taught linguistics and anthropology at Stanford University; University of California, Berkeley; City University of New York; and Naropa University.

Wim M.J. van Binsbergen was trained in sociology, anthropology, and linguistics at Amsterdam University (Municipal). He has held professorships in the social sciences at Leiden, Manchester, Durban, Berlin, and Amsterdam (Free University). At the latter institution, he took his cum laude doctorate (1979) and was the incumbent of the chair of ethnic studies (1990–8), prior to acceding to the chair of foundations of intercultural philosophy (Erasmus University, Rotterdam). Simultaneously, he has held senior appointments at the African Studies Centre, Leiden. He was president of the Netherlands Association of African Studies, 1990–3; and has been the editor of *Quest: An African Journal of Philosophy/Revue Africaine de Philosophie* since 2002. He did extensive field research in various regions of Africa and less extensively so in Asia. Over the decades, he has established himself internationally as a specialist on African ethnicity, African religion, ethnohistory, globalization, intercultural philosophy, comparative mythology, the Mediterranean Bronze Age, and transcontinental continuities between Africa and Asia in pre- and proto-history. His many scholarly books include *Religious Change in Zambia* (1981), *Tears of Rain* (1992), *Intercultural Encounters* (2003), *Expressions of Traditional Wisdom from Africa and Beyond* (2009), *Ethnicity in Mediterranean Protohistory* (with Fred Woudhuizen, 2011), *Black Athena Comes of Age* (2011), *Before the Presocratics* (2012), *Vicarious Reflections* (2015), *Religion as a Social Construct* (2017), *Researching Power and Identity in African State Formation* (with Martin Doornbos, 2017), and *Confronting the Sacred: Durkheim Vindicated* (2018). His published work is also freely available at http://www.quest-journal.net/shikanda. Wim van Binsbergen is married and has five adult children; he is a published poet, and a certified and practising diviner/healer in the Southern African *sangoma* tradition.

Index

academia, 130, 139, 206
Advaita, 40
ageism, 6, 83–4
aging, 82–8, 89–92, 95–7
Agrafiotis, Demosthenes, 170–3
Aldwin, Carolyn, 12
alienation, 105, 109
Alzheimer's disease, 97n2
Amida Buddha, 71–2
amithyatvat, 43n4
amnesia, 193, 206
animism, 10
anthropology: cultural relativism and, 19, 210, 212; as excavation, 157; language and, 181–4, 207–8; philosophical, 13; post-structuralism and, 217n5. *See also* ethnography; fieldwork
Apache, 6–8
apophatic modes of prayer, 53–5, 57–8, 60–1
Aristotle, 4, 5, 142, 173, 211
artifact (Zebra), 30–6, 38–40
Asad, Talal, 55
ašram model, 207
Assmann, Aleida, 12
astrology, 213
athletes, 141
atman, 33
authority: of elders, 189–90, 195, 197–8; in insurance companies, 127–8; in meditation centres, 134–6, 145–6; nomination of, 124; statistics and, 163–4; in technology companies, 138–9. *See also* gurus; sages
avidya, 108

Baker, Augustine, 49–50, 54, 56–7, 62n7
Bantu languages, 214, 221n22
baraka, 184–5
Barth, Fredrick, 67
Basso, Keith, 6–8, 149
Bateson, Gregory, 9–10, 21n6
becoming and unbecoming, 89–92
Benedictine monks, 45–62
Bergson, Henri, 90–1
Berlin Aging Study (BASE), 86
Berlin Wisdom Paradigm project, 82
blessings, 69, 184–5, 190
Blitz, 37–8
Bloch, Maurice, 12
Böhme, Jakob, 31, 37
Bordia, Prashant, 69
brain: activity of, 3; development of, 85; ecology of, 9–10; ego and, 42
Brefi Group, 155

Buddha, 71, 145, 146, 150–1n5
buddhi, 108
Buddhism: Africa and, 193, 203, 220n19; mythology of, 60; Pure Land, 67, 71; Shin, 71–2; Tibetan, 133–4; Zen, 70, 134. *See also* Buddha; meditation; meditation centres
Burke, Edmund, 58, 59–60

Cage, John, 55, 60
caregiving, 87–9, 95–6. *See also* nursing homes
Carr, Herbert Wildon, 91
Carson, Rachel, 162
cārvāka, 116, 117
Center for Practical Wisdom, 4
Chapman, John, 51–2, 57, 61n5
character, 144–5
charisma, 105, 106, 129
chie, 69, 72
Christianity, 197. *See also* Benedictine monks
Christman, John, 95
Cioran, E.M., 21n5
Cloud of Unknowing, The, 53–4, 55, 62n7
Cohen, Gene, 84
community, 45, 56–61, 106
consciousness: ecology of, 10, 21n6; enlightenment, 70, 103–5; evolution and, 5; integration of, 69; introception, 33, 39, 40, 42; prayer and, 52; self and ego, 38, 42; temporality and, 92–5; universe and, 215; yoga and, 103–5, 110, 112–13. *See also* ultra-meta-cognition
contemplation. *See* meditation; prayer
Cosmogony and Cosmology (PKD), 29–30, 36, 40, 41–2, 43n2

Cressy, Serenus, 49
Crites, Stephen, 92–4, 96
cultural relativism, 19, 210, 212
cybernetics, 9–10, 12
cyborgs, 94

dance, 10–12, 192
Daniel, Yvonne, 10–12
dark night of the soul, 47, 49, 60
death: aging and, 84–9, 97; ego, 34, 35, 38, 40; transcendence of, 192; yoga and, 109, 112
delusion: Buddhism and, 71–2; Philip K. Dick and, 27–30, 32, 38, 40, 43
dementia, 85
Derrida, Jacques, 227n43
dhāraṇīs, 114–16
Dick, Philip K. (PKD), 27–43; mystical experience of, 27, 39, 42–3; suffering and, 34–6, 38–9, 40–1
discourse: gerontological, 92, 95; places and, 6–8; postmodern, 13; prayer and, 50; psychology and, 18; scientific, 92, 182, 205, 214, 227n44; work of, 19. *See also* narratives
divination, 201–3, 213, 216, 223n29
Divine Life Society, 118
Downside Abbey, 45, 58. *See also* Benedictine monks
dreams, 9–10, 21n6
dualism, 94, 107, 108, 115–16. See also *sāṃkhya*
Durkheim, Émile, 210–11

Ecclesiastes, 28, 30
ecology of the mind, 9–10
Eden Alternative, 88
Egan, Harvey, 53–4
ego: brain and, 42; death of, 34, 35, 38, 40

Einstein, Albert, 226n41
elders: aging and, 82–3, 85–9, 95–7; authority of, 189–90, 195, 197–8; technology and, 148–9
Eliade, Mircea, 115
embodiment, 10–12, 82, 94, 96–7, 107. *See also* yoga
emic and etic analysis, 186, 203, 204. *See also* verbality
emotions: aging and, 86, 87; Buddhism and, 71, 78–9; intelligence and, 69–70; intentionality of, 5; passions, 21n5
enlightenment: authority and, 135; modernity and, 106; yoga and, 103–5, 107, 117; Zen narratives, 70
entrepreneurs, 149–50n2
environmentalism, 162
epiphanies, 193, 206
epistemology: fieldwork and, 183; scenario planning and, 162, 169, 173; of science, 212–13; shamans and, 8; yoga and, 105, 108–15, 118
ethics: character, 144–5; speech acts and, 7; technology and, 148; virtue, 142–3
ethnography: embodiment and, 107; limits of, 91; non-literate societies and, 179, 182–4, 192, 206–9. *See also* anthropology; fieldwork
ethos, 173
etic analysis. *See* emic and etic analysis
etymology of wisdom, 3
European Council in Lisbon, 170
European Economic Community (EEC), 171
evidential paradigm, 158–61, 164
evolution, 5, 18, 20n3. *See also* ecology of the mind
Exegesis, The (PKD): delusion and, 27–30, 32, 38, 40, 43; God and, 34, 37, 39; liberation and, 36; suffering and, 34–6, 38–9, 40–1. See also *Cosmogony and Cosmology*
exemplars, 122–51; authority of, 134–6, 138, 145–6; ethics of, 142–3, 144–5, 148; founder's paradox, 141–2; narratives of, 124–5, 128–34, 136, 138–40, 149, 150n3; power dynamics and, 147; presentations of, 127

Facebook, 148
faqirs, 185
feminism, 162
fetishization, 105–7, 109–10
fieldwork, 182–6, 208, 225–6n35
Fischer, Roland, 41–2
forbidden scholarship, 214, 228n46
forecasts, 155, 163–4. *See also* scenario planning
FORESIGHT, 155–6, 170–4
Foucault, Michel, 159
founder's paradox, 141–2

Gadamer, Hans-Georg, 166–7
Gage, Phineas, 85, 97n1
Gaski, Harald, 20–1n4
Gasquet, Aiden, 57
Gates, Bill, 139
Geertz, Clifford, 78–9
gender, 12–13, 169
Genesis, 43
genetics, 85, 97n2
gerontology, 95
Ginzburg, Carlo, 157–9, 169
globalization, 20, 105, 180, 184, 209–10, 225n35
God: and *The Exegesis*, 27, 34, 37, 39; ontology and, 108; prayer and, 46, 48, 50, 52, 53, 57–8
godmen, 117
Goffman, Erving, 131
gold mining, 223n28

Goodier, Alban, 57
Greece, 170–4
Greek Secretariat of Research and Technology (GSRT), 173–4
Grossman, Igor, 3–4
Guerlac, Suzanne, 90, 92
gurus, 103, 107, 113–14, 118, 166. *See also* sages

hagiography, 139
Hakuin, 70
hallucination. *See* delusion
healing, 9, 11, 36, 68, 90. See also *sangoma* cult
Heart Sutra, 43n4
hermeneutics, 166
heuristics, 18–19
historiography, 158, 169
Holmes, Sherlock, 158
holograms, 40
Homo sapiens, 3
Homo venatus, 158, 159
Ḫumiriyya, 184–91, 196–7, 204, 206–7

identity, 180, 209
Ignatius of Loyola, Saint, 48, 53
ignorance: meditation and, 71; prayer and, 60; scenario planning and, 168; yoga and, 108–10, 113–15, 117
infinity, 58–60
inflection, 5–6
Insole, Christopher, 57
insurance companies, 126–8, 143–5
intelligence: developmental, 84; emotional, 69–70; VALIS, 27, 33, 34, 37–8, 40
intentionality, 5
internet, 180, 225n35
intersubjectivity, 87, 88, 96, 97. *See also* subjectivity
introception, 33, 39, 40, 42
Islam, 184–5, 190–1, 211

Japan, 70–2, 169. *See also* Naikan
Japanese (language), 68
Jefferson, Thomas, 129
Jeste, Dilip, 85
Jesus, 41, 42
jinns, 184
Jobs, Steve, 139, 140, 148
John of the Cross, Saint, 49, 60
Julian of Norwich, 41

Kahn, Herman, 161–2, 167
Kaivalyadhama, 118
Kalanick, Travis, 140
kataphatic modes of prayer, 53–4
kinship, 189, 191–2, 203
Kuvalayananda, Swami, 118–19

landscape, 7–8, 184–5, 192, 204
language: anthropology and, 181–4, 207, 225n35; consensus and, 106; epistemology of, 111; poetic, 20–1n4; prayer and, 48, 50, 53, 60; reality and, 37, 40, 42; representation and, 216; transcendence of, 108, 224–5n32; truth enclaves and, 209, 226n41. *See also* discourse; etymology of wisdom; narratives; place names; proverbs; semiotics; verbality; *specific languages*
Levinas, Emmanuel, 87
liberation, 36. *See also* enlightenment; ultra-meta-cognition
lifespan, 6. *See also* aging
listening, 216
literacy, 179, 191, 205

Locke, John, 173
logos, 173
Lotus Sutra, 220n19
Louvain School, 207, 217n6
LSD, 21n6
Luhrmann, Tanya, 54

Malinowski, Bronislaw, 45–6
Mallinson, James, 104, 110
managers, 127–8, 131, 133, 138, 143
Manjushri, 69
mantras, 111–12, 114–16
maya, 30
medicine, 159–60
meditation: mindfulness, 71, 79; Naikan, 67–8, 72–9; Tibetan, 133; yoga, 112, 114–15; Zen, 70. *See also* meditation centres; prayer
meditation centres: Naikan, 67–8, 72–9; Tibetan, 133–6, 145–7
memory, 76, 78–9, 92, 95. *See also* amnesia
Meretoja, Hanna, 95
Merrell-Wolff, Franklin (FMW), 28, 33, 39, 40–2
metacognition, 5. *See also* ultra-meta-cognition
metonymy, 168
#MeToo, 147
mishirabe, 72
missionaries, 197, 222n27
modernity and modernization, 105–6, 162–3. *See also* postmodernity
money, 140, 142–3, 150–1n5
morality. *See* ethics
Morelli, Giovanni, 158
music and musicality, 11, 93–4, 95–6, 97, 192. *See also* song paths
Musk, Elon, 139
Mwali cult, 201, 202, 220–1n19
Mwendanyangula, 193
mysticism, 60, 114, 116. *See also* Dick, Philip K.; prayer

Naikan, 67–8, 72–9
narratives: evidential, 157–61; exemplary, 124–5, 128–34, 136, 138–40, 149, 150n3; of scenarios, 167; temporality of, 90, 92–6. *See also* discourse
nenbutsu, 71
nervous system, 4. *See also* brain
networks, 137–8
New Age movement, 180
Newland, Edward, 156
Nkoya, 191–8, 204, 206–7, 220nn18–19, 221n22
Normanton, Leander, 50
nuclear war, 161, 162
nursing homes, 88, 92, 96. *See also* caregiving
Nyambi, 193

objectivity, 31, 39–42, 201–2, 212
Olympic Games, 171–2
ontogeny, 97
ontology: *sāṃkhya*, 107–10; of time, 82, 88–97; Western, 211; yoga and, 103, 105–6, 115. *See also* reality; truth enclaves/domains
orientalism, 118
Ortega y Gasset, 89
Osho, 43n4
Oxford Scenarios Programme, 156

paradigmatic narratives, 130–2, 150nn3–4. *See also* exemplars
Pascual-Leone, Juan, 4–5
passions, 21n5
paterfamilias, 55
pathos, 173

Peirce, Charles Sanders, 104
Pelasgian culture, 196–7, 204, 219n12, 220–1n19, 221n21
performance, 19–20
phatic communication, 45–6
phenomenology, 83, 92–3, 96. *See also* time and temporality
philosophical anthropology, 13
phronesis, 4, 83, 142
place names, 7–8
Plato, 31, 35
Platt, Charles, 27
plausibility, 157, 168
poetry, 20–1n4
postmodernity, 94. *See also* modernity and modernization
post-structuralism, 217n5
pragmatics, 4, 5
prayer, 46; community and, 56–61; modes of, 53–7; roadmap of, 47–53. *See also* meditation
proverbs, 196
psychedelics, 21n6, 39, 41
psychic vitality, 86, 87
psychoanalysis, 160
psychology, 4, 5, 18, 68
puberty rites, 225n34
Pure Land Buddhism, 67, 71
purification, 112
puruṣa, 109, 111

quantum mechanics, 213, 227n43

reality: definition of, 31; lifeworld, 205; models of, 166; as projected framework, 30–4, 38, 40; self-awareness of, 33–4; suffering and, 34–6, 38–9. *See also* ontology; truth enclaves/domains
relativism, 19, 210, 212
representations: cave allegory, 31, 35; epidemiology of, 8; language and, 216; prayer and, 50–4; statistical, 163–4, 167; world-creation and, 209. *See also* discourse; narratives; semiotics
reputation, 139. *See also* authority
restlessness, 48–9, 51–2
Reynolds, David, 68
rites of passage, 96, 225n34
ritual: caregiving and, 88; dance, 10–12; Naikan and, 76; as orthopraxy, 19; Pelasgian culture and, 221n21; temporality and, 90, 96; transcendence and, 192. *See also* divination; rites of passage; *sangoma* cult
Royal Dutch Shell, 156, 165

sages: discourse of, 205; elders as, 85, 198; seeking, 3; yoga and, 114–16, 119. *See also* gurus
saints, 190–1. *See also specific saints*
Salk, Jonas, 5–6, 20n3
Salk, Peter, 5
samadhi, 41, 104, 112, 114
Sami, 20–1n4
sāṃkhya, 107–12, 115–17, 118
sangoma cult, 195, 198–204, 206–7, 214, 220–1n19, 222n26
scenario planning, 155–74; evidential paradigm, 158–61, 164; FORESIGHT, 155, 170–4; scenarists, 168–73; sophiology, 157–8, 163–4, 169. *See also* Wack, Pierre
Schloss, Jeffrey, 18–19
science, 212–14
secrecy: of puberty rites, 225n34; in Silicon Valley, 139; yoga and, 111–12, 115
self, 38, 41–2, 52, 89, 94–5
semiotics, 104, 108, 109, 112–18
senses, 111

shamanism, 8–10, 222n26
Sherman, Nancy, 5
Shields, Renée Rose, 96
Shin Buddhism, 71–2
Shinran, 72
silence, 45–7, 53–5, 58, 60–1, 181
Silicon Valley, 136–41, 147–9
Singleton, Mark, 104, 110
Sivananda, Swami, 118–19
skunkworks, 139
Smith, Jacqui, 86, 87
social relations: fetishization of, 105; language and, 117; Naikan and, 67, 70, 77, 79; ritual and, 10
Socrates, 150–1n5
song paths, 8–9
Sophia, 36, 157. *See also* Baker, Augustine
sophiology, 157–8, 163–4, 169
sorcery, 192, 197, 198, 202
space, 90–2. *See also* landscape; place names
Sperber, Dan, 8
Staley, David, 168–9
start-ups, 138, 140–1
storytelling. *See* narratives
Strawson, Galen, 94–5
subjectivity, 41, 91. *See also* intersubjectivity
sublime, 58, 59–60
suffering: Buddhism and, 71, 75; *The Exegesis* and, 34–6, 38–9, 40–1; knowledge and, 103; prayer and, 51
summum silentium, 46
Sutin, Lawrence, 29
sutras, 43n4, 109, 112, 220n19
symbols, 91, 113–14, 207, 214. *See also* semiotics
syphilis, 159–60
systems theory, 165

taboos, 205–6
Takahashi, Masami, 69
technology, 148–9. *See also* Silicon Valley
therianthropy, 224n29
Tibetan Buddhism, 133–4. *See also* meditation centres
time and temporality, 82, 88–97
Tolle, Eckhart, 52, 61n6
Toren, Christina, 97
Townsley, Graham, 8–9
tradition, 47
trance, 185, 223n29
transcendence, 192, 224–5n32
truth enclaves/domains, 184, 209–12, 214, 217n2, 226n41
Turner, Denys, 60
Turner, Victor, 207

ultra-meta-cognition, 27–9, 32–3, 35–6, 39, 41–2
unicorns, 140
Upanishads, 39, 103
Urgrund, 31–42; birth of, 35–8, 40; power of, 39. *See also* ultra-meta-cognition

VALIS, 27, 33, 34, 37–8, 40
Vedanta, 30
verbality, 205–7
verisimilitude, 168
virtue, 142–3
Vyasa, 109

Wack, Pierre, 156–7, 161, 163–7, 169, 170, 173
Watt, Ian, 168
Wei Wu Wei, 27, 28
Whicher, Ian, 103, 109
White, David Gordon, 113–14, 117
Wittgenstein, Ludwig, 181

world-creation, 209
Wozniak, Steve, 148

Yaminahua, 8–9, 10
yoga, 103–19; epistemology of, 105, 108–15, 118; fetishization and, 105–7; gurus, 103, 107, 113–14; renaissance of, 118
Yoga Sutra, 109, 112
Yoruba, 11
yoshi, 8–9, 10
Yoshimoto Ishin, 72, 79
youth, 90, 91, 113

Zebra (artifact), 30–6, 38–40
Zen Buddhism, 70, 134
Zuckerberg, Mark, 139

www.ingramcontent.com/pod-product-compliance
Lightning Source LLC
LaVergne TN
LVHW040150080826
844660LV00014B/909/J